Modelling Storage Systems

Computer Science:
Computer Architecture and Design, No. 5

Harold S. Stone, Ph.D., Series Editor

IBM Corporation
T.J. Watson Research Center
Yorktown, New York

Other Titles in This Series

Modelling Storage Systems

by
M. Satyanarayanan

UMI RESEARCH PRESS
Ann Arbor, Michigan

Produced and distributed by
UMI Research Press
an imprint of
University Microfilms, Inc.
Ann Arbor, Michigan 48106

Library of Congress Cataloging in Publication Data

Satyanarayanan, M.
  Modelling storage systems.

  (Computer science. Computer architecture and
design ; no. 5)
  "A revision of author's Ph. D. thesis, Carnegie-
Mellon University, 1983"—verso CIP t.p.
  Bibliography: p.
  Includes index.
  1. Computer storage devices—Mathematical models.
I. Title. II. Series.
TK7895.M4S28 1986   004.5   86-1312
ISBN 0-8357-1742-9 (alk. paper)

To my father and mother
from a loving son

Contents

Preface

An interconnection of memory devices, referred to as a *Memory Hierarchy,* is frequently used in computer systems to balance available tradeoffs in cost, speed, capacity, and longevity. This book presents a methodology that simplifies the performance analysis, by simulation, of such a memory hierarchy.

Drawing upon ideas from abstract data types and message-based communication, the book first shows that simulation models of memory devices can be developed independently of the hierarchies in which they will be used. The ability to separate hierarchy-specific information from device-specific information makes it possible to develop libraries of models for a variety of memory devices. During simulation, messages convey hierarchy-specific information between instantiations of the memory models.

The substantiation of these ideas occurs in three steps. First, the proposed methodology is shown to be versatile by developing models for a number of diverse memory devices. Next, practicability is established by an actual implementation that demonstrates the low computational overheads introduced by the methodology. Finally, the performance of a network file system is analyzed, using data gathered from an actual file system for driving the simulations. This data as well as the results of the simulations are interesting in themselves, but the analysis serves primarily to show that the proposed methodology is usable in solving real-life problems.

This work thus provides an affirmative answer to the question "Can one structure the modelling of complex memory systems in such a way as to permit the use of standard, off-the-shelf software?" Both system designers building actual computer systems and researchers analyzing alternative memory system designs should find this book useful.

The software described in chapter 5 (the tool implementation) is now being maintained and distributed by the SoftLab Project of the computer science department at the University of North Carolina, Chapel Hill. Readers may contact the Project Coordinator of the SoftLab project for details.

The research leading to this book was performed at the Computer Science Department of Carnegie-Mellon University. I found it a stimulating and supportive research environment and I am proud and fortunate to have been part of it.

The advice and constructive criticism of George Robertson and Bill Wulf undoubtedly improved the quality of this work. Sam Fuller, Dan Siewiorek, and Zary Segall also offered many useful comments and suggestions.

I have benefited from the work of others in a number of ways. Bjarne Stroustrup of Bell Labs wrote the *Class* package used here; Ivor Durham created the *Plot* program which was used to generate the graphs in this book; Louis Monier put together the *Mathlm* package for incorporating mathematics and special symbols into Scribe documents; and Ed Dehart installed file monitoring software in the PDP-10 operating system. As guardians of the computing facility, Howard Wactlar and Mike Accetta went out of their way on a number of occasions to provide me with the computational resources needed to do my work.

I would like to thank my friends in Pittsburgh for the good times we have shared. Louis and Nadine Monier, Dorai Ramprasad, Rick Snodgrass, Mark Sherman, and Jon Rosenberg were particularly helpful in cheering me up on the dismal days when nothing seemed to be going right.

Finally, for their constant support and encouragement of my educational endeavors I would like to thank my parents—I dedicate this work to them.

Part I

Introduction

1

Synopsis

1.1. The Problem

Memory plays an indispensable role in computing systems. Over the last three decades much effort has gone into the development of memory devices that span a wide range of cost, speed, capacity, and reliability. At a given level of technology, it is the case that the fastest devices cost the most and have the least capacity. However, to build reliable computing systems with high performance at a low cost, one needs cheap memory devices that are fast, reliable, and have large capacity. The traditional solution to this impasse has been to interconnect devices with differing characteristics in such a way as to achieve an acceptable compromise between the desired attributes. Such an ensemble of memory devices is referred to as a *memory hierarchy*.

Faced with a wide choice of memory devices and possible interconnection structures, the designer of a memory hierarchy can pose a number of questions. For example, given a specific hierarchy, what is its performance? Or, given a specific set of devices, what interconnection structure optimizes a particular performance measure? Alternatively, for a given cost constraint what hierarchy gives the best performance?

Finding answers to these and related questions forms the central problem in memory hierarchies. A survey of the literature shows that four alternative approaches are used in addressing this problem: analytical methods, queueing models, simulation studies, and direct experimentation. Simulation is the most frequently used method because it is flexible, able to model systems without oversimplification, and capable of predicting the performance of systems which are not yet implemented.

A large amount of work has been done on the development of simulation languages, and on techniques for reducing the execution times of simulations. In contrast, this book is concerned with a higher level of abstraction. It proposes a method of structuring simulation models of memory devices such that they make minimal assumptions about the environments in which they will be used. Such an approach to modelling makes it meaningful for libraries of performance models to be developed. This, in turn, would reduce the time and effort involved in exploring alternative memory organizations for a particular task—a virtue design engineers will surely appreciate.

1.2. The Thesis

The overall performance of a system depends on the intrinsic performance characteristics of its constituents, as well as on interactions between them. The thesis of this book is that, in the domain of memory systems, it is possible to separate hierarchy-specific and device-specific aspects of performance. Consequently, one can build a simulation model for the performance of a memory device independently of the hierarchies in which it will be used. During the course of simulation, communications between the device-specific performance models convey the hierarchy-specific information needed to obtain a complete performance model of a hierarchy.

The defense of this thesis occurs in a series of steps. It is first shown that simulation of memory hierarchies is a frequent activity and that the thesis, if true, would be a significant contribution. Then a methodology for modelling storage systems, based on the thesis, is proposed. This methodology draws upon ideas from abstract data types and message-based communication schemes. Potential criticisms of the methodology are then formulated and scrutinized. It is shown that the external behavior of memory devices can be characterized by two simple abstractions; further, only a small amount of information has to be communicated between the models for individual devices during simulation. These observations form the intuitive basis for accepting the thesis. The remainder of the dissertation is concerned with providing more substantive evidence to support the informal arguments.

There are two major ways in which the proposed methodology could potentially be inadequate. First, it may not be rich enough to model a wide range of memory devices. This is shown to be false by considering a large number of memory devices from the primary, secondary, and tertiary levels of storage and developing performance models for them. Models for a number of memory hierarchies are also considered, demonstrating that the models for the devices may indeed be used in a variety of environments. A second criticism is that simulations based on it are computationally too expensive. This argument is refuted by designing a tool based on the methodology, building an actual implementation, and measuring the overheads imposed by it.

Using the proposed ideas, a simulation study of an actual system is conducted. The purpose of this exercise is to develop further confidence in the thesis, and to obtain experience in the practical use of the methodology and tool. The system investigated is a network file system designed at Carnegie-

Mellon University. The simulations are driven by a model of file references derived from experimental observations of an existing file system in the same environment. Both the experimental observations and the simulation results are interesting and of value in their own right.

1.3. The Organization

The book is organized in four parts. Part I, consisting of chapters 1 and 2, provides a literature survey of the memory hierarchy problem and motivates this work.

Part II contains the main evidence supporting the thesis. Chapter 3 presents the proposed methodology and tool design; chapter 4 develops models for a wide range of memory devices and hierarchies; and chapter 5 describes an implementation of the tool and presents measurements of its overheads.

Part III deals with the application of the methodology and tool to a network file system. Chapter 6 describes the system, discusses the modelling assumptions and their rationale. Based on experimental observations reported in the literature, chapter 7 develops a synthetic driver for generating file system references. Further experimental observations, to obtain realistic parameter values for this driver, are also reported in that chapter. The results of a simulation study which uses the models of chapters 6 and 7 are presented in chapter 8.

Part IV consists of chapter 9, a summary which also describes interesting avenues of future research based on the work described here.

2

Background and Literature Survey

The purpose of this chapter is to provide context for this book, and to motivate the work described in the following chapters. The chapter begins with an examination of the properties of a hypothetical memory device. Memory hierarchies are then introduced as an attempt to alleviate the inability of any single memory device to meet the requirements of all conceivable applications. The diversity of such hierarchies and their widespread use in computer systems is noted. Techniques to evaluate the performance of memory hierarchies are presented next. The importance of simulation as a performance evaluation technique is established, and the absence of a formalism to permit compositions of simulation models of memory systems observed—a deficiency this work attempts to remove.

2.1. Memory Devices: Ideal and Nonideal

In the absence of real-world constraints, one could conceive of an ideal memory device. Such a device would cost nothing and would be capable of instantaneously storing or retrieving arbitrarily large quantities of data. In addition, it would be capable of storing data for indefinite lengths of time without corruption, would consume no power, and would occupy no physical volume. However, no known physical device possesses these properties to an extent adequate to be considered even near-ideal. The fundamental limitations encountered in the quest for ideal memory devices are discussed by Matick [77], Mead [80], and Keyes [81]. Since physically realizable devices are only approximations to the ideal, the choice of a memory device in an actual application is an engineering decision, based on the designers' judgment of what attributes of the memory are most critical for that application.

From the emphasis placed on them in the literature, it appears that access time, capacity, and cost are three critical properties for many applications. Figure 2-1 and table 2-1 (reproduced from Pohm [81]) indicate the positions occupied by a representative sample of memory devices along these three dimensions. In practice, those applications which require large capacity also

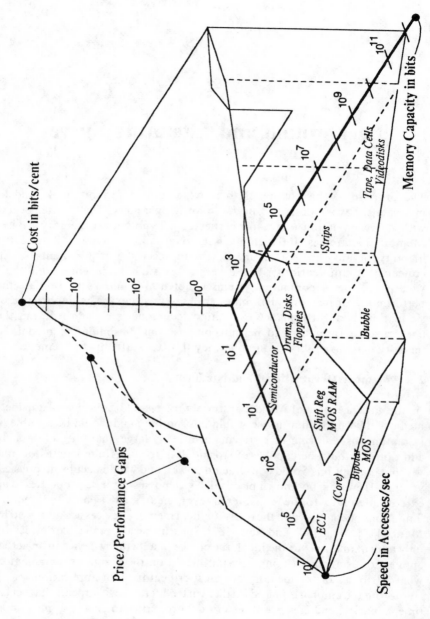

Figure 2-1. Speed/Capacity/Cost Design Space.

Source: Pohm, A.V., and Smay, T.A. "Computer Memory Systems." *Computer* 14, no. 10. © 1981 IEEE.

Table 2-1. Characteristics of Current Memory Devices.

Device Technology	Access plus Transfer Time	Memory Size (Bits)	Cents/Bit* (System Level)
Register (*Semiconductor flip-flops*)	0.1-10 ns	10^3-10^4	1-100
Cache (*Semiconductor RAM*)	10-100 ns	10^4-10^5	0.05-1
Main Memory (*Semiconductor RAM*)	70-500 ns	10^6-10^8	0.001-0.1
Backing Memory (*Fixed-head disks, bubbles*)	1-10 ms	10^7-10^9	2×10^{-3}-0.05
Secondary Memory (*Moving-head disks*)	20-100 ms	10^9-10^{11}	5×10^{-4}-5×10^{-3}
Mass Memory (*Videodisks, Automated tape handlers*)	10-100 sec	10^{11}-10^{12}	2×10^{-5}

*The cost of memory diminishes 20% or 30% a year. The values given are representative of 1984–1985.

demand long-term reliability. Consequently, although there is no fundamental physical basis for such a correlation, the devices with the largest capacities also offer the best long-term reliability.

Discussions of memory systems in the literature often use the terms *Primary, Secondary,* and *Tertiary* storage devices. One way to explain this taxonomy is to examine the number of levels of buffering used in accessing data from a device. Programs executing on a processor access data in primary memory. Data from secondary storage through one level of primary storage buffering before becoming programs. Accesses from tertiary storage devices usually buffering at a secondary storage device (often referred and then a level of primary storage buffering.

typically have fast access times, while tertiary storage devices have large capacity. Secondary storage devices have access times and capacities which are between those of primary and tertiary devices. This classification, while qualitative and imprecise, is still convenient in discussing memory systems.

The literature contains many surveys of memory devices and technologies. Probably the most comprehensive and recent of these are by Smith [78a, 81a]. Other surveys are by Hoagland [79] and Pohm [81]. Information on the rate of progress in different technologies can be found in Puthuff [78]. Matick [77] is probably the best source of detailed information on the principles of data storage technologies.

A review of contemporary devices and of past and projected future developments in this area supports two conclusions. First, no single memory device is adequate to fulfill the requirements of all existing applications. Second, while absolute improvements are continually being made in the characteristics of individual memory devices, the relative differences between them persist.

2.2. Memory Hierarchies

For applications where no single device possesses an acceptable combination of properties, one can construct a *Memory Hierarchy*—an interconnection of memory devices with differing characteristics, controlled by software, microcode, or hardware.* The overall properties of such an ensemble are dependent on the constituent devices, the connecting structure, and the policies used to manage the transfer of data between different components of the hierarchy.

One class of memory hierarchies arises from the use of secondary storage to provide user programs with an address space whose size is independent of the available primary memory. Systems incorporating paged virtual memory and segmented virtual memory [Denning70, Doran76] are members of this class. A survey of the literature in this area is provided by Smith [78b].

Caching schemes [Liptay68, Strecker76] are the source of another well-studied class of memory hierarchies. Using very fast, but expensive, technology for the cache and a slower, less expensive technology for main memory, a cache/main memory hierarchy yields a directly addressable

---

*The word "hierarchy" implies a total ordering of some property. One can partition a typical memory hierarchy into a number of equivalence classes, each consisting of memory devices with similar cost, speed and access times. A total ordering of a key attribute (typically access time) exists across these classes, and makes it appropriate to refer to the entire tem as a hierarchy.

memory that is almost as fast as the cache, but at a cost closer to that of the main memory. The attractiveness of this scheme is enhanced by the fact that the hierarchy management is carried out entirely in hardware and microcode—no software modifications have to be made in order to benefit from the presence of the cache.

Memory hierarchies are used at the secondary/tertiary storage levels too. In some installations where the space occupied by files created over a period of time exceeds the amount of on-line secondary storage available, migration schemes are used to move files from secondary storage to off-line tertiary storage. Johnson [75] and Accetta [80] describe file system designs which hide the distinction between secondary and tertiary storage from user software, and automate the file migration function. These designs constitute an application of the virtual memory and caching concepts to the secondary/tertiary storage levels.

The use of computer networks makes it possible to access files at remote sites. The CFS project at Carnegie-Mellon University [Accetta80] attempts to remove the distinction between local and remote files by permitting programs to transparently access files across a local network. Such a scheme can be viewed as a memory hierarchy in which the physical separation between storage devices is masked by memory management software.

The presence of memory hierarchies, in many guises, in contemporary computer systems suggests that:

1. Memory hierarchies are a viable means of overcoming the nonidealities of memory devices.

2. While specific designs and domains of application may change with time, the use of memory hierarchies in computer system design is likely to continue in the forseeable future.

2.3. Performance Evaluation of Memory Hierarchies

Performance evaluation techniques aim to provide designers with quantitative information on the properties of alternative memory hierarchy designs. By providing the means of judging whether a specific design meets the design criteria, they play an important role in the design of memory systems.

Each nonideal characteristic of memory devices is a potential yardstick by which devices can be evaluated. Given any memory system, it is reasonable to ask what its access time, capacity, reliability, and cost are. These questions are relatively simple to answer for individual devices. At worst, the answers may have to be given in functional form rather than as numbers: the access time to a disk, for example, is a function of the disk address requested, and the disk head's radial and rotational position with respect to the desired data block at the instant the request is made. In a memory hierarchy, however, the constraints of the connection scheme, the interaction between the memory devices, and the specific sequence of requests made to the hierarchy jointly conspire to make performance evaluation more difficult.

The performance of a memory hierarchy can be investigated either at the system level or at the individual device level. In the former case the performance characteristics of the hierarchy as a whole are of interest; the cost of a hierarchy and the access time to an arbitrary data item in it belong to this category. In the latter case, attention is focussed at individual components of the hierarchy, resulting in questions such as the queue lengths at devices, the utilization of devices, and the error rates at different points in the hierarchy.

The techniques used to evaluate memory hierarchies can be broadly classified into four groups:

- Analytic Techniques
- Queueing Models
- Simulation Studies
- Experimental Methods

We examine each method in the following sections.

2.3.1. Analytic Techniques

A significant amount of work has been done on the use of abstract characterizations of memory hierarchies to evaluate overall performance. Most often, these methods are used to design a memory hierarchy that has been optimized for some objective function such as cost or access time. To perform such mathematical analysis one needs analytic representations for:

1. the interconnection structure of the hierarchy,
2. the individual device characteristics,
3. the inter-level data management policies, and
4. the request stream presented to the hierarchy.

Differences in the choice of representations in each area accounts for the sizeable body of literature on analytic techniques for evaluating memory hierarchies.

The hierarchy is usually assumed to be a linear connection of N memory levels of differing capacities, with level *1* having the fastest access time and level N the slowest. Most formulations [Strecker78, Gecsei74a] permit accesses only between adjacent levels; a few [Mortenson76] make level *1* a distinguished level and permit all other levels to access it directly. It is also usually assumed that if a data item is available at some level *i,* it is duplicated at all lower levels $i + 1, i + 2, \cdots,$ N. Such hierarchies are called *nested hierarchies;* Mortenson [76] considers non-nested hierarchies. Another common assumption [Gecsei74a] is that references from external requestors are made only to level *1;* Welch [78] and Ramamoorthy [70] are among those who do not make this assumption.

Devices are represented in one of two ways. Some papers [Chandy69, Ramamoorthy70, Strecker78] assume that the space of available technologies is discrete and finite, each technology being characterized by an average access time and a cost per unit of storage. Others [Chow 74, Welch78] assume that the space of technologies is a continuum, with access speeds and unit costs related by some function. The specific function used is invariably a power function of the form $b(t) = b_0 t^{-\beta}$, where b is the cost per unit of storage, t the access time, and b_0 and β are constants. The primary reason for choosing this specific functional form is mathematical tractability. It has been argued, however [Chow74, Welch78], that such a function is a reasonable fit to empirical data presented by Lin [72] and Rege [76].

It is in the representation of program characteristics and hierarchy management policies that the literature shows the greatest diversity. The simplest approach combines the two factors into a single function, the *miss ratio function,* which specifies for all levels the relationship between the size of a level and the probability that an arbitrary request cannot find the desired data item in that level. A miss ratio function of the form $f(c) = f_0 c^{-\alpha}$ where f_0, α are constants, f is the miss ratio, and c is the capacity of a level, is used by Chow [74]. Based on work reported by Saltzer [74], a miss ratio function of the form $m(s) = b/(b + s)$, where b is a constant and s the capacity of a level, is used by Strecker [78]. Ramamoorthy [70] and Chandy [69] assume a static data distribution in the hierarchy, thus trivializing the data management policies. They also assume that the reference characteristics of a program can be specified by partitioning it into equal size blocks and giving the histogram of access frequencies of these blocks. Mortenson [76] assumes an independent reference model for programs, implying that a program can be partitioned into equal-sized pages of equiprobable access. This work examines hierarchy management policies along two dimensions: (1) when modifications to data are reflected to other copies of that data in the hierarchy, and (2) the effect of specific set of replacement policies. Salasin [73] examines three specific access techniques (sequential, random, and hierarchical linked-list) and derives miss ratios in each case. Woolf [71] assumes that a program consists of a sequence of non-nested loops of uniformly distributed length and a constant number of iterations, with the origins of the loops being uniformly distributed through the address space. The causal relationships between accesses at different parts of the hierarchy arising out of data management policies are specified in a four-dimensional array. A simpler, sequential program model is used by Welch [79].

The nature of questions answered by analytic techniques are typically of the form:

- Given a fixed cost and a minimum capacity, what is the fastest hierarchy one can obtain?

- Given a minimum desired access time and capacity, what is the cheapest hierarchy?

- In each of the above cases, how many levels should there be? What type of memory should be used at each level? What should be the capacity of each level?

Since these are formulated as optimization problems, the solution techniques used are typically those used in operations research: linear programming [Chandy69], integer programming (to handle modular memory sizes) [Ramamoorthy70], and nonlinear programming [Chow74, Strecker78, Chanson80].

All models discussed in this section depend on significant problem simplification to permit mathematical analysis. It is unlikely that real-life memory hierarchies will rigorously meet the assumptions used. However such methods are of value in obtaining an initial design point from which detailed investigations can be carried out using other techniques.

2.3.2. Queueing Models

A system made up of components that have finite delay characteristics and support multiple outstanding transactions can be represented as a queueing network. The usefulness of a specific representation depends on both the ease with which the queueing network can be solved and the accuracy of the solutions so obtained. Kleinrock [75a] gives a good introduction to the principles of queueing theory, and discusses its applications to computer systems [75b]. The work on queueing models of memory systems can be grouped into two broad classes: modelling of individual devices and modelling of hierarchies.

An example of a detailed queueing model of a device is that presented by Abate [68], for an IBM 2314 disk storage facility with one controller and multiple disk drives. The seek and data transfer delay distributions are assumed to be piecewise linear functions; the rotational delay is assumed to be a uniform distribution. Assuming a Poisson arrival process to the controller, the model is analyzed for the overall response time. A similar problem, with slightly different assumptions, is investigated by Finnin [78]. Assuming that disks have exponential times, that the controller has a constant service time, and that external requests are modelled by a Poisson process, the response time of the system is obtained. A queueing analysis of bubble memory devices organized in a major/minor loop configuration is presented by Bhandarkar [75]. Assuming a Poisson arrival process, and a geometric request size distribution, that work obtains the access time distribution as a function of traffic intensity (ratio of arrival rate to service rate) for different average record sizes. The effect of bidirectional shifting (where the direction of rotation of the minor loops can be decided on a per request basis) on the access time distribution is also studied.

An example of a simple analysis of a memory hierarchy using queueing theory is found in Tsuruho [78]; they examine a two-level hierarchy consisting of a tape-cartridge tertiary storage system with a disk drive as secondary storage. Poisson arrivals and exponential service times are assumed and a Markov chain analysis performed to obtain device utilizations, queue lengths, and waiting times. Misra [81] examines a similar two-level hierarchy but solves it by observing that the resulting model is analogous to one for a timesharing system analyzed in the literature [Scherr67]. A closed queueing network is used by Gecsei [74b] to model a multiprogramming system with a storage hierarchy. The results of the queueing analysis are used to determine the optimal hierarchy designs for two different objective functions.

Most work in this area ignores the differences between read and write requests to devices. However, Lavenberg [73] considers a hierarchy in which each level can service a number of different request types. Assuming a three-stage hierarchy with exponential service times at each stage, this paper uses a close queueing network to examine the performance of the system as a function of the level of multiprogramming, the computational requirements of individual programs, and the priorities assigned to different types of accesses. Distinguishing between read and write accesses, Mortenson [76] uses open and closed queueing networks to investigate the effect of data update policies in a linear hierarchy of exponential servers.

Some papers use queueing models at the individual device level, but apply other techniques to solve the queueing network obtained by representing the components of a memory hierarchy by these models. For example, Woolf [71] develops models for disks, data cells, and random access memories, assuming Poisson arrivals and exponential service times. A queueing network of a multiprogrammed, demand paged system is then constructed and solved by simulation. Harding [75] considers each level of a hierarchy to be an open queueing system with Poisson arrivals and a generalized service time. The paper obtains performance measures for each level as a function of a parameter which relates the utilization of that level in isolation to its utilization in the hierarchy. An iterative solution technique is used to obtain the value of this parameter. Kho [72] formulates three common I/O subsystem management problems in a queueing theory framework: shared buffer allocation for secondary storage devices, management of real memory in a demand paged environment, and utilization of shared I/O channels in a multiprogrammed system. A comprehensive queueing model of a paging algorithm is then developed and solved by simulation.

The type of solution technique used to solve queueing models usually depends on the extent to which simplifying assumptions have been used in the model formulation. Very simple models, such as those used by Tsuruho [78], can be analyzed to yield closed form solutions. More complex models can only be solved numerically by iterative or simulation techniques.

2.3.3. Simulation Studies

As a performance evaluation technique, simulation has the advantage that arbitrarily complex characteristics can be represented without simplifications that would introduce significant errors. Another advantage of simulation is that it is relatively simple to obtain transient characteristics as well as the actual distributions of the system parameters of interest in steady-state. Analytic and queueing methods are usually applicable only in the steady-state, and typically yield only the first and second moments of distributions. The price that is paid for this generality is the human time spent in developing the simulation programs and the computer time needed to run them: the more accurate the model, the greater these times usually are. Law [82] provides a good introduction to basic simulation techniques.

Given its generality, it is hardly surprising that simulation has been used as a tool in virtually every aspect of memory system design and analysis. Though significant programming effort is involved in a simulation, there is negligible discussion in the literature of building simulation models on top of existing ones. As described in the next chapter, this work proposes a methodology that will permit such compositions of simulators in the context of memory hierarchies.

The body of literature evaluating memory systems that use simulation is large, but relatively amorphous—there is no discernible overall structure which can be used to classify the work in this area. By sampling the literature, the rest of this section attempts to establish the fact that simulation is indeed used to analyze the entire spectrum of memory system issues.

Almost all studies of cache memory design have used simulation as a tool. Strecker [76], Bell [74], Agrawal [77], and Liptay [68], for example, use trace-driven simulation to investigate the effects of cache design parameters (such as cache width and set associativity), as well as replacement algorithms on performance. A similar application to translation buffers in virtual memory systems is described in Satyanarayanan [81b]. Using memory reference traces from a number of different numerical analysis programs, Joseph [70] examines the effects of page size and anticipatory paging on virtual memory systems. Rau [79] questions the usefulness of memory interleaving in computer systems that lack caches, and concludes that high degrees of interleaving are useful only in multiprocessor systems and in systems with caches.

In the domain of secondary and tertiary storage devices, simulation has been used both as a tool for performance evaluation as well as a means of validating queueing models. Wilhelm [77], for instance, uses simulation to validate a queueing model for disks, while Nakamura [78] and McBride [79] use it to analyze secondary storage subsystems. Nahouraii [74] describes a disk simulator for debugging user programs which contain time-critical input–output code.

Simulation also plays an important role in evaluating software issues. Stritter [77], for instance, uses trace-driven simulation to evaluate file migration algorithms, while Foster [75] studies the problem of optimal file assignment in memory hierarchies. Hulten [77] describes a simulation tool for investigating database performance. The evaluation of storage allocation policies on disks [Lyons74], and the comparison of disk scheduling policies [Teorey72] are other areas where simulation has been used.

2.3.4. *Experimental Methods*

The need to incorporate user and program behavior motivates experimental studies of computer systems. Such studies are used both as a means of validating predictions made by the methods discussed earlier, and as a source of data for developing these methods. Memory reference data, for example, is often used to drive simulations; confidence in queueing models, on the other hand, was first established by experimental validation. A serious shortcoming in this area of research is the lack of data from vendors on commercial computer systems—such data is usually considered proprietary and hence not published.

An example of direct experimental observation is the work reported by Oleinick [78] on memory interference in multiprocessor systems. Smith [76] presents data on disk head movement in actual computer systems and explains why the movement is much less than commonly assumed. Stritter [77], Smith [81b], Satyanarayanan [81a], and Revelle [75] describe observations of file properties and develop stochastic models to account for these observations. Lewis [73] analyzes page fault frequency in a two-level memory hierarchy and develops a model for it. Gaver [74] reports similar work in the context of a three-level hierarchy.

Another avenue of research in this area is the development of tools to measure computer system performance. A good survey of such tools can be found in Rose [78]. Bard [78] describes a data collection and analysis tool for use in a particular operating system environment. Smith [77] discusses techniques to compress memory reference traces without appreciable loss of information, thus reducing the cost of simulation.

Finally, techniques to process experimental data are presented in the literature. Stack processing as a means of evaluating many virtual storage organizations in one pass of a trace is introduced by Mattson [70]. Turner [77] describes how page fault frequencies and working set sizes can be derived from the reference stack depth distribution of programs.

2.4. Conclusion

As mentioned at the beginning of this chapter, memory devices are nonideal. The entire body of work on memory hierarchies has arisen in an attempt to circumvent these nonidealities. The need for evaluating alternative memory hierarchy designs has motivated many researchers to develop performance evaluation techniques. Simulation, though only one among many such techniques, has found widespread use because of its flexibility and potential for high accuracy. The next chapter develops a methodology which permits simulation models for hierarchies to be viewed as compositions of simulation models of individual devices or of other, smaller, hierarchies. The remainder of the book establishes the versatility and feasibility of such an approach.

Part II

Methodology

3

Methodology and Design Issues

From the discussions in the previous chapter, the versatility of simulation as a means of evaluating memory hierarchies and its widespread use are evident. Given this generality, it is reasonable to ask if the effort involved in performing a simulation can be reduced. "Effort" in this context refers to human intellectual effort. In an era of continually decreasing computing costs, it is appropriate to explore the possibility of trading-off computational efficiency for increased ease of use. In this chapter we examine a methodology that embodies such a trade-off and describe the design of a tool that implements this methodology.

3.1. Outline of the Methodology

The view advocated by this book is that separation of hierarchy-dependent information from device-dependent information yields a useful and realizable level of abstraction in the simulation of memory hierarchies. Corresponding to each device in the system is a *device module,* a collection of code and data that simulates the performance of this device. The contents of a device module are strictly local to that module and are not visible to any other element of the hierarchy. In this respect, device modules resemble abstract data types in modern programming languages. An arbitrary memory hierarchy may be represented as a directed graph whose nodes correspond to devices and whose arcs correspond to logical communication paths between the devices. The use of logical, rather than electrical or physical, communication paths characterizes the level of abstraction being considered: it permits expression of the essential characteristics of devices, free from obscuring details. For example, all disks which can perform DMA transfers to main memory have two logical communication paths—one for transfer of control and status information and the other for DMA transfers. For the range of simulations considered in this work, the exact electrical bus structures and the low-level control signals of these disks are irrelevant. Logical connectivity as well as other information needed for a simulation are expressed in a simple *hierarchy description.*

3.1.1. Utility of the Methodology

It is appropriate now to examine the benefits accruing from this approach. The cost of developing a simulator for a device (i.e., a device module) is amortized over the many hierarchy evaluations in which the module is used. Besides the direct lowering in the cost of a simulation, there is also a benevolent secondary effect: software intended for use over an extended period of time is usually better thought-out and better written than disposable software. In simulation this is reflected both as more efficient code and as a more accurate representation of actual device characteristics. The analogy of subprograms from the standard library of a programming language is applicable here.

The presence of a standard, formalized interface for device modules makes it possible for the person writing a module to be distinct from the persons who use it. Creating an accurate simulator for a device requires a deep understanding of the inner workings of that device. Such knowledge is most likely to be possessed by the designers of the device. It is not unreasonable to envisage a situation where peripheral manufacturers supply potential customers with device modules for each of their product offerings. Design engineers would use these device modules in simulations of the hierarchies they are designing, to decide on the suitability of specific devices.

By using this methodology, the gathering of simulation statistics may be automated to a significant extent. As discussed later in this chapter, some performance measures are common to all memory devices—these can be measured directly by the simulation tool, even without explicit code for them in the device modules. Device-specific statistics have to be collected explicitly by device modules. In neither case however, does the person performing the simulation have to spend any effort in obtaining raw performance data. Of course, the interpretation and analysis of such data still remains in his purview.

The technique of multigrain simulation can be employed in searching a design space for a memory hierarchy design optimized with respect to some objective function. The use of multiple grains of simulation reduces the total cost of such a search. Low-accuracy simulation models are used to identify the neighborhood of an optimum point; more accurate, but computationally more expensive, models are then used to locate the optimum. In a design space with many local optima, simulations of high accuracy should be performed to select the global optimum. An example of this approach is the work of Kumar and Davidson [Kumar80], where two levels of accuracy are used: an analytical model and a detailed simulation. The idea is conceptually extendable to multiple levels.

In the proposed methodology, a device module can incorporate models of different accuracy for that device. The selection of a specific level of accuracy for the module is done by parameterization: the accuracy parameter value specified in a given instantiation of a device module determines the level of accuracy of simulation for the device. A device module is thus analogous to a parameterized data type. This approach raises two interesting issues, which we will identify but not examine further.

1. How does one quantitatively characterize the grain of a given level of simulation? A bound on the accuracy of a specific set of performance measures is the most obvious characterization. However, a figure of merit that incorporates not only the accuracy but also the cost of the simulation would be more desirable. What would such a measure be?

2. To describe a multigrain search procedure, one needs a vehicle for expressing descriptions of the form: "Perform this simulation for t_1 units of time with device d_1 at grain g_1, device d_2 at grain g_2, and so on. Then continue the simulation with d_1 at grain g_1', d_2 at g_2', etc. until condition C is met." The design of such a metasimulation language would be an interesting exercise.

3.1.2. Feasibility of the Methodology

Having established the utility of this methodology, we now address the question of its feasibility. There are two potential sources of difficulty in applying this methodology:

1. *The methodology may be too constraining.* Perhaps only a small, uninteresting class of memory hierarchies are amenable to analysis in this manner.

2. *This approach may be computationally too expensive.* The partitioning of a simulation into individual simulations in device modules with extensive communication between them may result in computational overheads too large to justify the savings in human effort.

Each of these concerns is discussed separately in the following paragraphs.
Consider the operation of a typical device module during the course of a simulation. At some point in (simulated) time it receives a request for a certain operation from some other part of the hierarchy. It acts on this request, perhaps making requests to other devices and waiting for their responses, and after a (simulated) delay responds to the original request. Since the device module is written completely independently of the hierarchy in which it is used, it has to be able to respond reasonably to all possible potential requests. Unless the possible actions and responses are restricted to a small set, determined a priori, the coding of device modules will be very complicated.

Meeting this requirement in spite of the wide spectrum of available memory devices implies that a compact characterization of memory devices is necessary. Does such a representation exist?

The ability to insert an item of data and the ability to retrieve it when needed are essential functional capabilities of any storage system. The operations *Read* and *Write* are thus available on almost all memory systems. The physical organization of data may be one-dimensional, as in the case of a magnetic tape, or multidimensional, as in the case of a set of disk surfaces or a matrix of semiconductor memory cells. For all physical devices, however, each element of the set of available storage locations can be uniquely identified by an integer, its *address*. The interpretation of this integer is clearly device-specific: for a tape, this integer might directly identify the offset of a block of data from the beginning of the reel; for a disk, different fields of the integer might identify a cylinder, track, and sector address. In all such cases, however, it is appropriate to view memory as a one-dimensional array, whose entries are identified by integer addresses. From a performance point of view, ease of access to different elements of this array need not be the same—accessing a certain set of addresses, the *visible window,* may be much faster than accessing any other address. The visible window changes with time and usually depends on the most recently accessed address. On a disk, for example, the tracks over which the heads are currently situated constitute the visible window. In an automated tape library, the visible window is the set of data blocks on the currently mounted tape. Changing the visible window, the *Locate* operation, is supported by many memory devices. Seeks on disks and mounts of tapes are examples of Locate operations. Thus three operations—Read, Write, and Locate—are adequate to describe the basic actions of all physical memory devices. In comparison with these three operations, other device-specific operations occur infrequently so that it is valid to ignore them for performance analysis. Figure 3-1 illustrates the one-dimensional storage model.

Storage systems composed of both hardware and software require a slightly more complicated representation. Such systems are best represented by a two-level addressing scheme: the first level identifies a large item of data and the second level identifies a sub-item. An explicit access to a first-level item is necessary before the corresponding second-level sub-items can be accessed. The performance characteristics of these two classes of access are usually quite different. As an example, consider a file system in which integer file-identifiers are used to address files containing byte-addressed data. Opening a file usually takes much longer than accessing a byte within an opened file. Using the Locate operation for opening a file is inappropriate because this operation is needed to model random accessing of bytes within a file. Consequently, one needs another pair of primitives *Prepare For Read* and *Prepare For Write* to represent the act of accessing the first level of a two-level-

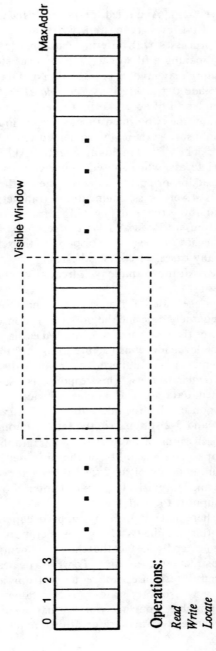

Figure 3-1. One-Dimensional Storage Model.

0 1 2 3

Visible Window

MaxAddr

Operations:
Read
Write
Locate

Note: The addresses in the visible window need not always be contiguous as shown above.

addressable memory system. A unified *PrepareForAccess* is likely to be inadequate because first-level read and write accesses may involve significantly different processes, with differing performance penalties. In a file system, for example, opening a file for writing involves storage allocation, while opening for reading may involve unmigration of data from an archive. For symmetry we include two operations *TerminateRead* and *Terminate- Write* to indicate completion of access to first-level data items.

Figure 3-2 illustrates the two-dimensional storage model. Note that file systems are not the only such systems. A segmented virtual memory system with dynamic linking can be viewed in this manner too. The initial linking of a segment is a first-level access, while subsequent references to it are second-level accesses. In transaction-oriented database systems, the opening of a file for transactions is a first-level access; augmenting a transaction with a page is a Locate (the visible window is the set of pages in the transaction); accesses to a page within a transaction are Read and Write operations.

All device modules have to be able to respond to the set of seven actions defined earlier. In many cases, of course, the responses may be trivial—a device module for a RAM, for example, will treat all operations other than Read or Write as no-ops.

The set of responses also forms a very small set. *Success* and *ErrorInOperation* adequately describe the possible responses of an arbitrary memory device to one of the seven actions discussed earlier. Storage systems which implement a one-level address structure using multiple physical levels (e.g., paged virtual memory) make it necessary for us to distinguish a special kind of error, *NonExistentAddress*. This response is used to indicate the absence of a requested data item at a given device, as opposed to an ErrorInOperation response, which would indicate a failure of some kind in the device. Tables 3-1 and 3-2 summarize the set of actions and responses.

Hopefully, the discussions of the preceding paragraphs give the reader confidence in the scope of applicability of the proposed methodology. A compact, abstract representation of the external behavior of a large class of storage systems does indeed exist. The next chapter provides a series of examples to further support these claims.

It is worth noting here that it is precisely our preoccupation with memory systems that permits this simplicity. Using this methodology on arbitrary digital systems is complicated by the fact that the components of such a system may have no simple abstract representation. To write a device module capable of providing meaningful responses to requests from another module, characterizable only by an arbitrary state-transition table, would indeed be very difficult if not impossible. Conversely, performance analysis of any class of objects with a compact behavioral representation is potentially amenable to this methodology.

Figure 3-2. Two-Dimensional Storage Model.

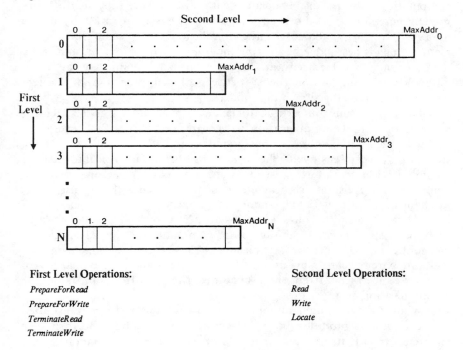

First Level Operations:

PrepareForRead

PrepareForWrite

TerminateRead

TerminateWrite

Second Level Operations:

Read

Write

Locate

Table 3-1. Summary of Actions.

1. PrepareForRead
2. PrepareForWrite
3. Read
4. Write
5. Locate
6. TerminateRead
7. TerminateWrite

Table 3-2. Summary of Responses.

1. Success
2. NonexistentAddress
3. ErrorInOperation

Being a simulation approach to performance analysis, all the computational overheads associated with discrete event simulation are present here too. The more accurate the models represented by device modules, the more expensive the simulation. The feasibility of this methodology is best judged by asking the following question: "In simulating the same memory hierarchy at the same level of accuracy, what is the difference in computational cost between this approach and a direct implementation of the simulation model?"

The dominating source of inefficiency in this approach is the need for explicit, formalized communication between device modules. Since every step of the simulation involves such communication, the overall cost of the simulation is very sensitive to the cost of this operation. Typical formalized communication mechanisms, such as message passing, involve two cost components: a constant overhead component, incurred with each use of this mechanism, and a variable component, dependent on the quantity of information transmitted in a given instance of communication. The large body of existing work on message-based communication indicates that the constant component can be kept reasonably low by careful implementation and, in extreme cases, by using microcode assistance. The quantity of information transmitted then becomes the deciding factor in the communication cost.

What is the minimum amount of information that must be transmitted between device modules in order to accurately model performance characteristics? It turns out that in addition to internally maintained state information, only four quantities are usually needed: (1) The operation to be performed; (2) the address at which the operation is to be performed; (3) the quantity of data to be transferred; and (4) the instant of time at which the request is made.

For instance, to simulate a disk one can keep track of the instant of time at which the last request was serviced and the position of the head (radial and circumferential) at that instant. With this state information and the mechanical characteristics of the disk, one can calculate the time delay to service the next request—the only information needed about the latter are the four quantities mentioned earlier. As another example, consider a cache. The internally maintained state is the set of addresses whose data is in the cache. Receiving a new request updates this state. To decide whether this request causes a hit or a miss, one need only know the address being accessed. An even simpler case is main memory; here no internal state has to be maintained. When presented with an address, the device simulator merely needs to check if this address is valid, and to respond after a constant time delay. Finally, consider a file system with an archive and a migration policy for automatic transfer of files to and from the archive. The internal state maintained by a device module for such a file system would be the set of unarchived addresses (i.e., file-identifiers) at a known instant of time, along with any information needed by the migration policy. When a request for a certain amount of data from a certain file arrives, the device module first simulates the effect of the migration policy on its old state to obtain the new state. The time of arrival of the request is of importance since migration algorithms are usually conditioned on time. The new state is then checked to see if it includes the requested file. Depending on the outcome of this test, a request is sent to a device module simulating the archive or to one simulating secondary storage. On receiving a response to this request, the device module for the file system simulates a time delay to account for overheads within itself, and then responds to the original request.

In a few cases, two additional pieces of information may be necessary:

1. Some devices, such as disks, are capable of transferring data to or from a device other than the driving device—processor-initiated disk DMA transfers to main memory are a typical example. In such a case the requestor has to specify two addresses: one specifying a location on the responding device, and the other specifying a location on the remote device, from or to which data is being transferred by the responding device.

2. In some cases it is necessary to view requests as members of a set of request groups, rather than as isolated entities. In a database system, for example, the response time to a read request from a transaction that has already locked the address to be read is likely to be shorter than the response time for a request from a transaction that is yet to acquire the necessary locks. The only way a device module can distinguish between two identical requests from different transactions is by having the identity of the parent transaction incorporated in the request. Generalizing this example, it is apparent that a means of identifying the parent group of each request in the system is necessary.

The current simulated time can be made available to device modules via calls to the simulation runtime system. Consequently, communications between device modules need only transmit the other five pieces of information. An implementation of this methodology could therefore assume that all communications are short and optimize the communication mechanism accordingly. In a later section this aspect is discussed in greater detail for one specific implementation.

While quantitative measures of computational cost can only be discussed in the context of specific implementations, we have established that, at least conceptually, the simulation of a memory hierarchy using the proposed methodology need not be dramatically more expensive than a monolithic implementation of the same simulation. The second potential obstacle to the feasibility of this approach is thus void.

3.1.3.   Address Translation

Until now, our discussions have implicitly assumed a homogeneous address space: there has been only one type of address in the system. This assumption is not valid for a number of interesting real-life hierarchies. For example, in a virtual memory system with a paging disk, there are three types of addresses: real, virtual, and disk. Depending on the outcome of certain events, some components of the hierarchy either respond immediately to a request, or perform an address translation, generate a new request using the translated address, wait for a response, and only then respond to the original request. In the virtual memory example, virtual addresses are translated to real addresses using page table lookup; the outcome of the translation may be a page fault. In that case, the disk address corresponding to the missing page is generated, and a request for this page is sent to the disk preceded, perhaps, by disk I/O to write out the page frame being replaced. The original request is responded to only after the disk I/O is complete.

The presence of address translation introduces a number of complications. First, it affects performance because the translation process itself generates requests; e.g., page table lookups cause delays even if the page is in main memory. Second, the information needed for translation resides as *data* in some memory device. For example, the contents of a page table entry determines the corresponding real address and the disk address. We would like to avoid keeping track of the data in memory devices because: First, it represents a huge amount of state information. If we are simulating a large-capacity device, the machine on which the simulation is being done may not have enough memory to maintain the state of the simulated device. Second, if we choose to selectively keep track only of those items of data we are interested in, we would have to impart this information to the device modules. This would complicate code and, perhaps, defeat the modularity and interchangeability goals we are striving after. Third, it would greatly increase the overheads involved in simulation, just to handle the few situations where the data is relevant.

We can circumvent these problems if we realize that address translation is not an intrinsic part of the behavior of any memory device, but arises because of the way in which devices are put together in a memory hierarchy. It is therefore reasonable to assign responsibility for simulating the effects of address translation to the designer of a hierarchy rather than to the authors of device modules. This permits device modules to be written independently of the contexts in which they will be used. If we adopt this view, we can represent address translation as an explicit node in the hierarchy description. Thus, address translation is represented as a pseudo-device for which the hierarchy designer writes the device module. The information needed for address translation is maintained as the state of this pseudo-device. To accurately model the performance penalty caused by translation, this pseudo-device may make requests to other memory devices. Such requests are treated by the device modules in exactly the same way that normal access requests are treated.

3.2. Tool Design: Description and Issues

In this section we discuss the design of a tool based on the principles discussed earlier. Because of the strong conceptual interdependencies between the different parts of this design, discussion of any part of the tool in isolation is not possible. To avoid excessive forward referencing, we therefore separate the discussion into two parts: a simplified overview in section 3.2.1, followed by detailed descriptions of each aspect of the tool in section 3.2.2.

3.2.1. Overview

Section 3.1 introduced the two main components of this tool: a *hierarchy description* and a set of *device modules*. The hierarchy description serves four functions:

1. It identifies the set of device modules used in a specific simulation (analogous to type declarations in a programming language).

2. It associates names (similar to the names of variables in a programming language) with specific instantiations of device modules, and performs the actual/formal parameter bindings.

3. It specifies the interconnections between modules.

4. It indicates the statistics to be automatically maintained by the tool.

Since the hierarchy description is primarily a syntactic exercise, we defer detailed discussion of it to section 3.2.2. Figure 3-4 is an example of a hierarchy description for the simple memory hierarchy of figure 3-3—this may not, of course, be fully comprehensible at this stage of the discussion.

Communication between device modules is message-based. Messages are transmitted between *Ports* on device modules. A port is a unidirectional, finite-length queue of messages. The input ports of a device module contain

Figure 3-3. A Simple Memory Hierarchy: CPU, Cache, Main Memory.

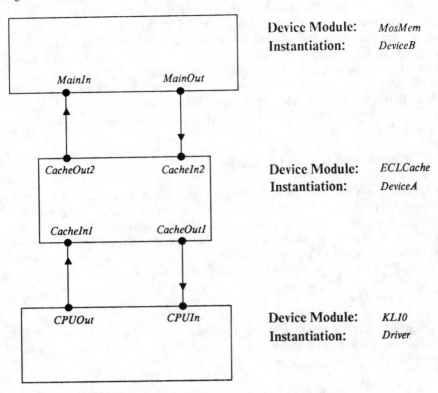

Device Module: *MosMem*
Instantiation: *DeviceB*

Device Module: *ECLCache*
Instantiation: *DeviceA*

Device Module: *KL10*
Instantiation: *Driver*

messages awaiting its attention. Its output ports contain messages awaiting transmission and are either the responses to messages received earlier or requests for action to other device modules. The inclusion of a queueing mechanism at this very basic level has two advantages:

1. Individual device modules do not have to re-implement this mechanism.

2. Queueing statistics, usually important performance measures, can be automatically collected by the simulation tool.

Real-memory devices are demand-driven: they are dormant until an external request activates them. This situation is modelled in the tool by associating a body of code and data, called an *Active Function,* with an input port. Each input port of a device module may have a different active function

Figure 3-4. The Hierarchy Description for Figure 3-3.

DeviceModules

```
        MosMem = "/usr/satya/devices/MosMem.dm";
        ECLCache = "/usr/satya/devices/ECLCache.dm";
        KL10 = "/usr/satya/drivers/KL10.dm";
```

Instantiations

```
        DeviceA: ECLCache(4096);          a 4K byte cache
        DeviceB: MosMem(1E6);  a 1 Mbyte main memory
        Driver: KL10;
```

Interconnections

```
        (Driver.CPUIn, DeviceA.CacheOut1);
        (Driver.CPUOut, DeviceA.CacheIn1);
        (DeviceA.CacheOut2, DeviceB.MainIn);
        (DeviceA.CacheIn2, DeviceB.MainOut);
```

Statistics

```
        DeviceA.CacheIn1;
        DeviceB.MainIn;
        Driver.CPUOut;
```

associated with it; one port may, however, be bound to at most one active function. When a message arrives at the head of the queue of an input port, an instantiation of the corresponding active function is created and its execution commenced. The activating message remains at the head of the queue until this instantiation terminates, or until the message is explicitly removed. An active function may be viewed as a procedure with one parameter, the activating message, which is invoked by the arrival of this message at the head of a queue. Multiple outstanding instantiations of an active function may coexist.

The ports of a device module have unique names within that module. Code inside the active functions of the module use these names to refer to the ports. Since device modules are written independently, and since a hierarchy may contain more than one instance of a specific device module, it would be unreasonable to demand that port names not be duplicated across modules. Consequently, in the hierarchy description, ports are identified by a two-component name, the first component specifying the name of the instance of a device module, and the second specifying the port name used within the module. For example, DISKA.DMAOut would be a port called DMAOut in a device module instantiated with the name DISKA.

Since a memory hierarchy is a passive entity, it has to be driven by requests from some external agency. These entities, called *driving functions,* are represented as pseudo-device modules in the tool. Section 3.2.2 discusses them in more detail.

We have, until now, avoided mention of the programming language in which device modules are coded. Any algebraic programming language such as Pascal, Simula, or ADA would be adequate. The internal state of a device is represented by variables global to all active functions in the corresponding device module. The bodies of the active functions are essentially procedure bodies in the underlying programming language. A preprocessor is used to convert port declarations and syntactic shorthand in the active functions into representations in the programming language. The specific programming language used is thus a degree of freedom left to the implementor of the tool.*

In concluding this overview, it is probably worth examining the behavior of a typical device module in response to a request, perhaps from a driving function:

> The message enters the queue of the input port of the device module connected to the output port of the driving function. It remains in the queue, advancing in FIFO order as the messages ahead of it are serviced, until it reaches the head of the queue. At this point the active function associated with this port is instantiated. This function processes the request, simulating time delays. It may make requests to other device modules by sending them messages through the output ports of this module. On receiving responses to all its outstanding requests, the active function sends a response to the originator of the message that triggered it. The active function terminates and its triggering message is destroyed. Now the device module has completed its simulation of one request. The next message in the queue gets to the head, thereby triggering another cycle of events. To simulate concurrency, an active function instantiation could remove its triggering message from the queue before it terminates.

3.2.2.   Design Details

3.2.2.1.   *Hierarchy Description.* The hierarchy description consists of four parts, each corresponding to one of the roles mentioned in section 3.2.1. The **DeviceModules** section is similar to the global-type declaration section of a programming language. It consists of a list of entries, each entry naming a device module and specifying the file where its definition can be found. The **Instantiations** section is analogous to a global-variable declaration section.

---

*Quite unintentionally, the portability of the methodology has been established within the scope of this work. The examples presented in the following chapter were created prior to an actual implementation, and use Pascal. The implementation, however, runs on Unix and supports device modules written in C.

Each entry in it names one or more instances of a device module with a particular set of actual parameter bindings. The connections between instances of device modules are specified in the **Interconnections** section. This is equivalent to specifying the edges of a graph whose nodes have been named in the **Instantiations** section. Edges may be optionally labelled for identification, and are defined by a tuple giving the source port name followed by the destination port name. Only one edge may be associated with a port. This implies that the in-degree of a node is at most equal to the number of input ports it has, while its out-degree is no more than the number of output ports in it. This restriction permits simplification in the routing of responses to messages and allows the method of handling differing data block sizes discussed in section 3.2.2.6. The **Statistics** section specifies the set of ports for which the user would like queueing statistics collected. Other implementation-dependent requests for statistics would also be placed here.

Figure 3-5 gives the BNF definition of the hierarchy description. In this definition non-terminals are italicized while terminals are in boldface. Plain text is used for prose definitions of those non-terminals whose formal definition would be impossible or confusing in BNF. The BNF, together with the description of this section, completely defines the hierarchy description. Figure 3-4 is an example of such a hierarchy description.

3.2.2.2. Device Modules. The contents of a device module must fulfil the following functions:

1. Name the device module and its formal parameters.

2. Define the communication interface between this module and its environment.

3. Represent the internal state of the device being simulated.

4. Define the active functions.

The BNF for device modules is defined in figure 3-6 and uses the same notational conventions as figure 3-5. The sections of a device module map into each of the four requirements listed above in the obvious way.

The **Port_Declaration** section identifies the ports in the module and specifies the following attributes for each:

1. Whether the port is an input port or an output port.

2. The maximum number of messages that can be queued at this port, excluding the message at the head of the queue. If this parameter is omitted, a default of zero is assumed.

Figure 3-5. BNF Definition of a Hierarchy Description.

```
HierarchyDescription  ::=
                DeviceModuleSection   InstantiationsSection   InterconnectionsSection   StatisticsSection


DeviceModuleSection  ::= DeviceModules DeviceModuleList
DeviceModuleList ::=          null | ModuleName = " FileName"; DeviceModuleList
ModuleName ::=        UniqueName
FileName ::= an implementation-dependent string identifying the file
                          containing the corresponding device module


InstantiationsSection  ::= Instantiations InstantiationList
InstantiationList ::=       null  |   ModuleInstanceList : ModuleName  ActualParmList;  InstantiationList
ModuleInstanceList ::= ModuleInstanceName   |   ModuleInstanceName , ModuleInstanceList
ModuleInstanceName  ::= UniqueName
ActualParmList  ::=  null  |  ( ParmList )
ParmList ::=          Parameter  |  Parameter , ParmList
Parameter ::= a scalar value in the underlying programming language


InterconnectionsSection  ::= Interconnections   ConnectionList
ConnectionList ::=  null  |   Connection ; ConnectionList
Connection  ::=
            Label :( ExternalPortname , ExternalPortname )  |  ( ExternalPortname , ExternalPortname )
ExternalPortname  ::= ModuleInstanceName . InternalPortname
InternalPortname ::= a UniqueName within a device module, identifying a port
Label ::= UniqueName


StatisticsSection  ::= Statistics PortList
PortList ::=          null  |   ExternalPortName ;   PortList


UniqueName ::= a unique string of letters and digits beginning with a letter
```

3.   The exact size of data quanta that may be transmitted through this
     port. If this parameter is omitted, data of arbitrary size may be
     handled. Section 3.2.2.6 discusses this parameter in more detail.

4.   The name of the response port for this port. This information is used
     to identify the responses to requests received on, or sent out of, this
     port. Section 3.2.2.7 explains this in more detail. If omitted, no
     default is assumed.

In certain cases, it may be necessary to leave the number of ports
unspecified until module instantiation time—this feature is particularly useful
in building device modules to which a variable number of identical devices
may be connected. To handle these cases, we support the notion of a *port
array*. As its name implies, a port array is a collection of ports with identical
attributes, indexed by an integer bounded by limits defined in the port array
declaration. All the elements of a port array share the same active function. A

Figure 3-6.   BNF Definition of a Device Module.

```
DeviceModule  : : =   HeaderSection   PortSection   StateSection   ProcedureSection  ActiveFnSection

HeaderSection  : : =   ModuleName : Device   FormalParms ;
ModuleName  : : =   UniqueName
FormalParms  : : =   null   |   ( FormalParmList )
FormalParmList  : : =   Parameter   |   Parameter , FormalParmList
Parameter  : : =   ParmName  :   ParmType
ParmName  : : =   a legal formal parameter name in the underlying programming language
ParmType  : : = a legal scalar type in the underlying programming language

PortSection  : : = Port_Declaration   PortList
PortList  : : =   null   |   PortDefinition   ; PortList
PortDefinition  : : =   PortIdent : ( PortType   QueuePart BlockSizePart   ResponsePart ActiveFnPart )
PortType  : : = Input   |   Output
QueuePart  : : =  null   |   , QueueLength =   positive integer
BlockSizePart  : : =   null   |   , BlockSize =   positive integer
ResponsePart  : : =  null   |   , ResponsePort =   PortName
ActiveFnPart  : : =  null   |   , ActiveFn = ActiveFnName
PortIdent  : : =   PortName [ LowerBound : UpperBound   ] | PortName
PortName  : : =   UniqueName
LowerBound  : : = integer
UpperBound  : : = integer

StateSection  : : = State _ Declaration
                            global type and variable declarations from underlying
                                            programming language

ProcedureSection  : : = Procedure _ Declaration  ProcedureList
ProcedureList  : : = null | List of procedure definitions in the programming language


ActiveFnSection  : : =   ActiveFn _ Declaration   ActiveFnList
ActiveFnList  : : =  null   |   ActiveFnDefn  ActiveFnList
ActiveFnDefn  : : =   ActiveFnName  : ActiveFn;   ActiveFnBody
ActiveFnName  : : = UniqueName
ActiveFnBody  : : =   a procedure body for a parmeterless procedure in the
                            underlying programming language, without the procedure header

UniqueName  : : = a unique string of letters and digits, starting with a letter
```

primitive function SelfPortIndex() allows an active function activation to determine the index of the port array element on which the message that triggered that activation was received. If a response port is specified for a port array, it must be of the same dimensionality as the latter. More details can be found in section 3.2.2.7.

The **State_Declaration** section is essentially the global-type and variable declaration sections of the underlying programming language. The **ActiveFn_Declaration** section defines the active functions, which are represented as parameterless procedure bodies in this programming language—the headers of these procedures are created by the simulation tool. The headers and bodies of the procedures which are called from the active function bodies are declared in the **Procedure_Declaration** section.

3.2.2.3. Message Formats. Messages are created by active functions in device modules and are sent from the output port of one device module to the input port of another. Corresponding to the two basic reasons for communication, making a request and indicating completion of service, are two types of messages: *Action Messages* and *Response Messages*. These messages differ in the fields they contain, in the way in which they affect statistics collection, and in the way certain message primitives treat them. In all other respects they are identical. Unless otherwise mentioned, the word "message" here refers to both kinds.

Each message is identified by a unique integer, its *MessageID*. This identifier is useful for routing responses and in debugging. When an active function is triggered, it acquires an *ActiveFunctionID* whose value is the same as the MessageID of the triggering message. This convention maintains and makes obvious the natural correspondence between messages and instantiations of active functions.

The causal relationship between messages and responses is indicated by the presence of a *CreatedBy* field in each message. This field identifies the active function instantiation that created it. Since the latter has the same ID as the MessageID of its triggering message, the CreatedBy field of the response has this same value too. Figure 3-7, for instance, indicates these causal relationships for a specific set of action messages and responses in a simple memory hierarchy. Nodes in the figure correspond to device modules, the arcs correspond to messages, and the numbers in parentheses indicate the MessageId and CreatedBy field values (in that order) for each message.

The complete sets of fields in action and response messages are presented in tables 3-3 and 3-4. The *Action* and *Response* fields take one of the values specified in tables 3-1 and 3-2, respectively. The *Address* field is an integer specifying an address in the device, at which the requested action is to be carried out. The *DataSize* field gives the number of bytes of data involved in the operation. For devices capable of DMA transfers, the *RemoteAddress* field specifies the remote device address to or from which data is to be transferred. The *Tag* field indicates request group membership—requests with the same tag field values are members of the same request group.

An *Empty Message* is a message in which all fields except the MessageID are zero. Such messages are used to indicate various status conditions by the simulation tool.

Note that it is not essential for an input port to have an active function associated with it. A message arriving at the head of the queue of such a port will merely remain there until the body of some active function in the module decides to receive a message from this port.

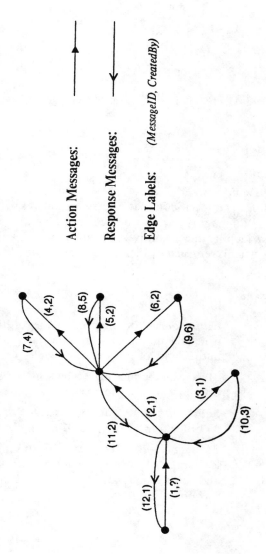

Figure 3-7. Using MessageID and CreatedBy Fields to Indicate Causality.

Action Messages:

Response Messages:

Edge Labels: *(MessageID, CreatedBy)*

Table 3-3.   Fields in an Action Message.

1. MessageId
2. CreatedBy
3. Action
4. Address
5. DataSize
6. RemoteAddress
7. Tag

Table 3-4.   Fields in a Response Message.

1. MessageId
2. CreatedBy
3. Response

3.2.2.4.   Message Primitives. This section presents the primitives provided for message handling. The specific format of these primitives will depend on the programming language in which device modules are coded. The descriptions below identify the primitives, list their parameters and their meanings, indicate what is returned by them, and explain what each primitive does.*

1. SendMessage

Parameters: *OutputPort*—the internal name of the port on which the message is to be sent. The port must be an output port of this device module.

Message—the message to be sent. This may be an action or response message.

SendType—one of two values **Blocking** or **NonBlocking.** If omitted, **Blocking** is assumed.

Result: *MessageID*—the ID created for this message. This is guaranteed to be different from the IDs of all past and future messages. A value of –1 indicates that this operation failed.

---

*Note that the tool implementation described in chapter 5 only supports the blocking version of these primitives. The parameters specifying blocking or nonblocking are therefore omitted in that implementation.

Semantics: Puts out *Message* on *Output Port* and returns the *MessageID* of the message. When the queue corresponding to *Output Port* is full, the action taken depend on the value of *SendType:* if **Blocking** is specified, the operation blocks until the queue has a free slot for this message; if NonBlocking is specified, a return code of –1 is returned immediately, without the message being queued.

2. ReceiveMessage

Parameters: *Input Port*—the name of an input port in this device module.

Receive Type—one of two values, **Blocking** and **NonBlocking**. If this parameter is omitted, **Blocking** is assumed.

Result: *Message*—the message at the head of *Input Port*. An empty message indicates that the operation failed.

Semantics: The message at the head of the queue corresponding to *Input Port* is returned as the value of this call. Note that the message is not removed from the queue. Thus, successive calls to the same input port will return the same message, unless that message is explicitly removed using the primitive **Remove-Message**. If the queue is currently empty, the action taken depends on the value of *Receive Type:* if **Blocking** is specified, the operation blocks until a message is available; if **NonBlocking** is specified, the operation terminates immediately and returns an empty message.

3. Receive Response

Parameters: *Input Port*—the name of an input port in this device module.

MessageID—the ID of an action message whose response is being awaited.

Receive Type—one of two values, **Blocking** and **NonBlocking**. If this parameter is omitted, **Blocking** is assumed.

Result: *Message*—the response message to the action message whose ID is *MessageID.* An empty message indicates that the operation failed.

Semantics: If a message in the queue corresponding to *Input Port* has a Created By field equal to *MessageID,* that message is returned as the value of this call. As in the case of **ReceiveMessage,** the message is not removed from the queue. If the queue is currently empty or if no message in the queue has the specified CreatedBy field value, the action taken depends on the value of *Receive Type:* if **Blocking** is specified, the operation blocks until the response is available; if **NonBlocking** is specified, the operation terminates immediately and returns an empty message. This primitive effectively permits non-FIFO sequencing of queue requests.

4. RemoveMessage

Parameter: *Input Port*—an input port of this device module.

Semantics: The message at the head of *Input Port,* if one exists, is removed. Blocking does not occur.

5. RemoveResponse

Parameter: *Input Port*—an input port of this device module.

    MessageID—the ID of an action message whose response is to be removed.

Semantics: If a response message to action message MessageID is present in *Input Port,* it is removed. Blocking does not occur.

6. SendResponse

Parameter: *Output Port*—an output port of this device module.

    Response—one of the values **Success, NonExistentAddress, ErrorInOperation.**

    SendType—one of two values **Blocking** or **NonBlocking.** If omitted, **Blocking** is assumed.

Semantics: A response message, with the response field set to the specified value, is created and sent to OutputPort. When the queue corresponding to *OutputPort* is full, the action taken depend on the value of *SendType:* if **Blocking** is specified, the operation blocks until the queue has a free slot for this message; if NonBlocking is specified, a return code of -1 is returned immediately, without the message being queued.

3.2.2.5.   Concatenated Queues. An output port of one device module is always connected to an input port of some other device module. Since input ports permit queueing, it may seem redundant to allow queueing at output ports as well. The need for the latter is best demonstrated by an example. Consider a device D_1, which has a port A on which it can provide concurrent service to a number of requests. Suppose that some fraction of these requests require D_1 to make requests via an output port B, to another device D_2. The input port of D_2 which is connected to B may or may not permit queueing. Consequently, the active function of D_1 that services A must be prepared to internally queue those requests which must be sent out on B. Permitting output ports to have queues simplifies the code in such active functions and, at the same time, permits the simulation tool to collect statistics on outbound requests.

Having permitted queueing at both input and output ports, it is necessary to define a semantics for such concatenated queues. Suppose an output port, A, of a device module is connected to an input port, B, of another device module. Let Q_A and Q_B be the queues at these ports, and S_A and S_B their respective maximum lengths. Figure 3-8 depicts this situation.

The view adopted here is that such a concatenation of queues behaves exactly like a single queue of size $S_A + S_B$. Neither output operations at A nor input operations at B can detect the fact that they are dealing with a concatenated queue. Thus, if Q_A and Q_B are initially empty, SendMessage operations at A cause the messages to be transmitted to B and queued there. Only when Q_B is full do messages queue up at Q_A. When a message is removed from Q_B, all the $S_B = 1$ messages left in Q_B move forward; the message at the head of Q_A is transmitted to the tail of Q_B, and the remaining S_A messages in Q_A advance too. If a SendMessage on A is blocked, it now becomes unblocked and its message joins the tail of Q_A. Similarly, if both Q_A and Q_B are empty, a ReceiveMessage or ReceiveResponse on B will be blocked until a message is sent on A; this message is transmitted to the head of Q_B immediately, thereby unblocking the blocked operation.

Figure 3-8. An Example of Concatenated Queues.

Note: Numbers indicate message slots.

Multiple blocked SendMessages or ReceiveMessages at a port are serviced in FIFO order. Multiple blocked ReceiveResponses are serviced in the order in which their awaited responses arrive.

3.2.2.6.   Disparate Block Sizes. When viewed at a sufficiently low level of detail, the data transfers from or to all memory devices occur in fixed size quanta. The magnitude of this quantum for each device is different, and depends on the data path widths and internal buffering capability of the device, and the level of abstraction at which the device is viewed.

For example, a hard-sectored disk may be logically capable of reading and writing 512-byte blocks at a time. Examined more closely, however, transfers in and out of the disk controller may be occurring on a 4-byte wide data path, with buffering in the controller. Does one represent this disk in a simulation as a device with a block size of 512 bytes or 4 bytes? The answer to this clearly depends on the accuracy of representation one is striving for. In a very accurate simulation, the overheads (in the simulated driver) of driving the disk with successive 4-byte blocks rather than one 512-byte block may be significant. This may be the case, for instance, if one wishes to examine the memory interference caused by I/O devices in a computer system. In other cases, such as simulating a file system, it may be perfectly acceptable to assume that disk transfers occur in 512-byte blocks. In cases where the mechanical characteristics of the disk dominate all other sources of performance degradation, it may even be reasonable to assume that the disk can transfer arbitrary-sized data blocks. In any case, the driver of the device must be aware of size of data blocks that may be transferred to or from that device.

The DataBlockSize parameter of an input port declaration indicates the size of data requests that may be handled via this port. Arbitrary-sized data handling capability is indicated by omitting this parameter. If a Read or Write action is requested on such a port for a DataSize value different from DataBlockSize, an ErrorInOperation response is generated by the active function for this port.

How does one provide a device module with information about the devices connected to its output ports, without making static assumptions about the memory hierarchies in which this device module may be used? A function **RemoteBlockSize** *(Output Port)* returns the DataBlockSize value of the port connected to *Output Port*. If this parameter is unspecified for the remote port, a value of –1 is returned. In the initialization phase of the simulation, device modules use this function to determine the data block sizes of their immediate neighbors. During simulation, an arbitrary-sized data transfer to a remote port with a fixed block size is done by performing an integral number of appropriately sized SendMessages and ReceiveResponses. In the disk example cited earlier, 128 successive 4-byte transfers would be used to achieve a 512-byte transfer. In general, CEILING *(Requested Data Transfer Size/Block Size of Remote Port)* transfers would have to be performed.

3.2.2.7. Simulation Statistics. There are two classes of performance measures for the components of a memory hierarchy: those applicable to all devices and those which are device-specific. Access time, for instance, is a measure which is meaningful for all memory devices. The average number of retries per operation, on the other hand, is meaningful only for devices with internal error retry capability.

The simulation tool automatically maintains statistics on a number of device-independent performance statistics. For each port specified in the **Statistics** section of the hierarchy description, the following measures are monitored:

1. The number of messages received or sent on this port.

2. The queue length distribution, and the first three moments of this distribution.

3. The waiting time distribution, and first three moments. The waiting time consists of two components: time spent in the body of the queue, and time spent at the head.

4. The service time distribution, and first three moments. The service time for a request is defined to be the time interval between the creation and termination of the active function instantiation corresponding to that request.

5. The response time distribution, and first three moments. This measure is maintained only for those ports which have a response port specified in their port declaration. The response time for a request received at an input port is taken to be the time difference between the instant at which the request arrives at this port, and the instant of departure, from the response port, of the first message whose CreatedBy field has the same value as the MessageID field of the request. In the case of an output port, the response time for an outbound request is the time interval between the queueing of the request at that port and the removal from the response port, of the first message whose CreatedBy field has the same value as the MessageID field of the request.

A port array and its response port, if specified, must have the same dimensionality—each port array element and its response port array element will have the same index.

For all device modules in the system, the simulation tool maintains the device utilization measure. This quantity is defined to be the fraction of total simulated time for which the device was busy servicing a request. It is equal to the fraction of simulated time for which at least one active function instantiation existed for this device.

For statistics other than those discussed above, the writer of a device module must include code for data collection in the active functions. The **Initialize** phase of the simulation, described in section 3.2.2.8, may be used to initialize the data structures for collecting performance measures; the reporting of this data is done in the **Terminate** phase, using the I/O facilities of the underlying programming language. By periodically writing out performance data on specially named ports of each device module and connecting these ports to suitable graphical interfaces, a dynamic picture of an ongoing simulation may be obtained.

3.2.2.8. Phases of Simulation. There are five clearly identifiable steps in the simulation process:

1. Establishing the internal consistency of all device modules.
2. Initiating the driving functions.
3. Performing the simulation.
4. Terminating the driving and quiescing the state of device modules.
5. Reporting simulation statistics.

The simulation tool operates in three phases: **Initialize, Simulate,** and **Terminate.** The transition from **Initialize** to **Simulate** occurs when the driving functions are initiated, while the transition from **Simulate** to **Terminate** occurs when the quiescing of the system is complete.

Each device module may have two distinguished input ports, with names **InitializePort** and **TerminatePort,** respectively. A driving function must, in addition, have an input port called **StartDrive.** Testing for the end of simulation is done by calling a system-provided Boolean function, **DoSimulate.** This function returns True as long as simulation is to continue and False when the simulation is to be terminated. The value returned by **DoSimulate** is altered by calling the function **TerminateSimulation**—after the first call to the latter function, **DoSimulate** will always return False. Both functions are available to all the device modules in the system.

With the control mechanism defined above, the simulation proceeds in the following manner:

1. An empty message is sent by the runtime system to all ports with the name **InitializePort.** The corresponding active functions are instantiated, and perform whatever initialization is necessary in their respective device modules. During this phase, messages may neither be sent nor received. This restriction prevents device modules from being caught in an inconsistent internal state. When all instantiated active functions terminate, the **Initialize** phase of the simulation comes to an end.

2. An empty message is sent to all ports in the system with the name **StartDrive.** The corresponding active function instantiations now start generating requests. The **Simulate** phase is now operative. The bodies of these active functions typically consist of a loop with a test of **DoSimulate** and a loop body to generate a request with a certain interarrival time. As long as **DoSimulate** returns True, the driving functions generate requests and simulation proceeds.

3. Based on suitable stopping criteria, some device module in the system calls **TerminateSimulation.** This may also occur when a preset simulation time limit expires. **DoSimulate** now returns False if called, and all driving functions fall out of their request generating loops. Since no further external requests are being presented to the memory hierarchy, the system slowly quiesces. When no active function instantiations exist, the system enters the **Terminate** phase.

4. An empty message is sent to all ports called **TerminatePort.** The reporting of user-defined statistics is now done by the active functions corresponding to these ports. When all such active functions terminate, system-defined statistics are reported and the simulation is complete.

4

Examples of Memory Devices
and Hierarchies

As its title indicates, this chapter illustrates the principles discussed in chapter 3 by presenting a variety of examples. In applying the methodology described in that chapter to a wide spectrum of memory devices and hierarchies, our aim is to substantiate the following claims:

- The separation of hierarchy-dependent information from device-dependent information is both possible and useful.

- The methodology is quite general in scope, and may be used in analyzing many different memory devices and hierarchies.

- The methodology proposes a level of abstraction, the device module, that is of significant use to the designer of a memory hierarchy.

The chapter is divided into two parts. The first part discusses a number of memory devices and develops device modules for them; the second part describes a number of nontrivial memory hierarchies and shows how the device modules of the first section may be used to build simulation models for these hierarchies. The code for the device modules also illustrates many aspects of the tool described in section 3.2.

4.1. Memory Devices

In this section we examine memory devices from various points in the space/cost/capacity design space. The discussion of each device is split into two parts: one describing the general characteristics of the device and the assumptions made in modelling it, the other discussing features of interest in the corresponding device module. In the interest of brevity we refrain from presenting actual code for device modules, except in sections 4.1.1 and 4.1.2.

Two simplifications have been made in presenting the code for the device modules. In cases where the body of a procedure would be long but straightforward, only the procedure header and semantic specification of the procedure are given. Many performance constants are embedded in the code rather than being defined as instantiation parameters.

The code for the device modules is formatted using the following conventions:

1. The underlying programming language is Pascal-like, with simple extensions where convenient. Since the methodology is language-independent, there is no loss of generality in using such a hypothetical language or in being loose about its syntax.

2. The keywords of the language (such as **if, then, begin**) are in boldface. Syntactic terms defined in chapter 3 (such as **ErrorInOperation, ResponsePort, QueueLength**) are also specified in boldface.

3. Built-in functions and predicates, as well as identifiers associated with the language runtime support or the simulation tool, are specified in small capitals. Examples are AND, GEQ, and RECEIVE MESSAGE.

4. Comments and labels for identifying the block structure are in italics.

5. Semaphores are used for synchronization of active function instantiations. The declaration of a semaphore has two parameters: its maximum value and its initial value. Starting from the initial value, each P on a semaphore decrements its current count until 0. An active function that now does a P on this semaphore enters a FIFO queue associated with the semaphore. A V on a semaphore increments its current count by one (up to the maximum value), and releases the first enqueued active function.

4.1.1.   Core Memory

4.1.1.1.   Description. The first memory device we discuss is a dual-ported* core memory unit, with differing cycle and access times. One connection to the device is a high-priority connection, intended for DMA accesses by I/O devices; the other is a low-priority connection for servicing CPU requests. Service to requests is non-preemptive: once a low-priority request is being serviced, no high-priority service can preempt it. However, as long as there are outstanding high-priority requests, they are serviced before any outstanding low-priority requests. Figure 4-1 illustrates the external connections to the device module for this device.

---

*The word "port" is used here in an electrical sense, rather than in the sense of chapter 3.

Figure 4-1. External Interface for Core Memory Device Module.

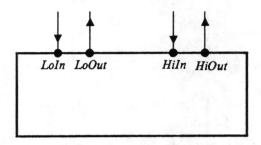

The differing cycle and access times imply that a device module for this device has to maintain, as state, the time of initiation of the last cycle. Service to a new request is delayed until the completion of the previous cycle. A write request is responded to as soon as the address decoding is complete. Read requests, however, are delayed by the access time before they are responded to.

In typical memory units of this type, accesses to and from the unit occur in chunks wider than a single byte. We refer to the width of this chunk as the *Data Width* of the device. With a data width of D, an address in the range 0 to $D - 1$ would access all the bytes in this range; an address in D to $2D - 1$ would access all the bytes in this range; and so on. Often the data width is chosen to be equal to the word width of the CPU. In a computer system with a 32-bit CPU, for instance, the data width of the main memory units would be 4. Since the machine instructions and the operands of a CPU are often whole words rather than single bytes, this grouping together of consecutive bytes reduces the number of accesses that have to be made to main memory.

Many mainframe computer systems use interleaving as a technique to increase effective memory bandwidth. When low-order interleaving of degree N is used (N invariably being a power of two), the integer defined by the low-order $\log_2 N$ bits of an address is used to index one of a set of N identical memory units. The set of addresses is thus uniformly distributed among the N different memory units. For many typically observed memory access patterns, the probability of accessing a specific memory unit is then close to $1/N$. Consequently, the effective cycle time of the interleaved set of memory units is about $1/N$ the cycle time of each individual unit. A detailed discussion of the performance enhancement achieved by interleaving can be found in Rau [79].

How are addresses presented to the set of memory units mapped into physical locations in these units? Suppose M_0, M_1, $\cdots$, M_{N-1} is a linear ordering of N identical memory units, each of size S and data width D. We assume that S is a multiple of D and that $Max = S$ DIV D. Then the assignment of addresses to memory units would be as indicated in table 4-1. The mapping

Table 4-1.   Address Assignment in an Interleaved Memory System.

M_0		M_1		M_{N-1}	
$0, 1, 2, \ldots$	$D-1$	$D, D+1, \ldots$	$2D-1$	$(N-1)D, \ldots$	$ND-1$
$ND, ND+1, \ldots$	$(N+1)D-1$	$(N+1)D, \ldots$	$(N+2)D-1$	$(2N-1)D, \ldots$	$2ND-1$
$\ldots\ldots$	$\ldots\ldots$	$\ldots\ldots$	$\ldots\ldots$	$\ldots\ldots$	$\ldots\ldots$
$(Max-1)ND \ldots$	$((Max-1)N+1)D-1$	$\ldots\ldots$		$(MaxN-1)D, \ldots$	$MaxND-1$

is thus characterized by four parameters: the size S, the data width D, the interleave factor N, and the index of each memory unit in the linear ordering. These four quantities are referred to by the names *Size*, *DataWidth*, *IFactor*, and *IOffset* in the code presented later in this section. In general, the set of addresses corresponding to a memory unit is defined by X_k, $X_k + 1, \cdots, X_k + $ DataWidth $- 1$, where $X_k = (k \times IFactor + IOffset) \times$ DataWidth, for integral values of k in the range 0 to Size DIV DataWidth -1.

4.1.1.2. The Device Module. The device module for this core memory has two pairs of ports: an input/output pair to be connected to a source of low-priority requests, and a similar pair for high-priority requests. Some of the interesting features of this module are:

- The use of parameters for size, cycle, and access times, and data width, as well as for describing the interleaving environment in which this unit is instantiated.

- The use of semaphores for resolving contention between high- and low-priority ports.

- Specification of block sizes and response ports.

- Use of a procedure common to two active functions.

- The use of the Initialize active function for variable initialization.

The code for the device module is shown in figure 4-2.

4.1.2. A Set-Associative Cache

4.1.2.1. Description. This section presents the device module for a set-associative cache memory, parameterized both in its physical characteristics and in its logical organization. Figure 4-3 depicts the external connections to this device module. The pair of ports CPUOut and CPUIn are for communication with a driver, typically a processor. MainIn and MainOut are ports for communication with the next lower level in the memory hierarchy, typically a MOS or core main memory unit.

Figure 4-4 illustrates the organization of a canonical set-associative cache with K sets and N entries per set. As in the case of main memory in section 4.1.1, accesses to the cache are often for a number of adjacent bytes rather than a single byte. Consequently, the entries in the cache store a number of consecutive bytes; this number is called the *Line Width L*, and is an instantiation parameter of the device module. To simplify computations, the number of sets K, the size of each set N, and the line width L are invariably

Figure 4-2. Code for the Device Module of Section 4.1.1.2.

```
CoreMemory: Device (Size, IFactor, IOffset, DataWidth: integer;
                                    CycleTime, AccessTime: real);

begin CoreMemory

    Port - Declaration
        LoIn: (Input, BlockSize=DataWidth, ResponsePort=LoOut,
                                            ActiveFn=LoActive);
        LoOut: (Output, BlockSize=DataWidth);
        HiIn: (Input, BlockSize=DataWidth, ResponsePort=HiOut,
                                            ActiveFn=HiActive);
        HiOut: (Output, BlockSize=DataWidth);

    State - Declaration
        LastTime: real;            Time of initiation of last access.
        IsBusy(1,1): semaphore;    Provides mutual exclusion between low
                                            and high priority ports.
        NoMoreHighs(1,0): semaphore;      Ensures non-preemptive priority
                                    access between high and low priority ports.


    Procedure - Declaration
        procedure HandleMessage(WhichMessage: Request; WhichPort:OutPort);

        Checks that WhichMessage is a valid request for this instantiation of the
        the device, and if so, presents a success response on WhichPort. If the
        address presented does not belong to this instantiation, a NonExistentAddress
        response is sent on WhichPort. If the quantity of data mentioned in
        WhichMessage differs from DataWidth, an ErrorInOperation is sent
        on WhichPort. Requests for actions other than Read and Write are
        responded to successfully, without any other checking.

        begin HandleMessage
        x: integer;

        if (WhichMessage.Action NEQ Read) AND
                        (WhichMessage.Action NEQ Write)
        then  SENDRESPONSE(WhichPort, Success)
        else
            if (WhichMessage.DataSize NEQ DataWidth)
            then SENDRESPONSE(WhichPort, ErrorInOperation)
            else
                if (WhichMessage.Address < 0) OR
                    (WhichMessage.Address DIV DataWidth) DIV IFactor >
                        (Size DIV DataWidth) DIV IFactor OR
                    ((WhichMessage.Address DIV DataWidth) MOD IFactor)
                            NEQ IOffset
                then
                    begin
                    Delay(a delay to account for address checking);
                    SENDRESPONSE(WhichPort, NonExistentAddress);
                    end
                else
                    begin the good case
                    x := TIME;
                    if (x - LastTime) < CycleTime
                    then Delay(CycleTime - x + LastTime);
                    LastTime := TIME;
                    if WhichMessage.Action = Read
                    then Delay(AccessTime);
                    SENDRESPONSE(WhichPort, Success);
                    end the good case;

        end HandleMessage;
```

Figure 4-2.   (concluded)

ActiveFn – Declaration

```
Initialize: ActiveFn;
    begin Initialize
    LastTime := -MAXREAL;    approximation to minus infinity
    end; Initialize


HiActive: ActiveFn;
    begin
    InMsg: Request;

    P(IsBusy);           indicate seizure of resource
    InMsg := RECEIVEMESSAGE(HiIn);     acquire the triggering message
    HandleMessage(InMsg, HiOut);         take care of it
    REMOVEMESSAGE(HiIn);         remove oneself
    if IsEmpty(HiIn)
    then V(NoMoreHighs);          allow one waiting low priority request in
    V(IsBusy);        release resource
    end HiActive;

LoActive: ActiveFn;
    begin
    InMsg: Request;
    if NOT IsEmpty(HiIn)
    then P(NoMoreHighs);          await emptying of high priority queue

    P(IsBusy);
    InMsg := RECEIVEMESSAGE(LoIn);
    HandleMessage(InMsg, LoOut);
    V(IsBusy);
    end LoActive;
end CoreMemory;
```

Figure 4-3.   External Interface for Cache Device Module.

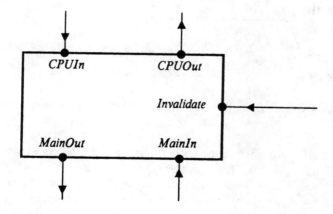

Figure 4-4.   Logical Organization of a Set-Associative Cache.

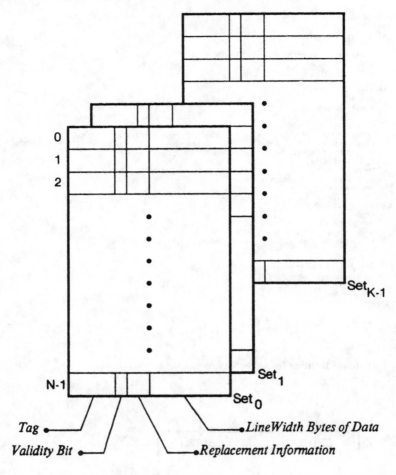

Tag

Validity Bit

Line Width Bytes of Data

Replacement Information

powers of two—the device module assumes that this is the case. The number of entries per set, N, is then related to the total cache size S, by $N = (S \text{ DIV } K) \text{ DIV } L$.

Associated with each cache entry is a validity bit indicating whether this entry is in use, and a tag field containing the starting address of the line of bytes held in this entry. For each possible address that may be presented to the cache, there is only one entry in each set where the data corresponding to this address may lie. Each such entry is called a *legal cache slot* for that address, and its index I_{Legal} in each set is given by $I_{Legal} = (\text{Address DIV } L) \text{ MOD } N$. To check for a cache hit, the tag field of the legal cache slot in every set has to be compared to the requested address. These comparisons are done in parallel by associative lookup hardware in the cache.

Read and write requests are treated in slightly different ways by the cache. A hit on a read request results in a response after a delay accounting for local access. A miss on read causes a legal cache slot to be selected for replacement, the algorithm used for this being an instantiation parameter of the device module. The required data is read from the device connected to the MainIn/MainOut ports and the original request responded to. This data is then filled into the cache slot chosen for replacement. Three possible replacement algorithms are provided for in the device module:

1. A Random replacement algorithm, which picks at random from the set of legal cache slots.

2. A FIFO algorithm, which picks the legal cache slot that was filled the earliest.

3. An LRU algorithm, which picks the legal cache slot that was least recently accessed.

A field in each cache entry contains the information needed by the replacement algorithm.

A miss on a Write causes no updating of the cache—the request is merely forwarded to the device on MainIn/MainOut, and the latter's response is conveyed back to the requestor. The behavior on a hit on Write depends on the parameter UpdateAlgorithm, which can take two values: *WriteThrough* and *WriteBack*. If WriteThrough is specified, a request is made to the device on MainIn/MainOut to write the same data at the same address, thus guaranteeing that there is never any data inconsistency between that device and the cache. If WriteBack is specified, the cache slot is merely marked as being *Dirty*—no actual writing to the MainIn/MainOut device is done. Only when a dirty cache slot is selected for replacement are its contents written back to the device on MainIn/MainOut. There is thus the possibility of temporary inconsistencies between the data in that device and the cache.

In a multiprocessor system, a write to memory by one processor must be made visible to all the processors in the system. This is trivially accomplished in the case of main memory since it is shared by all the processors. However, since caches are local to each processor, it is necessary to ensure that copies of the written data item in all other caches are invalidated. For this purpose, the device module has a port named Invalidate. When a write request is made on this port, the entry corresponding to this address, if present in the cache, is marked as being invalid. Because of consistency problems, WriteBack caches are seldom used in multiprocessor systems. Consequently, the device module does not attempt to correctly handle Invalidate requests in a WriteBack cache.

*4.1.2.2.   Device Module.** Since the number of sets is an instantiation parameter, the multidimensional array representation suggested by figure 4-3 is inconvenient to implement in most programming languages. Instead, the device module uses a single array and logically partitions it into sets. The variable TestSlot corresponds to the index of a legal cache slot, while CorrectSlot corresponds to its index in the array representation. There are as many CorrectSlot values for each TestSlot value as there are sets in the cache.

For the FIFO and LRU replacement algorithms, there has to be a way of indicating the relative times at which different cache entries were filled or accessed. The device module does this by keeping a count of the accesses made to it; since this is a monotonically increasing quantity, it can be used to timestamp the cache entry accesses. An actual timestamp could, of course, be used but would be relatively more expensive.

Other interesting aspects of this device module are:

- Parameterization of the physical characteristics as well as the behavior of the cache. This is handled by conditional executable code here, but conditional compilation could be used if compilation is deferred until instantiation time. The advantage of doing this is that the code would be more compact and efficient.

- Collection of device-specific statistics, in this case the hit ratios on reads and writes as well as the overall hit ratio.

- The use of the special active functions Initialize and Terminate to establish the values of some variables as well as for device-specific data collection.

- The assumption that the device connected to the MainIn/MainOut ports may have a fixed block size. This block size is determined in the initialization sequence and is used by procedure MainAccess to decide the number of iterations to perform in transferring data to or from that device.

- Use of the semaphore CacheBusy to ensure mutual exclusion between requests on the ports CPUIn and Invalidate.

- The presence of an input port MainIn without an associated active function—responses to requests on MainOut are explicitly removed from MainIn by procedure MainAccess.

---

*The code for this device is given in appendix A.

4.1.3. A Translation Buffer for Virtual Memory

4.1.3.1.   Description. A translation buffer (TB) is an associative memory used to speed up references to page table entries (PTEs) in a paged virtual memory system. A subset of the entries in the page table of the process currently executing on a CPU is present in the TB of that CPU. To translate a virtual address, the TB is first queried. If the PTE corresponding to this address is present there, the translation is completed using it; otherwise, the PTE is fetched from main memory, entered into the TB, and the translation then performed. If no free slots are available, the entering of a PTE into the TB will involve replacing an existing PTE. When the page table is altered, the TB has to be altered to maintain consistency: this may involve changing just a single entry, or clearing the entire TB. The latter event typically occurs when a process executing on a CPU is replaced by a process with a different page table. Since a TB is made with much faster technology than main memory and is physically closer to the CPU, significant performance improvements can be expected by its use in a virtual memory system. A more detailed discussion of translation buffers can be found in the work of Satyanarayanan [81b].

In view of the similarity in function between caches and TBs, it may be tempting to construct a device module for a generic set-associative device, capable of modelling a cache or a TB depending on the choice of values for instantiation parameters. Unfortunately a sufficient number of small, but important, differences render such an approach inadvisable—the hypothetical generic device module would have a large number of instantiation parameters and rather complicated code. Some of these differences are:

- On a miss, the address presented to the TB cannot be directly forwarded to main memory. The location of the origin of the page table in memory has to be used as a base, and the page number corresponding to the address to be translated used as an index into that table. Since the location of the page table may change dynamically (process switches may occur, for instance), it cannot be made an instantiation parameter. In a cache, this problem does not arise since the address presented to the cache can be used unchanged in accessing main memory.

- There is no notion of line width in a TB. Each TB slot corresponds to a PTE, and all the bytes in it must be returned if a hit occurs. The size of each entry defines the number of addressable pages.

- The frequency of modification of PTEs is much lower than the frequency of modification of data in a cache. Since WriteBack update algorithms enhance performance significantly only when Writes are frequent, the added hardware complexity and expense is unwarranted in the case of TBs. The device module therefore assumes that all modifications to the TB entries are also made immediately to the page table in main memory.

- In a multiprocessor system, the page tables of the processes executing in different processors are usually disjoint. Consequently, modifications made by a processor to its page table will not invalidate the information in the TBs of the other processors. Even if processors share the same page table, the frequency of page table modifications is usually low enough to make it feasible to maintain the consistency of the TBs by explicit actions by the processors. For example, when one processor modifies a PTE, it can impart this information to other processors via an interprocessor interrupt. Each interrupted processor can then invalidate the modified entry, if present, in its TB. In view of these considerations, the device module for the TB does not have an invalidate port associated with it, unlike the cache device module of appendix A.

In view of these differences we treat a translation buffer as a separate kind of device module, rather than as a special case of a cache device module.

4.1.3.2. Device Module. Figure 4-5 presents the external interface of the device module for a TB. The pair of ports AddrIn/ PTEOut are intended for communication with an address translation module. The organization of the TB is similar to that of the cache in figure 4-4. The PageSize parameter is used to determine the mapping from addresses to legal TB slots, which are similar to the legal cache slots discussed in section 4.1.2.1. In a TB of set associativity A and size S, the number of slots per set, K, is related to the PTESize, ρ, by the relation $K = (S \text{ DIV } \rho) \text{ DIV } A$. With a page size P, the index I_{Legal} of a legal TB slot for an address α is then given by $I_{Legal} = (\alpha \text{ DIV } P) \text{ MOD } K$. When a read request is received on port AddrIn, the TB examines all the legal slots for that address. After a delay to account for the lookup, a response of **Success** (in case of a hit), or **NonExistentAddress** (in case of a miss) is sent on port PTEOut. In the latter case, the address translation module is expected to look up the corresponding entry in main memory and enter it into the TB. On a write request, one of the legal slots corresponding to the address is selected and filled; if no empty legal slots are available, an LRU algorithm is used to select a legal slot for overwriting. The scheme for keeping track of LRU information is the same as that described in section 4.1.2.2. A Locate request with a negative address invalidates all the entries in the TB, while a positive address invalidates only the entry corresponding to that address, if present in the TB.

Figure 4-5.   External Interface of Translation Buffer Device Module.

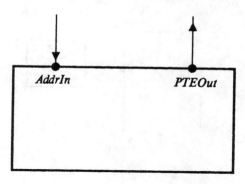

4.1.4.   A Disk Subsystem with Controller and Cache

4.1.4.1.   Description. In this section we describe a versatile device module, capable of modelling a wide family of moving head disk systems. As figure 4-6 depicts, a typical member of the family consists of a disk controller attached to a number of disks and an optional disk cache. The disk cache itself is outside the system being modelled and has to be represented by a suitable device module in a hierarchy description. To simplify the code, the device module assumes a cache with only one pair of ports, such as the translation buffer of section 4.1.3, rather than the more sophisticated cache model of section 4.1.2 which automatically generates a fill request in case of a miss. Though intended for an entirely different purpose, the translation buffer module of section 4.1.3.2 would serve as a suitable cache module, if instantiated with a PageSize equal to the sector size of the disk. Merely omitting the cache results in a conventional disk system. Modelling a single disk without a cache is also easily done by suitably instantiating this device module.

The controller is assumed to have enough internal buffer space to concurrently service up to twice as many requests as there are disks. The number two is arbitrary and may be made an instantiation parameter to obtain greater generality. Data transfers in and out of the system are assumed to occur on a device, called the *DMA Device,* which is distinct from the originator of requests. This reflects the typical situation where disk activity is initiated by a CPU, but data transfers actually occur by DMA to main memory. The more special case of the originator of requests also receiving the data is easily handled by suitably specifying the connections in the hierarchy description. Requests presented to the disk subsystem specify the address in the DMA device to or from which data is to be transferred.

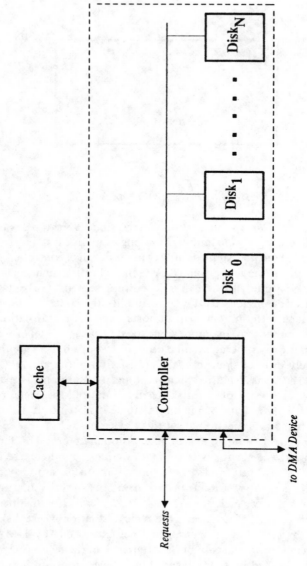

Figure 4-6. A Disk Subsystem with a Cache.

Note: Dotted line indicates boundary of system modelled.

The controller is used only in the initial and final processing of a request. Both these operations take a certain amount of controller time, specifiable at instantiation time. In between these phases of a request, while disk service is being awaited, the controller is free to service other requests. The specific sequence of events which occur when a request is serviced depends on the action requested, as described below:

Read   When the controller is free, it turns its attention to this request. The cache, if present, is checked, and if a hit occurs, the request is successfully terminated after transferring the requested sector to the DMA device. An error in cache access is treated as a cache miss, while an error in data transfer to the DMA device is reported to the originator of the request. If a cache miss occurs, or if no cache is present, the request is queued for service by the addressed disk. The controller is now free to service other requests. When the disk service is complete, this request again awaits the attention of the controller. Then data transfers to the DMA device and to the cache are performed concurrently. Errors in either of these operations are handled as mentioned earlier. This request has now been serviced fully.

Write   On acceptance for service by the controller, the data to be written is read from the DMA device. Errors in this operation terminate the request. If a cache is present, this data is written into it. Errors in this operation are ignored. The write request is then scheduled for the appropriate disk drive and the controller freed. On completion of disk service, the controller again attends to this request and sends a success response to the requestor. If read-after-write error checking were to be incorporated in the model, a read request for this data would have to be simulated at this point. For simplicity this is omitted from the code. The request is now complete.

Locate   When the controller is free to attend to this request it checks the cache, if present, for the requested data. On a hit, the request is successfully terminated. Otherwise the controller is freed and disk service awaited. The head of this disk is then moved to the desired cylinder, and if a cache is present, the addressed data is read into a buffer in the controller and the latter's attention awaited. The controller fills the cache, if present, with the data just read. If no cache is present, the **Locate** operation is merely a Seek operation. The request is now terminated.

An intelligent disk system, capable of batching requests and scheduling them to meet some objective function could be represented in this model, at the cost of additional complexity in the code.

Addresses presented to this system have the format shown in figure 4-7. Transfers to and from the disk are exactly one sector long—the byte offset field in the figure is only a convenience which allows addresses to be directly passed to byte-oriented caches.

4.1.4.2.   Device Module. Figure 4-8 illustrates the external connections to the device module for the disk subsystem. Requests for disk activity are presented on port ExternalIn, and responses to them are sent on ExternalOut. The cache, if present, is connected to the CacheOut/CacheIn pair of ports. DataIn/DataOut are the ports to which the DMA device is connected.

The features of interest in this device module are:

- There is a significant amount of concurrent activity being modelled. A semaphore on the controller, and semaphores on each disk ensure synchronization amidst this concurrency. The limitation on the available concurrency is enforced by ensuring that the number of requests in service is never greater than twice the number of disks present.

- Initialization and termination active functions are used to obtain information about devices connected to ports and about block sizes of devices, to establish random initial conditions for the disks, and for statistics collection.

- Device-specific statistics, the waiting and service times of the controller and disks, are collected in the device module.

- The actual data transfer occurs to or from a device other than the requestor. This requires the requestor to specify two addresses: the disk address, as well as the address on the DMA device. The latter is specified using the RemoteAddress field of the request message.

- There is a significant amount of total state, and the computation of time delays is non-trivial. Seek times, latency, queueing delays, and contention for the disks and controller are taken into account. The **Locate** operation is quite interesting, especially in the presence of a cache.

- The ExternalIn/ExternalOut queues have nonzero queue lengths. However, unless the disk system is heavily overloaded, most of the queueing will occur internally, at the disks.

Figure 4-7. Format of Address for Disk Subsystem.

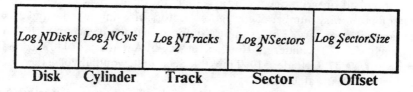

$Log_2 NDisks$	$Log_2 NCyls$	$Log_2 NTracks$	$Log_2 NSectors$	$Log_2 SectorSize$
Disk	**Cylinder**	**Track**	**Sector**	**Offset**

Note: Italic indicates field width in bits. Boldface indicates purpose of field.

Figure 4-8. External Connections to Device Module for Disk
Subsystem.

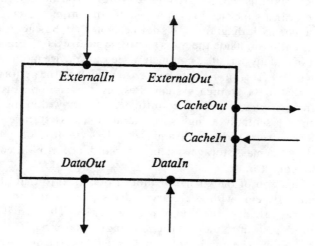

4.1.5. A Cartridge-Based Mass Storage System

4.1.5.1. Description. Having examined devices from the primary, secondary, and cache levels of the memory hierarchy, it is now appropriate to turn our attention to archival storage. The device we present here uses tape cartridges as the principal storage media, and is loosely modelled after the IBM 3850 Mass Storage System [Harris75, Misra81]. The logical organization and details of operation are, however, not necessarily the same in the two systems.

Externally, this device appears as a large collection of disks to and from which sector-level random access is possible. In fact, the request/response characteristics of this system are virtually identical to those of the canonical disk subsystem of section 4.1.4. The addressing structure here is identical to the one depicted in figure 4-7. The only difference is that, whereas that device could only read or write one sector at a time, the device presented here can transfer an arbitrary number of contiguous sectors, crossing cylinder and disk boundaries if necessary. For example, suppose that the device models 128 disks, each with 512 cylinders of 16 64-sector tracks. A request for 1102 sectors starting at Disk 37, Cylinder 510, Track 14, Sector 60, would involve the disk sectors specified in table 4-2.

This large virtual disk address space is realized using a small number of actual disks, called *Staging Disks,* a *Cartridge Repository* for storing tape cartridges not in active use, a few *Read/Write Stations* (RW stations) for cartridges, and a mechanical *Accessor Arm* capable of moving cartridges between the RW stations and the cartridge repository. The mechanical aspects of this device bear a superficial resemblance to an automated tape library. Figure 4-9 is a schematic diagram of this device. Note that the staging disks are represented as entities outside the mass storage system, even though they are logically part of it. This permits a completely separate device module, such as the disk subsystem of section 4.1.4, to be used in modelling the performance of this part of the mass storage system. Besides the components already mentioned are a *Controller,* which coordinates activity within the device, a *Buffer,* which is essentially a high-speed random-access storage device, a *Requestor,* which drives this system, and a *DMA Device* to/from which data is transferred by the mass storage system, in accordance with the commands issued by the requestor.

The organization of the virtual memory is identical to that of a paged virtual memory system, with the staging disks playing the role of main memory and the cartridges the role of paging storage. The virtual disks are identical in every respect to the real (i.e., staging) disks, except that there are far fewer of the latter. The number of cylinders per disk, the number of tracks per cylinder, the number of sectors per track, and the sector size are identical in the real and virtual disks. The granularity of the virtual/real address mapping is a cylinder: virtual disk–cylinder pairs are mapped into real disk–cylinder pairs. This mapping is performed by the controller using tables maintained by it internally. The specific mapping algorithm used is immaterial to this discussion; all that is necessary is to note the existence of the following capabilities:

Look Up   Given a virtual address, obtain the corresponding real address, if any.

Inv Look Up   Given a real address, obtain the corresponding virtual address, if any.

Enter Mapping Enter a new virtual/real mapping.

Table 4-2.   Example of a Request Traversing Cylinder and Disk Boundaries.

Disk No.	Cyl. No.	Track No.	Sector(s)
37	510	14	60
37	510	14	61
•	•	•	•
•	•	•	•
37	510	14	63
37	510	15	0 to 63
37	511	0	0 to 63
37	511	1	0 to 63
37	511	2	0 to 63
•	•	•	•
•	•	•	•
•	•	•	•
37	511	15	0 to 63
38	0	0	0 to 9

GetFreeCyl   Obtain a real address to map a virtual address on. This may involve invoking a replacement algorithm. We leave this algorithm unspecified here, but provide the following routines in connection with it:

> *NoteAccess*   Indicate that a given virtual address has just been used. This is for use by LRU-style replacement algorithms.
>
> *IsDirty*   Check if a given real cylinder has been modified since it was first bound to its current virtual address.
>
> *MakeDirty*   Indicate that a given real cylinder has been modified.

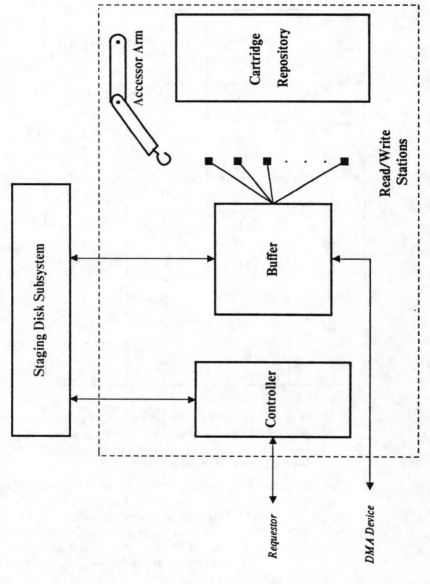

Figure 4-9. Organization of a Cartridge-based Mass Storage System.

Note: Dotted lines indicate boundary of system modelled.

The last two routines are used in implementing a write-back replacement scheme—a real cylinder selected for replacement has to be written back to the corresponding cartridges only if it has been modified (i.e., "dirtied") since it was copied from the cartridges to staging disks. Once a particular virtual cylinder is on a staging disk, no cartridge actions are needed to read or write that cylinder.

Each cartridge contains the images of an integral number of disk cylinders, and each cylinder image may be read or written independently of others on the same cartridge. Figure 4-10 illustrates the organization of data on a single cartridge.

A virtual disk is mapped onto an integral number of cartridges; this mapping is static and is determined by the disk and cartridge ids. If there are K cylinders per cartridge, and N cylinders per disk, the number of cartridges per disk, C, is given by CEILING (N/K). The mapping from disks to cartridges is then given by table 4-3.

Cartridges may be moved between a RW station and the repository in a constant amount of time by the accessor arm; direct movement of cartridges between RW stations is not possible. The time to read a cylinder image from a cartridge already located at a RW station consists of two parts. The first includes the time taken to move the tape so that the start of the desired cylinder image is at the RW head. This is itself made up of two subcomponents: (1) The time to initiate motion, which is a constant. (2) Time proportional to the number of cylinders between the current and desired head positions. The second part consists of the time taken to read/write the cylinder image. This is assumed to be a constant.

All transfers use the buffer either as the source or the destination. The possible transfers are those between the buffer and a staging disk, a cartridge on a RW station, or the DMA device.

External requests are for a number of contiguous virtual sectors. Internally, requests are handled a cylinder at a time, i.e., the virtual/real address mapping, accessing of the cartridge repository and/or the staging disks, and transfers to the DMA device are performed cylinder by cylinder. Partial cylinder transfers to the staging disk and to the DMA device may occur for the first and last cylinders involved in a request. Depending on the specific request, the following actions occur for each cylinder in the data transfer:

Read   If already present on the staging disk, this cylinder is read to the buffer, and from there to the DMA device. If not present on the staging disk, the data is transferred from a cartridge to the buffer and from there to the staging disk as well as the DMA device. If the cylinder chosen for replacement on the staging disk is dirty, it will have to be copied back to a cartridge via the buffer.

Figure 4-10. Organization of Data on a Tape Cartridge.

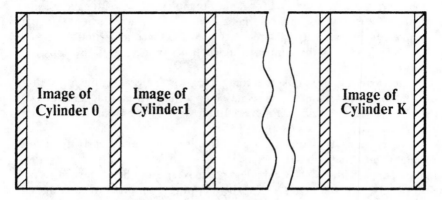

Note: Hatched region indicates head position prior to reading corresponding cylinder.

Table 4-3. Mapping of Virtual Disk Addresses to Cartridges.

Virt. Disk No.	Cyl. Nos.	Cartridge No.
0	0 to (K-1)	0
0	K to (2K-1)	1
•	•	•
•	•	•
0	(C-1)K to N	C-1
1	0 to (K-1)	C
•	•	•
•	•	•
1	(C-1)K to N	2C-1
•	•	•
•	•	•

Write   The data to be written is obtained from the DMA device and placed in the buffer. If only part of a cylinder is to be written, and that cylinder is not present on the staging disk, it is obtained from a cartridge. The cylinder is then written to the staging disk. If the existing real cylinder is dirty and is to be replaced, it has to be written back to a cartridge via the buffer.

Locate   A locate operation merely ensures that the desired cylinder is on the staging disk. It is thus identical to a **Read**, except that no data is transferred to the DMA device.

This system tries to maintain a high level of concurrency in the servicing of requests. Within limits dictated by the amount of available buffer space and RW stations, requests are serviced in parallel. One RW station and three cylinder-sized buffer regions are statically bound to each request in service, from its initiation to its termination. To ensure consistency, the virtual and real addresses involved in a data transfer can be locked. The locks are at the granularity of a cylinder and are held for the appropriate iteration of a cylinder-by-cylinder data transfer. Note that these locks are only for maintaining internal consistency and are not accessible to the requestor. The locking scheme used is extremely conservative in that cylinders to be read or written are locked—this is primarily for ease of exposition; an actual device would probably use a less restrictive locking scheme. Besides locking virtual and real cylinders, requests may obtain exclusive access to the controller, the accessor arm, and the cartridge being currently used by that request.

In addition to the concurrency between requests, there is significant parallelism possible in the servicing of a single request. Transfers between the buffer and a disk, a cartridge and the buffer, and the buffer and the DMA device, can all go on in parallel. In describing the sequencing of these activities, we note that there are four sources/destinations for data:

1. The external or DMA device.
2. The staging disk subsystem.
3. The cartridge subsystem.
4. The buffer.

There are also four possible data objects:

1. Data coming in from the outside.
2. The data on a cartridge, corresponding to a virtual cylinder.
3. A stale (i.e., dirty) real cylinder chosen for replacement.
4. The data on a cartridge corresponding to the not-to-be-modified part of a cylinder to be partially rewritten.

Table 4-4 enumerates the events that occur in one iteration of the cylinder-by-cylinder servicing of a request. There are two phases of operation. The controller is needed only to initiate and terminate the phases. The specific sequence of events depends on three factors: (1) the action requested (**Read, Write, Locate**); (2) whether the cylinder in question is already on the staging disk (*Hit, Miss*); and (3) whether a cylinder to be replaced is dirty or not (*Dirty, Clean*). In each phase, the actions corresponding to a particular case of this cross-product of possibilities occur in parallel.

4.1.5.2.   Device Module. As figure 4-11 indicates, the device module for the cartridge mass storage system has four pairs of ports: the ExternalIn/ExternalOut pair for communication with the requestor, the DMAIn/DMAOut pair for communication with the external source or sink of data, the StageIn/StageOut pair for control of the staging disks, and the BuffIn/BuffOut pair which provides DMA access to the staging disk subsystem.

The device module makes no assumptions about the performance characteristics of its staging disks: a completely separate device module, such as the one presented in section 4.1.4 is used to implement this function. The latter itself may make use of other device modules, in this case a disk cache. We thus have a situation in which the performance model for a complex device is composed of the performance models of simpler subsystems, a possibility alluded to in section 3.1.1.

There is address translation taking place within the device module: virtual disk addresses are translated to real disk addresses in the course of servicing a request. Since this translation is purely internal to the mass storage system, no explicit address translation module is present—it is implicit in the device module code.

Concurrent servicing of requests is supported up to a certain level, specified at instantiation time. The method used to control the level of concurrency is the same as that in the disk subsystem device module discussed in section 4.1.4.2. Messages are removed from port ExternalIn by their active functions until the maximum concurrency level is reached. Terminating active functions remove one message from this port if the current concurrency level is the maximum permitted.

The high level of concurrency makes the presence of output queues particularly useful. Even if the staging disk device module does not permit queueing at its input port, queueing statistics of requests sent out on port StageOut are automatically gathered because of the output queue present there.

Interactions between contenders for different kinds of resources can lead to deadlocks unless the demands on these resources are carefully constrained.

Table 4-4. Cartridge System: Activities in Transferring a Cylinder.

Read			Write			Locate		
Hit	Miss & Clean	Miss & Dirty	Hit	Miss & Clean	Miss & Dirty	Hit	Miss & Clean	Miss & Dirty
Acquire Controller and initiate operations in Phase 1.								
$Good_{Buffer}^{Disk}$	$Good_{Buffer}^{Cart.}$	$Good_{Buffer}^{Cart.}$ $Stale_{Buffer}^{Disk}$	New_{Buffer}^{Extern}	New_{Buffer}^{Extern} $Old_{Buffer}^{Cart.}$	New_{Buffer}^{Extern} $Stale_{Buffer}^{Disk}$ $Old_{Buffer}^{Cart.}$		$Good_{Buffer}^{Cart.}$	$Good_{Buffer}^{Cart.}$ $Stale_{Buffer}^{Disk}$
Relinquish Controller and await completion of processes End of Phase I.								
Acquire Controller and initiate operations in Phase II.								
$Good_{Extern}^{Buffer}$	$Good_{Extern}^{Buffer}$ $Good_{Disk}^{Buffer}$	$Good_{Disk}^{Buffer}$ $Stale_{Cart.}^{Buffer}$	New_{Disk}^{Buffer} *Mark Dirty*	New_{Disk}^{Buffer} *Mark Dirty*	New_{Disk}^{Buffer} $Stale_{Cart.}^{Buffer}$ *Mark Dirty*		$Good_{Disk}^{Buffer}$	$Good_{Disk}^{Buffer}$ $Stale_{Cart.}^{Buffer}$
Relinquish Controller and await completion of processes End of Phase II.								
Operations on one cylinder now complete								

Legend

A_i^j	Move the data item A from location i to location j
Good	The data on the virtual cylinder being read or located.
Stale	The data on the real cylinder which is dirty and being replaced.
New	The data to be written, being provided by the device on ExternalIn/ExternalOut.
Old	The data on a virtual cylinder corresponding to a to-be-partially-written cylinder.
Hit	The addressed virtual address is present on the staging disk.
Miss	The addressed virtual address is not on the staging disk.
Clean	The real cylinder chosen for replacement has not been written into since it was copied to disk, or has never been allocated.
Dirty	The real cylinder chosen for replacement has been written into since it was copied to disk.

Figure 4-11.   Device Module for Cartridge-based Mass Storage System.

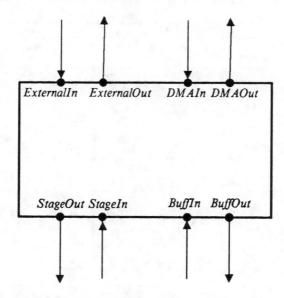

The code in the device module guarantees that a request never waits for locks while holding the controller. If the locks are not immediately available, the controller is relinquished before the wait on the locks is begun. This resource allocation discipline ensures that deadlocks cannot arise due to controller/lock interactions. Another potential source of deadlocks involves the accessor arm and a specific cartridge. The cartridge is always requested before the accessor arm, and this implicit linear ordering of resources makes deadlocks impossible.

   The device module makes a number of simplifying assumptions in order to make the presentation clearer and free from obscuring detail:

- The buffer is a memory device and should actually be represented externally by a device module. We choose, however, to incorporate the delay due to the buffer in the delay constants of the system. Assuming that this delay is a constant ignores the effects of contention in the buffer—probably a reasonable assumption since the buffer is a purely electronic device while all the other entities involve mechanical motion. Representing the buffer as an external device module would add a pair of input/output ports to the device module, and code to send and receive messages from the buffer; no major conceptual changes would be needed in the device module.

- As mentioned earlier, the exclusive lock requirements on both read and write accesses could be relaxed. The locking mechanism used is left unspecified—an actual implementation would have to address this issue.

- Not all requests to the mass storage system require use of a RW station and three buffer regions. The static binding of these resources to requests restricts the attainable level of concurrency. Making these resources allocatable on demand would ease this situation but would also require further efforts to avoid deadlocks.

- The address mapping algorithms and data structures are left unspecified.

- Each semaphore represents a resource, and queueing statistics for this resource are likely to be of interest. For example, the waiting times for the accessor arm and RW stations are important performance measures. For brevity we assume here that each use of a semaphore implicitly executes statistics collection code.

In conclusion, it is worth noting that even the partially specified device module for this rather complex device involves a significant amount of mental effort to understand. In constructing a device module for an actual device of similar complexity, only a person intimately familiar with the device could make sound judgments regarding which details of operation are important and which are not. A hierarchy designer who wishes to evaluate the effect of using this device on a memory hierarchy would clearly like to be spared the effort of writing the device module for it. The very complexity of this device module thus vindicates the claim made in chapter 3 regarding the utility of our methodology.

4.1.6. *A Transaction-Oriented Database System*

4.1.6.1. Description. As an example of a storage system composed of both hardware and software elements, we present here a model of a simple database system supporting read and write transactions. The device module discussed here implements only the software aspects of the system—the performance characteristics of the hardware elements are separately modelled using other device modules.

There are two levels of addressability in this model: the file level and offsets within files. Each file is identified by a unique integer called its *FileId*, and is composed of an integral number of fixed-length pages. All operations on files are at the granularity of a page: external requests should read or write entire pages. There is a fixed upper bound on the length of a file. Figure 4-12 depicts the format of an address in this system: the high-order bits, the FileId,

Figure 4-12. Address Format in Database System.

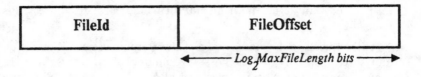

identify the file, while the low order bits, the FileOffset, specify the offset in bytes within the file. For convenience in address decoding, the page size and the maximum size of a file, in bytes, are assumed to be powers of two. In order to keep the device module simple, we assume that transactions are supported only on a per-file basis. Supporting transactions that guarantee atomicity across files would involve additional complexity. Initiating a read transaction is an indication by a user that he wishes to examine certain pages of a file without their contents being modified during the transaction. On the other hand, initiating a write transaction on a file is an indication that some pages of this file are to be modified, and that no other transaction is to be allowed to observe these pages while this transaction is incomplete. Starting with a null set, pages are added one at a time to a transaction; once incorporated in a transaction, a page remains included until the transaction is terminated. Changes to pages in a write transaction are not reflected in the file until the transaction is terminated. However, a write transaction which modifies a page and then reads it will see the altered version of the page. If a write transaction is aborted, none of its modifications are reflected in the corresponding file. Multiple read transactions or a single write transaction are permitted for each page of a file: locks on pages are used to implement this concurrency control policy. Since pages are individually added to transactions, deadlocks are possible. A rather harsh deadlock avoidance policy is enforced: just before a page is actually locked, a check is made to see if a deadlock would ensue; if so, the transaction requesting the page is aborted and all its locked pages released.

Some of the actions associated with a database system are not directly related to the storage function of the database. A clean representation of such actions within the framework discussed in chapter 3 does not exist. However, if such actions do not significantly impact the performance of the system, or if they occur only infrequently, the error incurred in ignoring them is likely to be small. Examples of typical database functions which are ignored here are:

- Abortion of transactions by users. It is assumed that all transactions terminate normally. Aborted write transactions do not require their modified pages to be reflected in the corresponding file. By treating all terminations as normal terminations we err on the side of underestimating performance.

- Allocation of transaction IDs. We assume that this allocation is done outside the device module, by the requestor.

- Actual error recovery procedures. All device errors are directly passed on to the requestor, without any recovery action being attempted. However, mechanisms for recovering from device errors typically impose a nontrivial performance penalty and this overhead is included in the device module.

Figure 4-13 illustrates the main components of the database system. The *File Store* is a large-capacity non-volatile device containing files. A *Stable Storage System* is implemented using the two devices labelled *Stable*$_1$ and *Stable*$_2$. These two devices contain identical copies of data and are always written in the same order. It is assumed that all data errors on both devices are detectable. If a data error occurs when trying to read one of these devices, the corresponding data item on the other device is used. If no data error occurs, but the two copies of a data item are different, it is assumed that a system crash occurred after writing the first copy and before writing the second. In such a case, the copy on the device written first is used. These two devices thus constitute a single logical storage device, whose probability of failure is very low. Stable storage is used to maintain critical housekeeping information for transactions, and for the pages of a file which have been modified by a write transaction still in progress. The database system runs on a processor whose main memory is represented by the *Buffer*. The stable storage devices and the file store use the buffer as the source or sink for DMA data transfers initiated by the database system. Note that the processor's memory reference behavior is not included in the device module. If contention in the buffer is likely to affect performance significantly, the hierarchy description should include an independent driver to represent the processor. To obtain the necessary correlation between the references generated by that driver and the request currently in service by the database system, a communication path between these two devices is necessary. In the interests of simplicity, we assume that contention is not a limiting factor and hence ignore the processor altogether. The processing overheads for requests are directly incorporated as delays in the device module for the database system.

The FileId, FileOffset pair presented to the database system has to be mapped into actual storage addresses on the file store device and the stable storage device. Since this constitutes address translation, we could leave this function to be performed by the hierarchy designer. However, that would merely defer the discussion of this topic to a later part of this chapter. Consequently we incorporate the address translation into the device module for the database system, using rather simple mapping functions.

Assuming contiguous storage allocation, a FileOffset can be used directly as an address offset in any memory device with a uniform address space, such

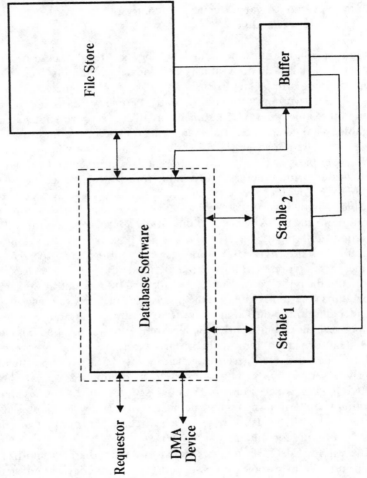

Figure 4-13. A Transaction-oriented Database System.

Note: Dotted lines indicate boundary of system modelled.

as a main memory device. For devices with a structured address format, such as a disk, the FileOffset has to be mapped into address components. However, if each address component has a maximum value that is a power of two, and if the address is obtained by a simple concatenation of components, the mapping is trivial: different fields of the integer representing FileOffset directly correspond to the different address components of the device. The disk subsystem of section 4.1.4 and the cartridge subsystem of section 4.1.5 use such an addressing structure. Hence the FileOffset can be interpreted unchanged by such devices; different fields of this integer will correspond to a disk number, cylinder number, etc. We assume that the addressing structure of the file store and stable storage devices conform to this format. Such devices may effectively be viewed as having a uniform address space.

With the assumption made above, a FileId identifies a contiguous set of bytes located at some point in a uniform address space. In defining a mapping between FileIds and the origins of the corresponding files, the following assumptions are made:

- Storage for files with consecutive FileIds is allocated consecutively. So, the storage for the file F_{i+1} will immediately follow the storage for file F_i.

- The length of a file is a uniformly distributed random variable between 0 and the maximum permitted length.

- Every file is an integral number of pages long.

- Explicit file creation and deletion operations are ignored. Modifications to files are assumed to be inplace updates.

To avoid storing a large table of FileId/origin mappings, the origin of a file is treated as a random variable and dynamically generated as needed. This random origin generation occurs when a transaction is initiated on a file not currently being used. The same file origin is used throughout the transaction. Other transactions initiated on this file while the first transaction is incomplete also use this origin. Only when all transactions using a given file are terminated is the binding between a FileId and an origin destroyed. A later transaction using the same file will cause a new origin to be generated. This mapping strategy ensures that short-term correlations in the file access patterns are reflected as correlated address reference patterns to the file store. Long-term correlations in file access are not accurately reflected. The accuracy of this model thus depends on the extent to which long-term correlation in access patterns affects the performance of the file storage device—for typical storage devices such as disks, this is unlikely to be a serious shortcoming.

On the basis of the assumptions listed above, it is relatively simple to obtain the distribution function for the origin of a file. Let O_i be the origin, and S_i the size, of the file with FileId i. Then the following relations hold:

$$O_0 = 0$$
$$O_1 = S_0$$
$$O_2 = S_0 + S_1$$
$$O_3 = S_0 + S_1 + S_2$$
$$\cdots$$
$$\cdots$$
$$O_N = S_0 + S_1 + S_2 + \cdots + S_{N-1}$$

Each S_i is an independent, identically distributed random variable. By the Central Limit Theorem, for large N, O_N is well approximated by a normal distribution whose mean and variance are N times the mean and variance of S_i. Since S_i is assumed to be a uniform distribution in the range 0 to the S_{Max}, the maximum file length, the mean of S_i is $S_{Max}/2$ and its variance is $S^2_{Max}/12$. Consequently O_N is normally distributed with a mean of $N \cdot S_{Max}/2$ and a variance of $N \cdot S^2_{Max}/12$. For simplicity we assume that these expressions are valid for all N—some error is incurred for small values of N. Figure 4-14 is a sketch of the distribution of file origins with FileId as a parameter.

As discussed earlier, the stable storage devices are used for holding short-lived data items. Using the same address mapping as for the file store is unlikely to be realistic. We therefore adopt a much simpler mapping strategy. Housekeeping information is assumed to be stored on one half of a stable storage device, while its other half is used for the modified pages of a write transaction. When a transaction is initiated, a page is selected at random from the first half and bound to the transaction. For the duration of the transaction, all housekeeping accesses are to this address. Each addition of a page to a write transaction causes a new address to be allocated, at random, from the second half. Accesses to this page by this transaction are directed to this address. This address mapping scheme is economical in terms of storage, yet correlations in the input request stream are reflected in corresponding correlations in the access patterns to stable storage.

The operations supported by the database system map in a fairly obvious way onto the primitive actions listed in chapter 3. The opening of a file for a read transaction or a write transaction is modelled by **PrepareForRead** and **PrepareForWrite** respectively. Adding a page to a transaction is a **Locate**, while actual reading and writing are done by **Read** and **Write**. Termination of read and write transactions is specified by **TerminateRead** and **Terminate-Write**, respectively.

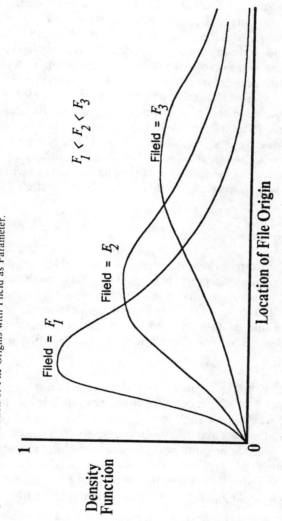

Figure 4-14. Distribution of File Origins with Fileld as Parameter.

4.1.6.2.   Device Module. Figure 4-15 shows the device module for this transactional database system. The requests that drive this system are presented on port ExtIn and are responded to on port ExtOut. Data transfers between the requestor and the device module take place via the DMAOut/DMAIn port pair. The BufIn/BufOut port pair is used for communication with the buffer. The file storage device and the stable storage devices are assumed to be capable of performing DMA transfers to the buffer: the communication paths necessary for this are not part of the device module, but will be specified in the hierarchy descriptions in which this device module will be used. FileStoreIn/FileStoreOut is the port pair on which the database system sends requests to and receives responses from the file storage device. Communication with the two stable storage devices is done on the port pairs Stable1Out/Stable1In and Stable2Out/Stable2In. Note that it is not necessary that these two devices be identical: the only assumptions made about them in the device module are that they have equal capacities, and that their addressing formats meet the conditions specified in section 4.1.6.1 for the file store device.

4.1.7.   A Simple Driver

4.1.7.1.   Description. Typically, memory hierarchies are driven by a processor which issues memory references for fetching instructions and operands, and for storing results. A full description of the memory reference stream from such a driver would include the specific sequence of memory addresses, the amount of data involved in each transfer, and the time interval between successive references. Chief among the factors which determine the reference stream are:

- *The architecture of the processor.* The instruction set of the processor determines how higher-level functions are represented. In a register-oriented architecture, for instance, most instructions would use data in registers, thereby avoiding many memory references. As another example, an architecture with an instruction set restricted to fixed length operands (typically the word size of the processor) would present only word-sized operand references. More general instruction sets would make operand references of varying lengths.

- *The specific program execution.* Both the program being executed and the data used for the execution greatly influence the reference stream. Only an actual trace of a program execution can capture the precise reference stream for that execution. The same program with different data, or in the case of nondeterministic programs, even the same data, will yield a different reference stream.

Figure 4-15.   Device Module for Transaction-oriented Database System.

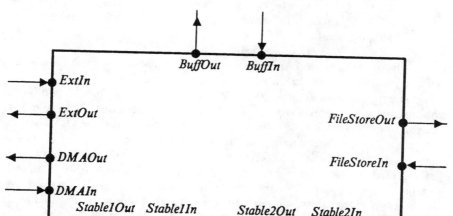

- *The implementation of the processor.* Two implementations of an architecture may yield different reference streams even when running the same deterministic programs with identical data. Differences in processor technology, data path widths, degree of parallelism (especially pipelining), and microcode implementation of architectural features, account for this variation.

In choosing a memory reference stream for driving a simulation, there are two approaches that can be taken:

- *Use the memory reference trace of an actual program.* The architecture and implementation of the processor on which the program is run for trace collection should be the same as the processor driving the memory hierarchy. The simulation is performed by reading in a trace file containing these recorded references and using them to drive the simulation. This approach accurately models the performance of the hierarchy for the specific reference stream used, but involves extensive input-output overhead in simulation.

- *Synthesize a model which exhibits "typical" characteristics.* For a specific program execution, the performance predictions made by using this approach cannot be as accurate as one obtained by using a trace. However, in analyzing the behavior of the hierarchy with respect to a large number of programs with similar general characteristics, the results obtained by this method may be quite acceptable. Since no input/output operations are involved in generating references, the overheads incurred in using such a driver are much less than in one using a trace file.

The driver described here supports both approaches: when instantiating the device module, one of the two methods may be specified.

The trace model assumes a simple processor architecture with two types of instructions: *Short* instructions and *Long* instructions. Both type of instructions begin with a memory fetch for the instruction itself. After this there is a constant delay to account for instruction decoding. In the case of a short instruction, this is followed by a sequence of operand fetches, a constant execution delay, and then a sequence of result stores. The number of operand fetches and result stores, and the amount of data involved in each are specified in the trace entries corresponding to these events. Long instructions model situations where execution is interspersed amidst operand fetches and result stores. For example, string comparison and block transfer instructions may perform comparisons or transfers a byte at a time. For such instructions, there is a constant execution delay to initiate the instruction, and a delay proportional to the length of the operand after each operand fetch. There is no limit to the number of operand fetches or result stores, or on the order of their occurrence in a long instruction.

The trace file consists of a sequence of triples. Each triple defines one memory reference, and contains the type of the reference, the address to which the reference is made, and the length of the data transferred. There are four reference types: a short instruction fetch, a long instruction fetch, an operand fetch, and a result store. Characterizing the behavior of the processor by just two types of instructions is a simplification for expositional purposes. To model an implementation of an actual architecture, one may represent each opcode in the instruction set by a different trace entry type and incorporate execution delays to correspond to each different instruction in the device module.

The synthetic reference model is built upon a model proposed by Woolf in his dissertation [Woolf71]. A program is assumed to consist of an infinite sequence of non-nested loops whose origin is randomly distributed in the address space. The length of a loop is exponentially distributed to account for the fact that short loops are observed to be much more frequent than long ones. The number of iterations of each loop is a uniformly distributed random number bounded by a value specified when instantiating the module. All memory references are one word long, and all instructions consist of an instruction fetch, a decode delay, two operand references, an execution delay, and a result store. The body of the loop is assumed to consist of straight-line code. The set of operand and result addresses used are random—however, the same sequence of random addresses is used for each iteration of a loop. Only when a new loop is commenced is a new set of random addresses generated. Locality in instruction, operand, and result references is thus exhibited, and the set of addresses referenced in a loop can be viewed as the current working set. Changes in the working set are modelled by the fact that the loop origin and the operand and result addresses are randomly relocated after completing a loop execution.

4.1.7.2.   Device Module. Figure 4-16 presents the external interface of the device module for this driver. The MemRefOut/MemRefIn port pair is connected to a memory device. The simulation tool sends a message to port StartDrive to initiate activity. The body of the active function corresponding to port StartDrive performs the actual generation of requests. An interesting feature of this device module is the use of an instantiation parameter to determine the accuracy of modelling (trace-driven versus synthetic reference generation).

4.2.   Hierarchies

Using the device modules developed in the previous section, we examine three different memory hierarchies in this section. These hierarchies encompass hardware-only hierarchies as well as hierarchies incorporating a significant amount of software control. For each hierarchy we present an overview and prose description, followed by hierarchy descriptions for two different configurations. Hierarchy-specific device modules which are needed for address translation or connectivity reasons are described in the corresponding subsections.

4.2.1.   A Multiprocessor System

4.2.1.1.   Description. As a simple but nontrivial application of the principles outlined in chapter 3, consider the simulation of a multiprocessor system with a cache per processor, and a shared, interleaved main memory. Figure 4-17 illustrates a four-processor system connected to an eight-way interleaved main memory subsystem via an interconnection unit. For simplicity, we omit I/O devices from this discussion—the primary effect of their inclusion would be to increase memory traffic (and hence contention) in the system. The interconnection unit performs two important functions. (1) It provides the logical connection paths for the multiprocessor system. (2) It routes addresses presented by processors to the appropriate memory units. The memory unit to which a particular address is routed depends on the address, the degree of interleaving and on the blocksize of the memory units.

The device modules of sections 4.1.1, 4.1.2, and 4.1.7 can be used to represent the main memory units, caches, and the processors. A device module has to be created for the interconnection unit. Figure 4-18 shows the external interconnections for such a device module. The use of port arrays

Figure 4-16. Device Module for the Simple Driver.

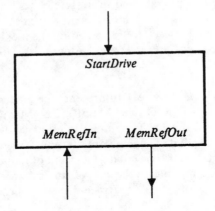

Figure 4-17. A Multiprocessor System with Interleaved Memory
and Caches.

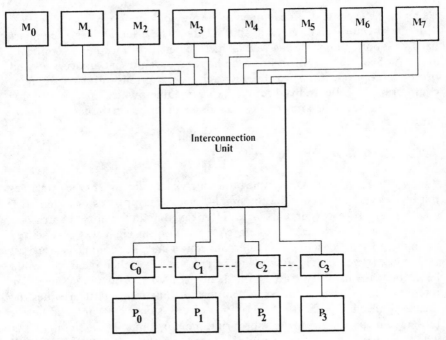

P_i = Processor i

M_i = Memory Unit i

C_i = Cache for processor i

------- = Cache Invalidation Connections

Figure 4-18. Device Module for Multiprocessor Interconnection Unit.

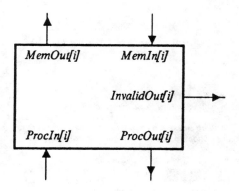

allows the precise configuration of the system to be deferred until instantiation time. The port array ProcIn provides one input port for each processor in the system. Main memory requests by processors (or their caches, if present) are presented on these ports. The requests received on ProcIn ports are forwarded to the appropriate memory units on the MemOut ports. Responses from the memory units are received on the MemIn ports and conveyed back to the requesting processor (or its cache) on the ProcOut ports. As in figure 4-16, cache entry invalidation information is usually distributed by means of direct connections between caches. From a logical point of view, however, this function can be assigned to the interconnection unit. The port array InvalidOut is used to send invalidation signals to all the caches in the system when a write on a memory location is performed.

4.2.1.2. Hierarchy Description. As an example of how the same set of device modules can be used to simulate different hierarchies, we present two different multiprocessor systems in this section. The first, illustrated in figure 4-17, is a four-processor eight-way interleaved system with a write-through cache per processor. The hierarchy description for this system is presented in figure 4-19. The instantiation parameters values have been chosen arbitrarily—in an actual simulation they would correspond to the characteristics of the devices being simulated.

The second configuration is shown in figure 4-20 and its hierarchy description is given in figure 4-21. In this system, there are two processors directly connected to a four-way interleaved memory system, without intervening caches.

4.2.2. A Multiprogrammed Virtual Memory System

4.2.2.1. Description. In this section we consider a multiprogrammed uniprocessor system with paged virtual memory. Figure 4-22 shows one

Figure 4-19. Hierarchy Description for a Multiprocessor System— 1.

DeviceModules
>   CoreMemory = *File specification of the device module in Section 4.1.1.2* ;
>   Cache = *File specification of the device module in Appendix A.1* ;
>   GenericCPU = *File specification of the device module in Section 4.1.7.2* ;
>   ICUnit = *File specification of the device module in Section 4.2.1.1*

Instantiations
>   P0, P1, P2, P3: GenericCPU(false, 0.5E-6, 2, 0, 0, 2**16-1, 4, 10, 1000);
>   *Specifies drivers, in synthetic mode, for a machine with 0.5 microsecond instruction*
>   *decode time and a 2 microsecond instruction execution time, with a 16 bit*
>   *address space. The word size of the machine is 4 bytes. The average*
>   *loop length is 10 instructions, and the maximum loop count is 1000 iterations.*

>   M0: CoreMemory(8096, 8, 0, 4, 1E-6, 0.75E-6);
>   *Defines an 8K byte core memory, occupying first position in an 8-way*
>   *interleaved set. Accesses are in 4-byte chunks. The cycle time is one*
>   *microsecond, and the access time in 750 nanoseconds.*

>   M1: CoreMemory(8096, 8, 1, 4, 1E-6, 0.75E-6);
>   M2: CoreMemory(8096, 8, 2, 4, 1E-6, 0.75E-6);
>   M3: CoreMemory(8096, 8, 3, 4, 1E-6, 0.75E-6);
>   M4: CoreMemory(8096, 8, 4, 4, 1E-6, 0.75E-6);
>   M5: CoreMemory(8096, 8, 5, 4, 1E-6, 0.75E-6);
>   M6: CoreMemory(8096, 8, 6, 4, 1E-6, 0.75E-6);
>   M7: CoreMemory(8096, 8, 7, 4, 1E-6, 0.75E-6);

>   C0, C1, C2, C3: Cache(1028, 16, 2, 3, 4);
>   *Defines a 1K byte write-through cache with a line width of 16 bytes.*
>   *An LRU replacement algorithm is used, and 4-byte wide accesses are supported.*

>   CrossBar: ICUnit(8, 4, 4);
>   *An interconnection unit for a 4-processor, 8-way interleaved system,*
>   *with 4-byte wide memory accesses.*

Interconnections
>   (CrossBar.MemOut[0], M0.HiIn);
>   (CrossBar.MemIn[0], M0.HiOut);
>   (CrossBar.MemOut[1], M1.HiIn);
>   (CrossBar.MemIn[1], M1.HiOut);
>   (CrossBar.MemOut[2], M2.HiIn);
>   (CrossBar.MemIn[2], M2.HiOut);
>   (CrossBar.MemOut[3], M3.HiIn);
>   (CrossBar.MemIn[3], M3.HiOut);
>   (CrossBar.MemOut[4], M4.HiIn);
>   (CrossBar.MemIn[4], M4.HiOut);
>   (CrossBar.MemOut[5], M5.HiIn);
>   (CrossBar.MemIn[5], M5.HiOut);
>   (CrossBar.MemOut[6], M6.HiIn);
>   (CrossBar.MemIn[6], M6.HiOut);
>   (CrossBar.MemOut[7], M7.HiIn);
>   (CrossBar.MemIn[7], M7.HiOut);

>   (CrossBar.InvalidOut[0], C0.Invalidate);
>   (CrossBar.InvalidOut[1], C1.Invalidate);
>   (CrossBar.InvalidOut[2], C2.Invalidate);
>   (CrossBar.InvalidOut[3], C3.Invalidate);

Figure 4-19. (concluded)

```
(CrossBar.ProcIn[0], C0.MainOut);
(CrossBar.ProcIn[1], C1.MainOut);
(CrossBar.ProcIn[2], C2.MainOut);
(CrossBar.ProcIn[3], C3.MainOut);


(CrossBar.ProcOut[0], C0.MainIn);
(CrossBar.ProcOut[1], C1.MainIn);
(CrossBar.ProcOut[2], C2.MainIn);
(CrossBar.ProcOut[3], C3.MainIn);

(C0.CPUOut, P0.MemRefIn);
(C1.CPUOut, P1.MemRefIn);
(C2.CPUOut, P2.MemRefIn);
(C3.CPUOut, P3.MemRefIn);


(C0.CPUIn, P0.MemRefOut);
(C1.CPUIn, P1.MemRefOut);
(C2.CPUIn, P2.MemRefOut);
(C3.CPUIn, P3.MemRefOut);
```

Statistics

List of ports on which statistics are to be collected.

Figure 4-20. A Multiprocessor System without Caches.

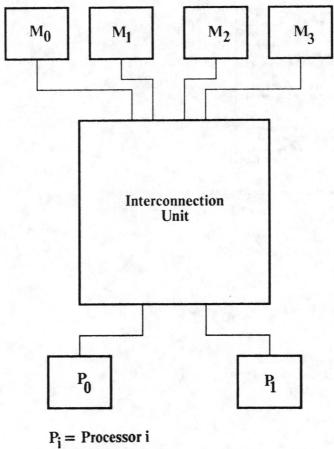

P_i = **Processor i**
M_i = **Memory Unit i**

Figure 4-21. Hierarchy Description for a Multiprocessor System— 2.

DeviceModules
>   CoreMemory = *File specification of the device module in Section 4.1.1.2 ;*
>   GenericCPU = *File specification of the device module in Section 4.1.7.2 ;*
>   ICUnit = *File specification of the device module in Section 4.2.1.1*

Instantiations
>   P0, P1: GenericCPU(false, 0.5E-6, 2, 0, 0, 2**16-1, 4, 10, 1000);
>   *Specifies drivers, in synthetic mode, for a machine with 0.5 microsecond instruction*
>   *decode time and a 2 microsecond instruction execution time, with a 16 bit*
>   *address space. The word size of the machine is 4 bytes. The average*
>   *loop length is 10 instructions, and the maximum loop count is 1000 iterations.*

>   M0: CoreMemory(8096, 4, 0, 4, 1E-6, 0.75E-6);
>   *Defines an 8K byte core memory, occupying first position in an 4-way*
>   *interleaved set. Accesses are in 4-byte chunks. The cycle time is one*
>   *microsecond, and the access time in 750 nanoseconds.*

>   M1: CoreMemory(8096, 4, 1, 4, 1E-6, 0.75E-6);
>   M2: CoreMemory(8096, 4, 2, 4, 1E-6, 0.75E-6);
>   M3: CoreMemory(8096, 4, 3, 4, 1E-6, 0.75E-6);

>   CrossBar: ICUnit(4, 2, 4);
>   *An interconnection unit for a 2-processor, 4-way interleaved system,*
>   *with 4-byte wide memory accesses.*

Interconnections
>   (CrossBar.MemOut[0], M0.HiIn);
>   (CrossBar.MemIn[0], M0.HiOut);
>   (CrossBar.MemOut[1], M1.HiIn);
>   (CrossBar.MemIn[1], M1.HiOut);
>   (CrossBar.MemOut[2], M2.HiIn);
>   (CrossBar.MemIn[2], M2.HiOut);
>   (CrossBar.MemOut[3], M3.HiIn);
>   (CrossBar.MemIn[3], M3.HiOut);

>   (CrossBar.ProcIn[0], P0.MemRefOut);
>   (CrossBar.ProcIn[1], P1.MemRefOut);

>   (CrossBar.ProcOut[0], P0.MemRefIn);
>   (CrossBar.ProcOut[1], P1.MemRefIn);

Statistics
>   *List of ports on which statistics are to be collected.*

Figure 4-22. A Multiprogrammed Virtual Memory System.

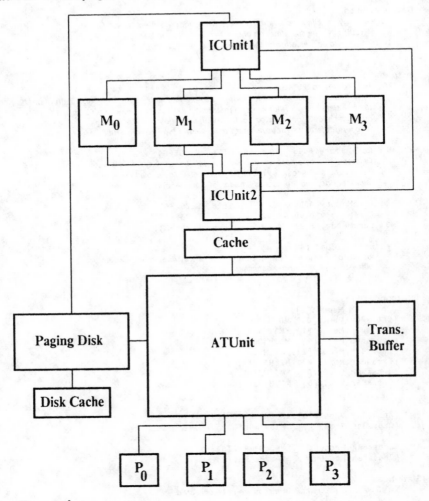

P_i = Process i
M_i = Memory Unit i

example of such a system, with a translation buffer, a paging disk with a disk cache, and an interleaved main memory system with a cache. The paging disk has DMA access to the main memory system. The virtual to real address mapping is performed by the unit labelled ATUnit in figure 4-22. This unit represents both the software and microcode support needed for paging.

The body of the device module for the ATUnit will depend on the design decisions in the virtual memory system and on the scheduling policies for multiprogramming. Figure 4-23 shows the external interface of such a device module, based on the following set of assumptions:

- There is a fixed level of multiprogramming in the system, represented by a set of nonterminating processes. From a performance point of view, a process is represented as a stream of memory references.

- Processes are nonpreemptible. Execution of a process begins as soon as the processor is free to service it, and continues until a page fault occurs. The process gives up the processor while paging I/O is being performed for it. On completion of the I/O activity, the process joins a FIFO queue of processes waiting to run. Page faults are the only events in the system that cause a process to relinquish the processor.

- In an actual virtual memory system, the handling of a page fault involves the execution of instructions in the page fault handler of the operating system. This results in memory references which are completely unrelated to the processes being multiprogrammed. One can model this situation accurately by postulating a memory reference stream corresponding to the page fault handler—references from this stream are serviced when a process encounters a page fault. For simplicity, we completely ignore all such memory references. This would be realistic if the entire page fault handler were implemented in microcode, and main memory used only for storing page tables.

- The page tables themselves are not paged. It is assumed that each process may have a different virtual address space, and that the translation buffer is cleared on context switches.

- The location of page tables in main memory, and of page images on the paging device are left unspecified. Functions to provide this information are assumed to be present.

- Only paging I/O is done on the paging device. Nonpaging I/O can be modelled by assuming that each memory reference has a small probability of initiating I/O activity as a side effect.* For simplicity we ignore all I/O except that needed for paging.

---

*This view is not purely hypothetical—in architectures like the PDP-11, device registers are addressable as memory locations. A write to a device register initiates I/O activity on that device.

Figure 4-23. Device Module for Address Translation Unit.

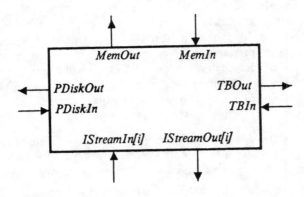

4.2.2.2. Hierarchy Description. As in section 4.2.1.2, we consider two different configurations in order to demonstrate the ease with which related, but different, memory hierarchies may be represented in the proposed methodology. The first configuration is depicted in figure 4-22. The driver presented in section 4.1.7 can be used for the memory reference streams in this configuration. We assume that all processes are identical. Nonidentical processes can be modelled by choosing different instantiation parameters for the instruction stream. The cache, translation buffer, and main memory units are instances of the devices presented in sections 4.1.2, 4.1.3, and 4.1.1, respectively. The paging disk is a one-disk instantiation of the disk subsystem discussed in section 4.1.4; its cache is represented by the same device module as the translation buffer, but with different instantiation parameters. Connections to the interleaved memory units are made using the interconnection unit described in section 4.2.1.1. There are two such units, one for processor accesses and the other for DMA disk accesses. DMA accesses are directed to the high-priority ports of the memory units, while processor requests are serviced by the low-priority ports. The hierarchy description for this configuration is shown in figure 4-24.

As figure 4-25 illustrates, the second configuration differs from the first in the following ways:

- The main memory is noninterleaved and does not distinguish between high-priority and low-priority requests.
- The paging device has two disks but no cache.
- The level of multiprogramming is half that of the first configuration.

The hierarchy description for this configuration is given in figure 4-26.

Figure 4-24. Hierarchy Description for a Virtual Memory System— 1.

DeviceModules
CoreMemory = *File specification for device module of Section 4.1.1.2*
Cache = *File specification for device module of Appendix A.1*
Process = *File specification for device module of Section 4.1.7.2*
ICUnit = *File specification for device module of Section 4.2.1.1.*
TBuffer = *File specification for device module of Section 4.1.3.2*
DiskSubSys = *File specification for device module of Section 4.1.4.2*
VirtMemATUnit = *File specification for device module of Section 4.2.2.1*

Instantiations
PO, P1, P2, P3: Process(false, 0.5E-6, 2, 0, 0, 2**32-1, 4, 10, 1000);
*Specifies drivers, in synthetic mode, for a machine with 0.5 microsecond instruction
decode time and a 2 microsecond instruction execution time, with a 32-bit
address space. The word size of the machine is 4 bytes. The average
loop length is 10 instructions, and the maximum loop count is 1000 iterations.*

MO: CoreMemory(65536, 4, 0, 4, 0.75E-6, 0.75E-6);
*Defines an 64K byte memory, occupying first position in an 4-way
interleaved set. Accesses are in 4-byte chunks. The cycle time and
the access time are both 750 nanoseconds.*

M1: CoreMemory(65536, 4, 1, 4, 0.75E-6, 0.75E-6);
M2: CoreMemory(65536, 4, 2, 4, 0.75E-6, 0.75E-6);
M3: CoreMemory(65536, 4, 3, 4, 0.75E-6, 0.75E-6);

SysCache: Cache(8096, 32, 2, 3, 4);
*Defines a 8K byte write-through cache with a line width of 32 bytes.
An LRU replacement algorithm is used, and 4-byte wide accesses are supported.*

TransBuffer: TBuffer(8096, 2, 4, 512);
*Specifies a 8K byte, 2-way associative translation buffer for a
page size of 512 bytes and page table entries of 4 bytes.*

DiskCache: TBuffer(65536, 128, 512, 512);
Defines a fully associative memory, with 128 sector-sized entries.

PagingDisk: (1, 512, 16, 64, 512, 0.0001, 0.0001, 50, 0.001, 0.0001);
*Defines a single disk with controller. The disk has 512 cylinders,
each with 16 tracks of 64 512-byte sectors. The controller takes
100 microseconds to initiate and terminate requests. The disk rotates
at 50 revolutions per second (i.e. 3000 rpm). Initiating disk head
movement takes 1 millisecond, after which it takes 100 microseconds
for the head to cross each track.*

ATUnit: VirtMemATUnit(4, 512, 4, 2**32-1, 2**18-1);
*Address translation module for 4-process system, with a page size of 512 bytes.
The virtual address space is 2**32 bytes. There are 256K bytes of real memory.*

ICUnit1, ICUnit2: ICUnit(4, 1, 4);
Interconnection unit with a fanin/fanout of 1/4, with accesses being 4 bytes wide.

Figure 4-24. (concluded)

Interconnections

```
(P0.MemRefOut, ATUnit.IStreamIn[0]);
(P1.MemRefOut, ATUnit.IStreamIn[1]);
(P2.MemRefOut, ATUnit.IStreamIn[2]);
(P3.MemRefOut, ATUnit.IStreamIn[3]);

(P0.MemRefIn, ATUnit.IStreamOut[0]);
(P1.MemRefIn, ATUnit.IStreamOut[1]);
(P2.MemRefIn, ATUnit.IStreamOut[2]);
(P3.MemRefIn, ATUnit.IStreamOut[3]);

(ATUnit.TBOut, TransBuff.AddrIn);
(ATUnit.TBIn, TransBuff.PTEOut);
(ATUnit.MemOut, SysCache.CPUIn);

(ATUnit.MemIn, SysCache.CPUOut);
(ATUnit.PDiskOut, PagingDisk.ExternalIn);
(ATUnit.PDiskIn, PagingDisk.ExternalOut);

(PagingDisk.DataOut, ICUnit2.ProcIn[0]);
(PagingDisk.DataIn, ICUnit2.ProcOut[0]);
(PagingDisk.CacheOut, DiskCache.AddrIn);
(PagingDisk.CacheIn, DiskCache.PTEOut);

(SysCache.Invalidate, ICUnit2.InvalidOut);
(SysCache.MainOut, ICUnit1.ProcIn[0]);
(SysCache.MainIn, ICUnit1.ProcOut[0]);

(ICUnit1.MemOut[0], M0.LoIn);
(ICUnit1.MemIn[0], M0.LoOut);
(ICUnit1.MemOut[1], M1.LoIn);
(ICUnit1.MemIn[1], M1.LoOut);
(ICUnit1.MemOut[2], M2.LoIn);
(ICUnit1.MemIn[2], M2.LoOut);
(ICUnit1.MemOut[3], M3.LoIn);
(ICUnit1.MemIn[3], M3.LoOut);

(ICUnit2.MemOut[0], M0.HiIn);
(ICUnit2.MemIn[0], M0.HiOut);
(ICUnit2.MemOut[1], M1.HiIn);
(ICUnit2.MemIn[1], M1.HiOut);
(ICUnit2.MemOut[2], M2.HiIn);
(ICUnit2.MemIn[2], M2.HiOut);
(ICUnit2.MemOut[3], M3.HiIn);
(ICUnit2.MemIn[3], M3.HiOut);

(ICUnit2.InvalidOut, SysCache.Invalidate);
```

Statistics

List of ports on which statistics are to be collected.

Figure 4-25. A Second Configuration of a Multiprogrammed
Virtual Memory System.

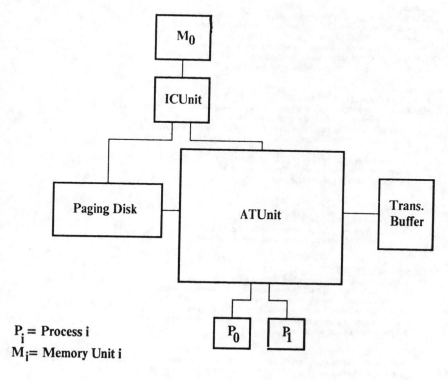

P_i = Process i
M_i= Memory Unit i

4.2.3. A Database System

4.2.3.1. Description. Section 4.1.6 presented the device module for the software in a transaction-oriented database system. In this section we consider the composition of hardware and software elements needed to accomplish the database storage function defined by the assumptions of section 4.1.6.

All the necessary device modules, except one, have been presented in earlier sections of this chapter. The sole exception is a driver for generating transaction requests. The device module for such a driver would have to perform the following functions:

- Generate and keep track of transaction IDs.
- Present requests for: the opening and closing of files, the adding of pages of a transaction, and the reading and writing of pages in a transaction.
- Interleave requests from different transactions.

Figure 4-26.. Hierarchy Description for a Virtual Memory System— 2.

DeviceModules
> CoreMemory = *File specification for device module of Section 4.1.1.2*
> Process = *File specification for device module of Section 4.1.7.2*
> ICUnit = *File specification for device module of Section 4.2.1.1*
> TBuffer = *File specification for device module of Section 4.1.3.2*
> DiskSubSys = *File specification for device module of Section 4.1.4.2*
> VirtMemATUnit = *File specification for device module of Section 4.2.2.1*

Instantiations
> P0, P1: Process(**false**, 0.5E-6, 2, 0, 0, 2**32-1, 4, 10, 1000);
> *Specifies drivers, in synthetic mode, for a machine with 0.5 microsecond instruction decode time and a 2 microsecond instruction execution time, with a 32-bit address space. The word size of the machine is 4 bytes. The average loop length is 10 instructions, and the maximum loop count is 1000 iterations.*

> M0: CoreMemory(262144, 4, 0, 4, 0.75E-6, 0.75E-6);
> *Defines an 256K byte memory. The cycle time and the access time are both 750 nanoseconds.*

> TransBuffer: TBuffer(8096, 2, 4, 512);
> *Specifies a 8K byte, 2-way associative translation buffer for a page size of 512 bytes and page table entries of 4 bytes.*

> PagingDisk: (2, 512, 16, 64, 512, 0.0001, 0.0001, 50, 0.001, 0.0001);
> *Defines 2 disks with a controller. The disk has 512 cylinders, each with 16 tracks of 64 512-byte sectors. The controller takes 100 microseconds to initiate and terminate requests. The disk rotates at 50 revolutions per second (i.e. 3000 rpm). Initiating disk head movement takes 1 millisecond, after which it takes 100 microseconds for the head to cross each track.*

> ATUnit: VirtMemATUnit(2, 512, 4, 2**32-1, 2**18-1);
> *Address translation module for 2-process system, with a page size of 512 bytes. The virtual address space is 2**32 bytes. There are 256K bytes of real memory.*

> ICUnit1: ICUnit(2, 1, 4);
> *Interconnection unit with a fanin/fanout of 1/4, with accesses being 4 bytes wide.*

Interconnections
> (P0.MemRefOut, ATUnit.IStreamIn[0]);
> (P1.MemRefOut, ATUnit.IStreamIn[1]);
>
> (P0.MemRefIn, ATUnit.IStreamOut[0]);
> (P1.MemRefIn, ATUnit.IStreamOut[1]);
>
> (ATUnit.TBOut, TransBuff.AddrIn);
> (ATUnit.TBIn, TransBuff.PTEOut);
> (ATUnit.MemOut, ICUnit1.ProcIn[0]);
> (ATUnit.MemIn, ICUnit1.ProcOut[0]);
> (ATUnit.PDiskOut, PagingDisk.ExternalIn);
> (ATUnit.PDiskIn, PagingDisk.ExternalOut);
>
> (PagingDisk.DataOut, ICUnit1.ProcIn[1]);
> (PagingDisk.DataIn, ICUnit1.ProcOut[1]);
>
> (ICUnit1.MemOut[0], M0.LoIn);
> (ICUnit1.MemIn[0], M0.LoOut);

Statistics
> *List of ports on which statistics are to be collected.*

As in the case of the program reference stream generator discussed in section 4.1.7, these functions could be accomplished either by using a trace from an actual database system or by synthetic generation of references.

For brevity, we refrain from discussing details of an actual device module for driving the database system. We assume that such a device module exists, and that its external interface is as specified in figure 4-27. Requests are communicated to the database software on the DataBaseOut/DataBaseIn port pair; control of local devices, if needed, is performed on the LocalOut/LocalIn port pair. A buffer is shared by the requestor and the database system; data transfers in response to driver requests occur to or from this buffer. If present, the local device (typically a disk) performs DMA data transfers to or from this buffer, under the control of the driver.

The device module for the database software already incorporates address translation: no separate address translation is necessary, as long as the stable storage and file storage devices have a uniform address space, as discussed in section 4.1.6.

Figure 4-27. External Interface for a Database Driver.

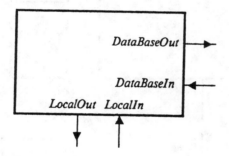

4.2.3.2. Hierarchy Description. Figure 4-28 illustrates a configuration of the database system, using the cartridge mass storage system of section 4.1.5 as the file storage device, and disks (D2 and D3) as the stable storage media. The cartridge store staging subsystem, D4, has two staging disks with a disk cache. The driver has a disk, D1, as a local storage device. In the hierarchy description shown in figure 4-29, it is interesting to note how the same disk subsystem device module, instantiated with different parameters, provides the device modules for all the disks in the system.

The second configuration is simpler and is presented in figure 4-30. The file store is now a set of eight disks (without a cache), and the stable storage devices are random access memories. The requestor has no local device to control. As expected, the hierarchy description for this configuration (fig. 4-31) is much simpler than for the first configuration.

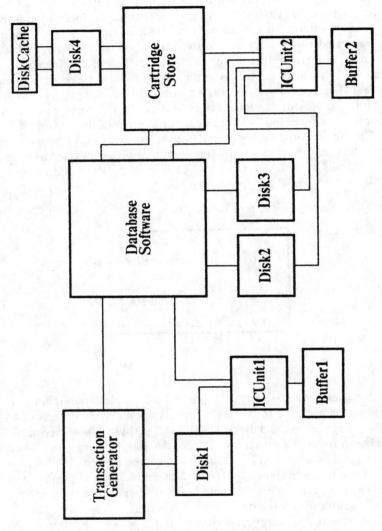

Figure 4-28. A Database System with a Cartridge File Store and Disk Stable Storage.

Figure 4-29. Hierarchy Description for a Database System—1.

DeviceModules

    CoreMemory = *File specification for device module of Section 4.1.1.2*
    ICUnit = *File specification for device module of Section 4.2.1.1*
    TBuffer = *File specification for device module of Section 4.1.3.2*
    DiskSubSys = *File specification for device module of Section 4.1.4.2*
    CartridgeSys = *File specification for device module of Section 4.1.5.2*
    TODBS = *File specification for device module of Section 4.1.6.2*
    TGenerator = *File specification for the hypothetical transaction generator*

Instantiations

    TGen: TGenerator(*with suitable instantiation parameters*);

    DBSoftware: TODBS(65536, 512, 1048575, 262143, 1024, 8);
        Defines a database system with 512-byte pages, handling files up to
        64K bytes. The stable storage devices are 1 Mbyte each in size
        and the buffer has 256K bytes of storage. Transaction identifiers
        take values in the range 1 to 1024. Upto 8 requests may be
        queued at the ports of this device module.

    CartridgeStore: CartridgeSys(256, 2, 4, 256, 8, 16, 512, 4);
        A cartridge store supporting 256 virtual disks with 2 real disks.
        The real and virtual disks have 256 cylinders with 8 tracks per cylinder.
        Each track has 16 sectors of 512 bytes each. Upto 4 requests can be
        serviced concurrently by the system.

    Disk4: DiskSubSys (2, 256, 8, 16, 512, 0.0001, 0.0001, 50, 0.001, 0.0001);
        Defines 2 disks with controller. Each disk has 256 cylinders,
        with 8 tracks of 16 512-byte sectors. The controller takes
        100 microseconds to initiate and terminate requests. The disk rotates
        at 50 revolutions per second (i.e. 3000 rpm). Initiating disk head
        movement takes 1 millisecond, after which it takes 100 microseconds
        for the head to cross each track.

    Disk2, Disk3: DiskSubSys(1, 128, 1, 16, 512, 0.0001, 0.0001, 50, 0.001, 0.0001);
        Single-platter disks with 128 cylinders each. Each cylinder has 16 sectors
        of 512 bytes each. The mechanical and electrical constants are same as
        for Disk4.

    Disk1: DiskSubSys(1, 512, 16, 32, 512, 0.0001, 0.0001, 50, 0.001, 0.0001);
        A disk with 512 cylinders of 16 tracks each. Each track has 32 sectors
        of 512 bytes each. The mechanical and electrical constants are same
        as for Disk4.

    DiskCache: TBuffer(65536, 128, 512, 512);
        Defines a fully associative memory, with 128 sector-sized entries.

    Buffer1, Buffer2: CoreMemory(262144, 1, 0, 4, 1E-6, 1E-6);
        256K byte random access memories with 1 microsecond cycle and access
        times, and a datawidth of 4 bytes.

    ICUnit1: ICUnit(1, 2, 4);
        Unit for connecting two requestors with one 4-byte wide memory.

    ICUnit1: ICUnit(1, 4, 4);
        Unit for connecting four requestors with one 4-byte wide memory.

Figure 4-29. (concluded)

Interconnections
```
(TGen.DataBaseOut, DBSoftware.ExtIn);
(TGen.DataBaseIn, DBSoftware.ExtOut);
(TGen.LocalOut, Disk1.ExternalIn);
(TGen.LocalIn, Disk1.ExternalOut);

(Disk1.DataOut, ICUnit1.ProcIn[0]);

(Disk1.DataIn, ICUnit1.ProcOut[0]);

(DBSoftware.DMAOut, ICUnit1.ProcIn[1]);
(DBSoftware.DMAIn, ICUnit1.ProcOut[1]);
(ICUnit1.MemOut[0], Buffer1.LoIn);
(ICunit1.MemIn[0], Buffer1.LoOut);

(DBSoftware.FileStoreOut, CartridgeStore.ExternalIn);
(DBSoftware.FileStoreIn, CartridgeStore.ExternalOut);
(DBSoftware.DMAOut, ICUnit2.ProcIn[2]);
(DBSoftware.DMAIn, ICUnit2.ProcOut[2]);
(DBSoftware.Stable1Out, Disk2.ExternalIn);
(DBSoftware.Stable1In, Disk2.ExternalOut);
(DBSoftware.Stable2Out, Disk3.ExternalIn);
(DBSoftware.Stable2In, Disk3.ExternalOut);

(Disk2.DataOut, ICUnit2.ProcIn[0]);
(Disk2.DataIn, ICUnit2.ProcOut[0]);
(Disk3.DataOut, ICUnit2.ProcIn[1]);
(Disk3.DataIn, ICUnit2.ProcOut[1]);

(CartridgeStore.DMAOut, ICUnit2.ProcIn[3]);
(CartridgeStore.DMAIn, ICUnit2.ProcOut[3]);
(CartridgeStore.StageOut, Disk4.ExternalIn);
(CartridgeStore.StageIn, Disk4.ExternalOut);
(CartridgeStore.BuffIn, Disk4.DataOut);
(CartridgeStore.BuffOut, Disk4.DataIn);

(DiskCache.AddrIn, Disk4.CacheOut);
(DiskCache.PTEOut, Disk4.CacheIn);
```

Statistics
List of ports for which statistics are to be maintained.

Figure 4-30. A Database System with a Disk File Store and RAM Stable Storage.

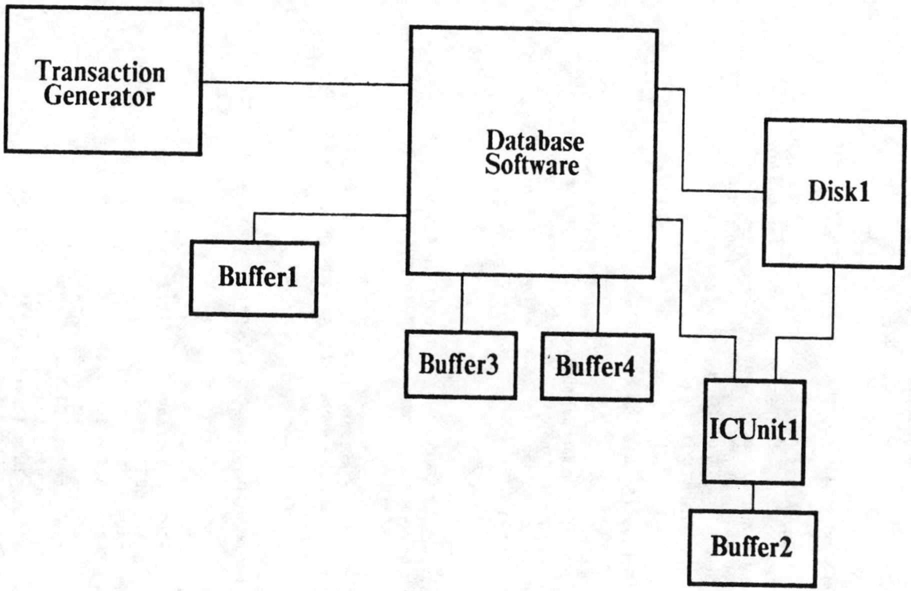

Figure 4-31. Hierarchy Description for a Database System—2.

DeviceModules

CoreMemory = *File specification for device module of Section 4.1.1.2*
ICUnit = *File specification for device module of Section 4.2.1.1*
DiskSubSys = *File specification for device module of Section 4.1.4.2*
TODBS = *File specification for device module of Section 4.1.6.2*
TGenerator = *File specification for the hypothetical transaction generator*

Instantiations

TGen: TGenerator(*with suitable instantiation parameters*);

DBSoftware: TODBS(65536, 512, 1048575, 262143, 1024, 8);
*Defines a database system with 512-byte pages, handling files upto
64K bytes. The stable storage devices are 1 Mbyte each in size
and the buffer has 256K bytes of storage. Transaction identifiers
take values in the range 1 to 1024. Upto 8 requests may be
queued at the ports of this device module.*

Disk1: DiskSubSys (8, 512, 16, 64, 512, 0.0001, 0.0001, 50, 0.001, 0.0001);
*Defines 8 disks with controller. Each disk has 512 cylinders,
with 16 tracks of 64 512-byte sectors. The controller takes
100 microseconds to initiate and terminate requests. The disk rotates
at 50 revolutions per second (i.e. 3000 rpm). Initiating disk head
movement takes 1 millisecond, after which it takes 100 microseconds
for the head to cross each track.*

Buffer1, Buffer2: CoreMemory(262144, 1, 0, 4, 1E-6, 1E-6);
*256K byte random access memories with 1 microsecond cycle and access
times, and a datawidth of 4 bytes.*

Buffer3, Buffer4: CoreMemory(1048576, 1, 0, 4, 1E-6, 1E-6);
*1M byte random access memories with 1 microsecond cycle and access
times, and a datawidth of 4 bytes.*

ICUnit1: ICUnit(1, 2, 4);
Unit for connecting two requestors with one 4-byte wide memory.

Interconnections

(TGen.DataBaseOut, DBSoftware.ExtIn);
(TGen.DataBaseIn, DBSoftware.ExtOut);
(DBSoftware.DMAOut, Buffer1.LoIn);
(DBSoftware.DMAIn, Buffer1.LoOut);

(DBSoftware.FileStoreOut, Disk1.ExternalIn);
(DBSoftware.FileStoreIn, Disk1.ExternalOut);
(DBSoftware.DMAOut, ICUnit2.ProcIn[0]);
(DBSoftware.DMAIn, ICUnit2.ProcOut[0]);
(DBSoftware.Stable1Out, Buffer3.LoIn);
(DBSoftware.Stable1In, Buffer3.LoOut);
(DBSoftware.Stable2Out, Buffer4.LoIn);
(DBSoftware.Stable2In, Buffer4.LoOut);

(Disk1.DataOut, ICUnit1.ProcIn[1]);
(Disk1.DataIn, ICUnit1.ProcOut[1]);

(ICUnit1.MemOut, Buffer2.LoIn);
(ICUnit1.MemIn, Buffer2.LoOut);

Statistics
List of ports for which statistics are to be maintained.

5

Tool Implementation

Having established the wide range of applicability of the ideas developed in chapter 3, we now turn to an implementation of the tool described there. The primary purpose of this implementation is to demonstrate that it is possible to build a practically useful tool based on the proposed methodology. Objectives such as robustness, a good user interface, and ease of use, while certainly important in a production version of the tool, have been de-emphasized in favor of ease of implementation.

The chapter begins with a discussion of the software environment on which the implementation is based. The overall design of the implementation and its main components are then presented. Techniques to enhance computational efficiency are also described, along with timing measurements of the most frequently used operations. The concluding section of the chapter examines the ways in which the tool could be improved.

The design, coding, and debugging of this implementation were accomplished by one individual in two months of full-time work. The fact that the tool works and is capable of performing the simulations described in the following chapters lends credibility to the claim that the proposed methodology is a feasible one. A more refined and efficient implementation would indeed be a valuable tool for designers of memory hierarchies.

5.1. The Implementation Environment

Two factors were paramount in choosing a machine and an operating system to build the implementation on: (1) a large address space, to permit detailed simulations of complex systems, and (2) a collection of software tools that would simplify the efforts of the implementor.

Of the systems available to the implementor,* a VAX-11/780 running

---

*A PDP-10 running TOPS-10, a PDP-20 running TOPS-20, a VAX-11 running VMS, VAX-11s running Unix, and the Alto and PERQ personal computers.

Unix was judged to best meet these requirements. Though the use of Simula as the language for coding the implementation would have been convenient in view of its data abstraction facilities and its support for discrete-event simulation, there is no compiler or interpreter available for this language on the VAX-11 at present. As an alternative, the implementation language was chosen to be the C language, with a preprocessor facility that supports data abstraction and discrete-event simulation through a language extension called *Classes.** Two features of Simula which are missing in this language are automatic garbage collection, and strong type checking. The absence of the latter feature was not found to be a major hindrance in implementing the tool—perhaps the debugging would have been simpler, since more errors would have been detected at compile time. The lack of garbage collection did not prove to be a drawback either: there are only a few, easily identifiable, points at which heap storage is freed in the implementation, and it is simple to explicitly free storage at these points. An advantage of using C is that Unix itself is coded in C, and there are thus no problems with interlanguage calling conventions in making use of operating system primitives.

In order to appreciate the implementation strategies used, it is necessary to understand how the class mechanism works, and how simulation primitives are represented within this framework. The next section presents a brief overview of these topics. The documents describing the class mechanism (see [Stroustrup81] and [Stroustrup80]) discuss these issues more comprehensively and in greater depth. A familiarity with the C language is assumed throughout this chapter; Kernighan [78] is the canonical reference on this subject.

5.1.1.   The Class Mechanism

Support for the language features described in this section is provided by a special preprocessor phase located between the macro expansion phase and the other phases of the standard C compiler. The presence of this preprocessor is completely transparent to all other phases of the compiler. During a compilation, portions of the source code which make use of the class mechanism are transformed into underlying data representations and operations in C, while other parts of the source program are left unchanged. The preprocessor only performs syntactic transformations—the semantics of the source program is not altered.

---

*These are similar, but not identical to classes in Simula.

A *Class* is essentially an abstract data type—a collection of data and procedures that operate on this data. Figure 5-1 presents a self-explanatory example, illustrating the use of the class mechanism to define a stack of characters. There are three separate source files: **stack.h**, defining the class; **stack.c**, containing the code for functions of the class; and **main.c**, containing a program which uses the class. The latter two files can be compiled independently of each other, each including the first file as an initial prefix to their contents.

The salient language features illustrated by this example are as follows.

Information Hiding. Only those parts of a class definition that follow the keyword *public* are visible to users of that class. All the data items and functions defined in a class are, however, accessible within the bodies of the member functions of that class. In the example, only the functions *push* and *pop* are accessible in the body of *main*, but the bodies of these functions may use all the entities defined in the class *StackOfChars*. Changes may be made to the private parts of a class and to the bodies of its member functions without modifying the programs which use the class.

Initialization/Termination. The functions *new()* and *delete()* have a special significance: they cannot be explicitly called, but are implicitly invoked by the runtime system. The *new()* function of a class is called immediately after the storage for an instance of that class is allocated, and performs whatever initialization is necessary. Before storage for a class object is freed, the *delete()* function for that class is called, in order to perform termination operations. The *new()* function can take parameters—this provides a means of defining a class with instantiation parameters.

Allocation and Naming. A class definition does not cause storage allocation; it is only a template for the creation and use of a certain kind of object. In this respect a class definition is identical to a *struct* definition in C. A class object can either be created on the stack, by declaring a variable of that class, or on the heap, as a result of an explicit allocation request. In the example, *MyStack1* is a class object allocated on the stack, while *MySPointer* is a pointer to a similar object allocated on the heap. A notation identical to that for *struct* references is used in naming entities within a class. *MyStack1.pop()*, for example, refers to a pop operation on the stack object *MyStack1. MySPointer->pop()*, on the other hand, refers to a similar operation on the stack object whose address is in *MySPointer.*

Figure 5-1. A Simple Example Using the Class Mechanism.

```
/*----------------------Start of file "stack.h"----------------------*/
#define SIZE 100      /* compile-time constant definition */
class StackOfChars
        {
                void new(int); /* initialization */
                void delete(); /* de-initialization */
                int     stacktop; /* where to put the next pushed element */
                char    contents[100]; /* the actual contents */
        public:
            void        push(char);
            char        pop();
        };
/*----------------------End of file "stack.h"----------------------*/




/*----------------------Start of file "stack.c"----------------------*/
#include <stack.h>      /* Provide the class definition */

        /* Now define the functions associated with this class */

void StackOfChars.new()
        /* Called by run time system just after creation of data structure */
        {
        stacktop = 0;
        };

void StackOfChars.delete()
        /* Called by run time system just before deletion of data structure */
        {
        if (stacktop != 0)
                printf("Attempt to delete non-empty stack\n");
        };

void StackOfChars.push(char c)
        {
        if (stacktop == SIZE)
            printf("Stack full, can't push\n");
        else
            contents[stacktop++] = c;
        };

char StackOfChars.pop()
        {
        if (stacktop == 0)
            printf("Can't pop empty stack\n");
        else
            return(contents[--stacktop]);
        };

/*----------------------End of file "stack.c"----------------------*/




/*----------------Start of file using the class "stack"----------------*/
#include <stack.h>        /* provide the class definition */
                          /* code for the class functions will be linked in
                                    at load time */

main()
    {
    char x;
    class StackOfChars MyStack1; /* this will be allocated on main's stack */
    class StackOfChars *MySPointer; /* pointer to a stack to be allocated on
                                    the heap */
```

Figure 5-1.   (concluded)

```
MySPointer = new class StackOfChars;  /* heap allocation */

/* typical use of MyStack1 */
MyStack1.push(x);
x = MyStack1.pop();

/* typical use of MySPointer */
MySPointer->push(x);
x = MySPointer->pop();


delete MySPointer; /* get rid of heap object */
};
/*------------------End of file using the class "stack"--------------------*/
```

The notion of a *derived class* provides a means of using an existing class as a partial definition of a new class. If C_B is a class derived from class C_A, then all the public data items and functions defined in C_A are available to the functions of class C_B—they can also be made public to C_B. C_A is referred to as the *base class* of the derived class C_B. A base class may be viewed as an abstraction which captures the properties common to all classes derived from it. In the simple example shown in figure 5-2, the stack of characters defined in figure 5-1 is used as a base class for a data structure that has an operation, *TopOfStack*, which allows nondestructive examination of the topmost element of the stack. In all other respects the derived class *NewStack* is identical to the base class *StackOfChars*.

5.1.2. Support for Discrete-Event Simulation

Two features of the class mechanism are useful in writing simulation programs. First, the passage of simulated time is maintained. Events may be scheduled to occur in the future. Second, multiple loci of control are permitted. This simplifies the description of the activities of a number of different entities at the same instant of simulated time.

The abstraction of an independent locus of control is embodied in a *task*. A task is a predefined class whose *new()* function is executed concurrently with the *new()* functions of other tasks. The most frequently used operations provided for tasks by the runtime system are: sleeping until woken by another task, suspending execution for a specified length of time, and waiting for one or more tasks to terminate. The execution of a task is begun, on creation, by an implicit call to its *new()* function, and continues until the function terminates. No timeslicing is done by the runtime system—a task continues execution until it voluntarily requests suspension. Using task as a base class, one can construct a model for an autonomously functioning entity in a

Figure 5-2. A Simple Example of a Derived Class.

```
#include <stack.h> /* to obtain definition of StackOfChars */

class NewStack: public StackOfChars
    {
    public:
        char TopOfStack();
    };

char NewStack.TopOfStack()
    {
    char c;
    c = pop();
    push(c);
    return(c);
    };
```

simulation. Further details on the class mechanism and the support provided for simulation can be found in the original documentation ([Stroustrup81] and [Stroustrup80]).

5.2. Outline of Implementation

In this section we present an overview of the implementation strategy, identify the components comprising the tool, and trace the transformation of a hierarchy description and the device modules used by it into an executable module which will perform the simulation. In the rest of this chapter all references to the C language refer to the extended version of that language, incorporating the class mechanism. Similarly, references to the C compiler are to be understood to include the class preprocessor.

The tool has three main components: (1) a library of class definitions and associated functions; (2) a preprocessor for device modules; and (3) a preprocessor for hierarchy descriptions.

Each device module is transformed into a class, using the definitions in the library as base classes in the transformation. The functions defined as part of these base classes, along with a few functions for initialization, termination, and error handling, together constitute the runtime system for the simulation. Underlying this runtime system is the support for task management and scheduling of events in simulated time.

Dmprep, the device module preprocessor, takes a device module specification with the syntax defined in figure 3-6, parses it, and uses the base class definitions to construct a class definition for the device module. Each device module is a separate file and is transformed by *dmprep* into two files: one containing the class definition and the other containing the bodies of the functions defined for this class. A naming convention is adopted for these files:

- The suffix ".dm" indicates a file containing a device module definition.
- The standard Unix suffix ".c" is used for files containing actual C code.
- A suffix ".h" is used for the class definition files. These files are included as prefixes of ".c" files and hence have the standard Unix suffix for included files.

Figure 5-3 depicts the steps involved in the processing of a device module file, *X.dm*. Using the collection of base classes, *dmprep* converts *X.dm* into two files, *X.h* and *X.c*. *X.c* is then used as input to the C compiler, yielding the file *X.o*, which contains the compiled code for all the functions specified in *X.h*. The *X.h* file is used not only in *X.c*, but also in the ".c" files of all hierarchy descriptions which use this device module. *X.o* is used by the Unix linker in the final step of creating the executable module for a simulation.

A hierarchy description is converted by *hdprep* into two files: one containing the C source code for the main program of the simulation, and the other containing the dependency relationships between the various source program files used in constructing the final executable module. The latter file is in a format acceptable to the *make* program. This program is a standard Unix tool, typically used for building a large system in a series of steps from a number of different source files and language processors—details on it can be found in Feldman [78]. The main advantage of using *make* is that only those source files which have been altered since the last time the system was built are recompiled—unnecessary recompilations are avoided.

Figure 5-4 illustrates the processing of a hierarchy description. The file naming conventions adopted here are:

- The suffix ".hd" indicates a file containing a hierarchy description.
- ".c" files contain C source code.
- ".o" files are files containing compiled C code.
- ".out" is the suffix used for the final output module—execution of this file performs the simulation described by the corresponding hierarchy description.
- A file with the suffix ".make" is in a format acceptable to *make* and contains the instructions needed to build the ".out" file.

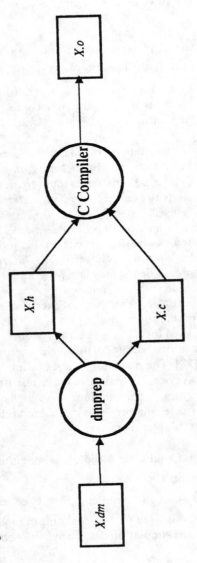

Figure 5-3. Steps in Processing a Device Module.

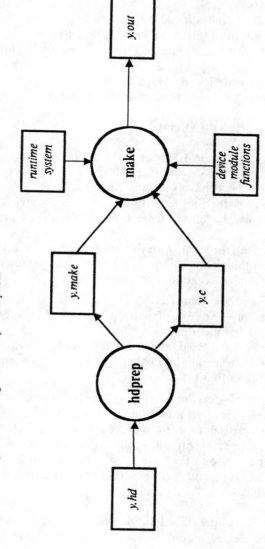

Figure 5-4. Steps in Processing a Hierarchy Description.

In figure 5-4, a hierarchy description file *y.hd* is converted by *hdprep* into the files *y.c,* containing the main program for the simulation, and *y.make.* Driven by *y.make, make* first applies *dmprep* to those ".dm" files which have been altered since the last time *y.out* was constructed. It then compiles *y.c* using the base class definitions and the ".h" files of the device modules referred to in *y.hd.* The output of this compilation is then linked with the ".o" files of the referenced device modules to yield *y.out.* Executing *y.out* performs the simulation.

Based on the overview provided in this section, the next two sections describe the details of the transformations effected by *dmprep* and *hdprep.*

5.3. Processing a Device Module

Using the example in figure 5-5 this section discusses how a device module is converted into a C class. This example is a contrived one, and is not representative of the behavior of any memory device—it does, however, incorporate many of the tool features discussed in chapter 3. The syntactic conventions adopted in this implementation are evident from figure 5-5:

- The input is free form, with line breaks, spaces, and tabs being legal wherever a blank is permitted. Text within the character pairs "/*" and "*/" are construed as comments and ignored.

- The underscore character, "_," is of special significance to the preprocessor. For ease of parsing, it is used as a prefix to all the keywords of the device module. For instance, the keywords **PortDeclaration, ResponsePort**, and **BlockSize**, which are depicted in boldface in the examples in appendix A are expressed with a leading underscore in figure 5-5.

- The names of procedures defined in the procedure declaration section also have a leading underscore. This permits easy recognition of procedure calls embedded in procedure and active function bodies— the need for recognizing such calls is discussed later in this section. For the same reason, the names of runtime procedures, such as DOSIMULATE() and SELFPORTINDEX(), are also preceded by an underscore.

Figure 5-6 shows the class definition file (i.e., the ".h" file) generated by *dmprep* for the device module file of figure 5-5. There is a single class definition, named after the device module name and derived from the base class *BasicDevMod.* The latter class contains the data structures and functions needed for keeping track of device statistics and other housekeeping

Figure 5-5. An Example of a Device Module.

```
Example: _Device(int parm1, real parm2, char *parm3, int parm4);

/* Comments such as this one can appear anywhere and are ignored */
/* The input is free-format: no line ending conventions apply, and arbitrary
amounts of whitespace may appear wherever a blank is permitted */


_PortDeclaration
     ScalarPort2: (_Output, _BlockSize=parm4);
     ScalarPort1: (_Input, _QueueLength=parm1, _BlockSize=parm4, _ActiveFn=AFn1,
                                    _ResponsePort=ScalarPort2);
     ArrayPort2[10]: (_Output);
     ArrayPort1[10]: (_Input, _ActiveFn=AFn2, _ResponsePort=ArrayPort2);

_StateDeclaration
     int StateVar1;
     char StateVar2[100];
     char *StateVar3;
     class PreDefinedClass StateVar4;
     struct PreDefStruct StateVar5;

_ProcedureDeclaration
     void _Function1()
         {
         Body of procedure Function1
         };


_ActiveFnDeclaration
     AFn1: _ActiveFunction
         {
         Body of active function AFn1
         };

     AFn2: _ActiveFunction
         {
         Body of active function AFn2
         };
```

information. Each instantiation parameter is represented as a variable of the same name and type as the parameter, and is thus accessible within the bodies of all the functions defined in the class. There is also a one-to-one correspondence between the instantiation parameters of the device module and the second to the last parameters of the *new()* function. The first parameter to the function is the instantiation name of the device module. The state variables of the device module are represented as variables of the class definition, thereby making them globally accessible to all the functions defined in the class. Note that there is no public part to the class definition—names defined within the class definition are thus accessible only to the functions of the class.

Figure 5-6. The ".h" File Corresponding to Figure 5-5.

```
class Example: public BasicDevMod
        {
        void new (char *, int, real, char *, int);
        int parm1;
        real parm2;
        char * parm3;
        int parm4;
        class OutPort *ScalarPort2;
        class InPort *ScalarPort1;
        class OutPort *ArrayPort2[PORTARRAYMAX];
        class InPort *ArrayPort1[PORTARRAYMAX];
        int StateVar1;
        char StateVar2[100];
        char *StateVar3;
        class PreDefinedClass StateVar4;
        struct PreDefStruct StateVar5;
        void Function1 (int, int);
        int AFn1(int, int);
        int AFn2(int, int);
        };
```

Each port definition in the device module is represented as a pointer to a port in the class definition; the actual instantiation of this port is done by the *new( )* function. Port arrays are represented as arrays of pointers to ports. C permits only compile-time constant array bounds, but the dimensionality of a port array may be an instantiation parameter. Consequently, an implementation-dependent limit is enforced on the size of a port array, and is used as the bound of the corresponding port pointer array. The *new( )* function, however, only creates as many port array elements as are actually specified.

Functions defined in the **PortDeclaration** section are made functions of the class definition, with two extra trailing parameters. Active functions, which are essentially parameterless procedures, are also declared as functions of the class definition with two parameters. The need for the extra parameters in both cases is explained later in this section.

The ".c" file generated when the ".dm" file of figure 5-5 is used as input to *dmprep* is shown in figure 5-7. The preamble consists of a series of included files specifying macro definitions for input-output and other basic facilities of C, base class definitions of the tool, and the class definition for this device module (i.e., the ".h" file of figure 5-6).

The bodies of all the functions defined in the class definition file follow this sequence of included files. The first of these is the *new( )* function, constructed by *dmprep*. Each formal parameter to this function has the same

Figure 5-7. The ".c" File Corresponding to Figure 5-5.

```
#class
#include <sys/types.h>
#include <sys/times.h>
Other included files

void Example.new (char *_instName, int _parm1, real _parm2,
    char * _parm3, int _parm4): (_instName)
    {
    int __i;
    parm1 = _parm1;
    parm2 = _parm2;
    parm3 = _parm3;
    parm4 = _parm4;
    ScalarPort2 = new class OutPort("ScalarPort2", this, 1, parm4, 0);
    ScalarPort1 = new class InPort(AFn1, "ScalarPort1", this, parm1, parm4, 0);
    ScalarPort1->BindRport(ScalarPort2);
    if (10 > PORTARRAYMAX) simerr(2);
    for (__i = 0; __i < PORTARRAYMAX; __i++)
            ArrayPort2[__i] = NULL;
    for (__i = 0; __i < 10; __i++)
        {
        ArrayPort2[__i] = new class OutPort("ArrayPort2", this, 1, -1, __i);
        }
    if (10 > PORTARRAYMAX) simerr(2);
    for (__i = 0; __i < PORTARRAYMAX; __i++)
            ArrayPort1[__i] = NULL;
    for (__i = 0; __i < 10; __i++)
        {
        ArrayPort1[__i] = new class InPort(AFn2, "ArrayPort1", this, 1, -1, __i);
        ArrayPort1[__i]->BindRPort(ArrayPort2[__i]);
        }
    }


void Example.Function1 (int _TrigMsgId, int _TrigPortIndex)
        {
        Body of active function Function1
        }

int Example.AFn1(int _TrigMsgId, int _TrigPortIndex)
        {
        Body of active function AFn1
        }

int Example.AFn2(int _TrigMsgId, int _TrigPortIndex)
        {
        Body of active function AFn2
        }
```

name, prefixed by an underscore, as the corresponding parameter defined in the device module declaration. This disambiguation is needed in order to be able to refer to both the device module parameters as well as the formal parameters of the *new()* function. The series of assignments statements at the beginning of the *new()* function perform the binding of device module parameters to instantiation-specific values.

The ports declared in the device module are then created in the *new( )* function and their addresses stored in the corresponding port pointers of the class definition. Defaults for unspecified port parameters are provided by *dmprep* in the calls to create ports. If a response port is specified for a port, a call is made to the runtime system to establish this relationship. The code for creating the scalar ports *Scalar Port1* and *Scalar Port2* in figure 5-7 illustrates these steps.

Following the *new( )* function are the bodies of the functions declared in the **ProcedureDeclaration** and **ActiveFn** sections of the device module. The major transformation performed here by *dmprep* is to suffix two extra formal parameters to each such function definition. The first of these parameters is the message ID of the triggering message. This information is needed in order to correctly set the **CreatedBy** field values of outbound messages, as discussed in section 3.2.2.3. The second parameter provides the information used by SELF PORT INDEX( )—it specifies the index of the port array element on which the triggering message currently being serviced was received. This parameter is ignored in the case of messages received on scalar ports. The appending of these two parameters is transparent to the author of the device module. With a view to simplifying the recognition of procedure calls, *dmprep* adopts the convention that all functions defined in the **ProcedureDeclaration** and **ActiveFn** sections, as well as the simulation runtime functions accessible to the user, have an underscore as the first character. A number of other minor transformations performed by *dmprep* within function bodies are not discussed here, in the interests of brevity.

The functions which are used, but not defined, in the code in figure 5-7 correspond either to standard C functions, or to the runtime functions defined in section 3.2.2. As mentioned earlier, the latter are implemented as function definitions of the collection of base classes defined in the included file *simtool.h* and are linked in when creating the executable module for simulation. One of these base classes, which is itself derived from the primitive class *task,* is used to represent the triggering of an active function. An instantiation of this class is created when a message reaches the head of an input queue; the body of the *new( )* function for this class consists merely of a call to the active function specified for the port on which the triggering message arrived. Each such message thus triggers a new locus of control. When the call to the active function terminates, this locus of control vanishes. An important optimization, related to this aspect of the tool, is discussed in section 5.5.

Dmprep itself is constructed with the aid of two versatile Unix tools—the parser generator *Yacc* [Johnson75b], and the lexical analyser generator *Lex* [Lesk75]. Using the BNF defined in figure 3-6, and a set of action routines written in C for performing the transformations described above, these tools provide the control structure for parsing and scanning input. A number of restrictions have been placed on the input to *dmprep* in order to simplify the action routines and to avoid writing a full parser for C. These restrictions are quite superficial, and do not detract from the usefulness of this implementation as a proof of the feasibility of the proposed methodology. A sample of the most important of these restrictions follows:

- The underscore character has a special significance, described above, outside comments and quoted strings. The names of user-defined procedures, and the keywords and runtime functions of the tool begin with this character. If an underscore is needed in any other context, it should be represented by two successive underscores.

- Port arrays cannot be arbitrarily large, as discussed earlier.

- There is an upper limit on the lengths of the names of procedures, ports, and instantiation parameters.

- Function declarations should specify the types of all parameters as well as the type of value returned by the function—defaulting, as permitted by C, is not supported.

- There is a limit on the number of parameters for a user-defined function.

- The calls to runtime system and user functions must specify only numbers or identifiers of the appropriate type as actual parameters. More complex forms, such as array elements and function values, should first be assigned to a variable of the correct type and that variable used in the call.

- Variables declared in the **StateDeclaration** section cannot have initial values specified. Initialization, if necessary, can be done in the **Initialize** phase of the simulation.

5.4. Processing a Hierarchy Description

As mentioned in section 5.2, the preprocessor *hdprep* takes a hierarchy description as input and produces two output files: one being the main program to initiate the simulation, and the other being a command file for the *make* program to construct the executable module for simulation. Figure 5-8 is an example of a short hierarchy description. Except for the fact that keywords are preceded by an underscore (a convenience for easy parsing), the syntax of the example conforms to that presented in figure 3-5 in chapter 3. The rest of this section explains the actions of *hdprep* with reference to this example.

Figure 5-8. An Example of a Hierarchy Description.

```
_DeviceModules
DevMod1: "devmod1";
DevMod2: "/usr/satya/sim/devmod2";

_Instantiations

Driver: DevMod1(10, 10);
Receiver: DevMod2(1,1,1);

_Interconnections
(Driver.DriveOut, Receiver.PortA);
(Driver.ResponsePort, Receiver.PortB);

_Statistics

(Driver.DriveOut); (Receiver.PortA);
```

The ".make" file for this example is presented in figure 5-9. The commands in this file instruct *make* to: (1) ensure that each device module which is used in the ".hd" file, and which has been altered since that module's last compilation, is processed by *dmprep* and then by the C compiler, and (2) compile the main program, and link it with the runtime system and the compiled function bodies of the device modules used in the ".hd" file.

Figure 5-10 shows the ".c" file created by *hdprep* for the ".hd" file of figure 5-8. As in the ".c" file created by *dmprep,* the preamble consists of commands to include files containing C macro definitions, base class definitions, and the class definitions corresponding to those device modules which are specified in the **DeviceModules** section of the hierarchy description. Following this is the body of the main program, the first part of which examines the command line switches and sets global variables that control the simulation. There are three legal switches:*

-d *integer*   indicates that debugging output corresponding to a level of *integer* is desired. The higher this value, the more profuse and detailed the debugging output. A value of zero, the default, suppresses debugging output. The primary use of this is to debug the simulation runtime system, but it may also be of value in debugging device modules.

-t *integer*   sets the simulation time limit to *integer*. The simulation will terminate either at this time, or when there are no more active functions alive in the system, whichever occurs earlier. If omitted, a default of infinity is used.

---

*Section 8.5 describes additional options which were added after actual usage experience with the tool.

Figure 5-9. The ".make" File Corresponding to Figure 5-8.

```
.SUFFIXES:
S = /usr/satya/sim
testhd.out:     testhd.hd $S/simtool.o devmod1.o  /usr/satya/sim/devmod2.o
        ccc testhd.c $S/simtool.o devmod1.o /usr/satya/sim/devmod2.o  -o testhd.out

$S/simtool.o:   $S/simtool.h $S/simtool.c
        ccc -c $S/simtool.c

devmod1.o:      devmod1.dm $S/simtool.h $S/simext.h
        dmprep devmod1
        ccc -c devmod1.c

/usr/satya/sim/devmod2.o:       /usr/satya/sim/devmod2.dm $S/simtool.h $S/simext.h
        dmprep /usr/satya/sim/devmod2
        ccc -c /usr/satya/sim/devmod2.c

devmod1.dm:

/usr/satya/sim/devmod2.dm:

$S/simtool.h:

$S/simext.h:

testhd.c:
```

Figure 5-10. The ".c" File Corresponding to Figure 5-8.

```
#class
#include <basic.h>
#include <stdio.h>
other included files


main(argc, argv)
int argc;
char *argv[];
        {
        Code to scan command line switches

        Code to construct runtime data structure in Figure 5-12

        Start simulation and await completion
        }
```

−p   turns on the profiling monitor. In conjunction with a Unix
                postprocessor, this enables an execution time profile of a
                simulation to be obtained. This feature was originally
                incorporated in order to improve the performance of the
                simulation tool itself, but can also be used to identify efficiency
                bottlenecks in device modules.

Next, a data structure containing all the device module instantiations in the hierarchy description is created. As figure 5-11 shows, this data structure is a circularly linked list of the device module instantiations, with the global variable *GlobRoot* serving as a handle. The *new()* function of each such device module instantiation, in turn, creates a circularly linked list of input ports and output ports associated with that module. Following the creation of device module instantiations are a series of calls to runtime functions which perform the bindings specified by the **Interconnections** section of the hierarchy description. Finally, for each port specified in the **Statistics** section, a Boolean variable in its class instantiation is set. Whenever a message passes through a port, the runtime system checks this variable to see if data collection is necessary.

At this point, the data structure rooted at *GlobRoot* contains all the information specified in the hierarchy description. An instance of the class *Simulate*, derived from the class *task*, is now created. The *new()* function of this class takes the data structure mentioned above as an implicit parameter, and performs the simulation as described in section 3.2.2.8.

5.5. Efficiency of the Tool

Though most of the development time for this implementation has been spent on design and debugging, efficiency has not been completely ignored. The most obvious and easy-to-fix sources of computational inefficiency have been identified, and modifications made to the design to improve its performance. This section discusses the techniques used for improvement and presents timing measurements of the most frequently used operations of the tool.

Profiling measurements made with an early version of the implementation indicated that more than 70% of the execution time was spent in the Unix memory allocator. The design of this routine is such that all storage, allocated or freed, is stored on one list which is sequentially searched each time storage is requested. Consequently, if a long series of allocation requests is made, the total time spent in searching this list grows asymptotically as the square of the number of such requests. In practice, since storage is sometimes freed, the performance penalty is not quite so bad. However, in the hope that appreciable improvement would still result, the design was altered to manage storage allocation internally and minimize calls to the Unix memory allocator.

Three frequently encountered sources of storage allocation requests were identified to be:

- Messages.
- Data structures used by the runtime system to hold information at a port about a message for which a response is still outstanding. This is needed in order to collect response time statistics.

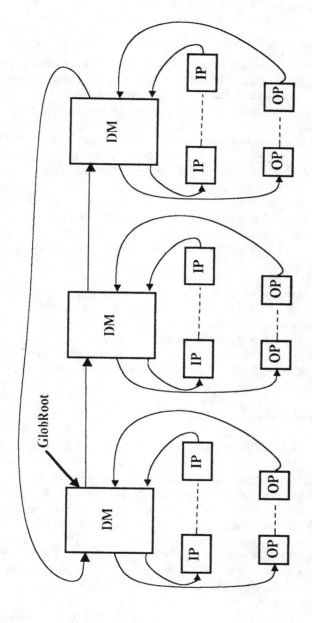

Figure 5-11. The Data Structure Built by *hdprep*.

DM = Device Module
IP = Input Port
OP = Output Port

- Data structures for holding information about device module instantiations which are blocked on a RECEIVER RESPONSE() operation.

A caching scheme is used to minimize the allocation requests due to the second item listed above: instead of a simple linked list of awaited responses, a fixed length array is used as a cache. A trivial hash function based on the message ID is used to generate a cache entry index—if empty, that entry is used to hold information regarding the outstanding request. If the entry is not free, the linked list is used as before. With a 90% cache hit ratio, this technique was observed to reduce the time required for a SEND MESSAGE() operation from an average of over 2000 microseconds to about 500 microseconds.

Another improvement in the design is the use of an internally maintained free list for each of the three entities listed above. Freeing such an entity no longer results in its storage being reclaimed by Unix—the freed entity merely gets added to the corresponding internal free list. Allocations are made from this list and the Unix allocator is called only when the free list corresponding to a desired entity is empty. With this technique, the time for allocating a message, after a typical sequence of allocations and deallocations, is reduced from about 270 microseconds to 70 microseconds. Comparable improvements are observed in operations involving the other entities.

The creation of a task-based class requires memory allocation for the data in the class as well as private stack space. For obscure "implementation reasons," the task management system of C does not permit deletion of task-based classes. Such classes can be put into a state from which they can never be reactivated, but they remain on the task scheduler's dispatch list and occupy the storage allocated to them. Such a restriction is obviously incompatible with an implementation strategy that makes each triggering of an active function a new instance of a task-based class—the memory requirements for a long simulation could exceed the available storage! For the reasons discussed earlier in this section, even if adequate memory were available, the allocation of a long sequence of task-based classes, without any freeing, would result in unacceptable Unix memory allocator performance. For instance, a sequence of 1000 active function triggerings was observed to require, on the average, more than 100 milliseconds per activation—a figure that is certainly too high for the simulation tool to be of any practical use. The implementation therefore associates, with each input port, a linked list of instantiations of the task-based class representing the triggering of an active function. The elements on this list are either busy executing the active function body, or are asleep awaiting work—they are never in a terminated state. When triggering is to be done, this list is searched for an idle element to be woken up and assigned to this instantiation of the active function. Only if no such element is available, is a new task-based class instantiation created and linked to the end of this list. The number of such elements created at an input port of a device in the course of a simulation thus corresponds to the high-water mark of the concurrency level of the device, as a result of requests received at that port. With this design, the average time for an activation and termination of an active function, assuming a concurrency level of about five, is about 1500 microseconds.

Finally, since statistics collection is done on every message transmitted, the code for it is inline rather than in procedures, as in the first implementation. Measurements are not available to indicate exactly how much time is saved by this.

5.5.1. Operation Timings

Table 5-1 shows the observed times for the two most frequently used operations of the simulation tool—SEND MESSAGE() and RECEIVE MESSAGE(). Each measurement was made by performing 1000 iterations of an operation and obtaining the average time per operation. The Unix timing facility has an accuracy of about 1/60 of a second, and hence the average times presented here are at a resolution of about 1/60 of a millisecond. The overheads incurred in loop housekeeping during measurements have been taken into account in these times.

The time for these operations is not a constant, but is dependent on which of a certain set of actions has to be performed by the runtime system. For instance, the time for sending a message between two ports for which no statistics collection has been specified is less than the time for the case when statistics collection is specified for one or both ports. The main factors which increase the time for SEND MESSAGE() are:

- Statistics collection.

- The presence of a response port for the receiving port. Further, the hit ratio in the cache of awaited responses is a critical factor is determining the operation time. When statistics collection is disabled at the receiving port, the presence or absence of a response port is immaterial.

- The presence of an active function at the receiving port—this involves triggering of an instantiation of the active function. The time for the operation also increases with the high-water mark of the concurrency level of this device module.

The time given for a RECEIVE MESSAGE() operation assumes that a message is always available at the port where the operation is performed—if blocking

Table 5-1. Typical Timings of Operations.

	Operation	Qualifications	Time(μs)
1.	SendMessage	No statistics No triggering	130
2.	SendMessage	With statistics No response port No triggering	210
3.	SendMessage	With statistics With response port 90% cache hit ratio No triggering	490
4.	SendMessage	No statistics With triggering Concurrency level 5	1500
5.	ReceiveMessage	No Blocking	60

were necessary, the time observed would be longer. For each entry in table 5-1, the third column specifies the conditions under which the time given in the fourth column was observed.

5.6. Conclusion

This chapter has attempted to illustrate the design strategy used in one implementation of the tool described in chapter 3. In the preceding sections, an effort has been made to strike a reasonable balance between the conflicting goals of providing adequate detail, and being clear: it is hoped that the end product convinces the reader that a reasonably efficient implementation of the simulation tool can indeed be built.

A production version of this tool would have to address two main issues: (1) removing the restrictions on the input format of the device module; and (2) making the primitive operations more efficient than they are now.

The first of these is a purely syntactic issue, and there is no reason to doubt that this improvement can be made. Confidence in the ability to effect the second improvement is engendered both by the fact that very little time has been spent on this issue in the current implementation, and by the existence of message-based systems with efficient task creation and termination mechanisms. For instance, the Echoes experiment [Kazar80] on the Cm* multiprocessor demonstrates that a task with a private stack but the same address space as its parent can be created on a remote processor in about 1000 microseconds. Communication between processors on Cm* is microcoded and hence efficient; however, those processors are LSI-11s, which are about five times slower than the VAX-11/780 used in this simulation tool implementation. With microcode support, and more careful design and coding, there is reason to expect the time for a SENDMESSAGE() operation with triggering to be well below 500 microseconds in a production version of this tool.

Part III

Application

6

Cooperating File Systems
for a Local Network

The preceding chapters have put forth a methodology for modelling storage systems, and have established that it is both versatile and feasible. The latter half of this book, composed of chapters 6, 7, and 8 describes the application of the proposed ideas to the performance analysis of an actual system. Use of the methodology and tool in an in-depth case study serves a number of functions:

- It further confirms the practicality of the proposed methodology.

- By providing experience in using the tool, it gives feedback to the design and implementation process. The features needed to make a system usable are often recognized only during actual use of the system.

- It provides an opportunity to obtain a realistic estimate of the overheads imposed by the tool in simulations.

- The specific system examined is one whose performance characteristics are not known a priori. The modelling of the system and analysis of simulation results thus provide implementors with an understanding of the performance tradeoffs in this design.

This chapter is divided into two main parts: section 6.1 describes the design of the system being studied, while section 6.2 discusses the models used to represent the system components and the assumptions made in developing them. Based on experimental observations of an actual file system, chapter 7 develops a device module for driving file system simulations. Using this driver and the device modules described here, chapter 8 reports the results of simulations which examine the effect of various design parameters on system performance. The latter chapter also evaluates the tool and the methodology in light of the experience gained by using them.

6.1. Description of the System

The system chosen for study consists of a collection of autonomous file systems connected by a local network, and cooperatively providing a variety of services related to the long-term storage of data. This system was originally designed for use in the Computer Science Department at Carnegie-Mellon University. The goals addressed by the design are as follows:

- From the viewpoint of users, the entire facility appears to be a single logical entity. The physical distribution of data and functions between different components is transparent to users.

- Hardware limitations, such as limited storage capacity at a network node, are only reflected in reduced performance. Users at such nodes are able to use the full functionality of the system.

- There is a clear separation of the storage, naming, and authentication functions, and it is possible to use any of these functions independently of the others. This separation simplifies the design of protected subsystems tailored to specific tasks such as database management and program development.

- The protection mechanism is flexible and easily managed, and permits the granting and revocation of access rights at the file level.

- The nodes of the network span a broad range of hardware and software. Some of the nodes correspond to existing timesharing systems, while others are personal computers being developed in the SPICE project [Spice80].

- It is recognized that the preceding goals may sometimes conflict with the philosophies of existing software. To maintain compatibility with the existing file systems on certain nodes, it may be necessary to restrict the set of functions available to these nodes. However, the file systems at the personal computer nodes will support the full functionality of the design.

At the present time the actual implementation meets only a subset of these goals and differs in some details from the original design described in the works by Accetta [80] and Thompson [81]. For purposes of analysis, however, we consider the latter. Sections 6.1.1 to 6.1.3 briefly describe this design, focussing on those aspects of the system which are germane to its performance.

6.1.1. Overview

Communication between file systems takes place over a 3-Mbit Ethernet, using the IPC protocol described by Rashid [80]. This protocol provides for the reliable and protected transport of messages between processes executing on the same or different hosts. It also subsumes functions such as flow-control, priority transmission of emergency messages, and the disassembly of messages into packets and their reassembly.

One of the file systems, designated the Central File System (CFS), is the logical repository of all shared data in the system. Each of the other file systems, referred to as a Local File System (LFS), is a client of the CFS and contains two kinds of files: local and global. The union of the global files of all the LFSs constitutes the shared data in the system; the global file address space is common to all the LFSs.

Also present on the network, but visible only to the CFS, is an archive facility using videodisks [Bulthuis79] to provide a very large, write-once, storage capacity—sufficient to store all the global files created in the system over its expected lifetime. The archive consists of a library of videodisks, disk drives for reading and writing videodisks, and an automated selection mechanism to transfer videodisks between the library and a drive. The archive is completely automatic, and requires no human intervention for its functioning. Figure 6-1 is an illustration of the overall system configuration.

Every file created on the CFS has a permanent copy created on the archive. The LFSs, in turn, act as local caches for the files in the CFS, thus resulting in a three-level memory hierarchy. Analogous to the situation in hardware caches, the transfer of files between the CFS and the archive, and between an LFS and the CFS is invisible to users. This hierarchical organization of the file systems is depicted in figure 6-2.

It has been mentioned earlier that the LFSs differ in their software and in the hardware on which they run. For the purpose of detailed examination, modelling, and simulation we examine one specific type of LFS: the Spice File System (SFS), which runs on the SPICE personal computers. The SFS is explicitly designed to operate in this environment whereas the other LFSs have to be retrofitted for compatibility. Consequently, SFS comes closest to meeting the design goals listed earlier, and offers a functionality not exceeded by any other LFS. Modelling the most general case makes it relatively simple to model more specialized LFSs if the need arises. In the rest of this study, unless otherwise specified, the term "LFS" will be synonymous with "SFS."

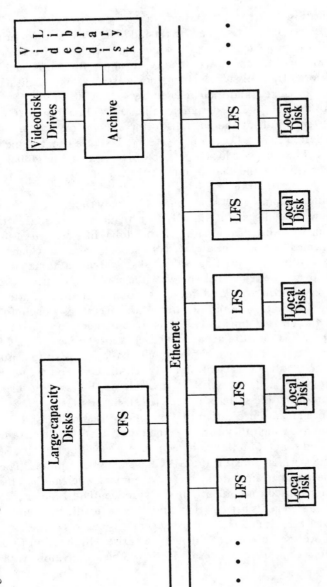

Figure 6-1. Configuration of LFS, CFS, and Archive.

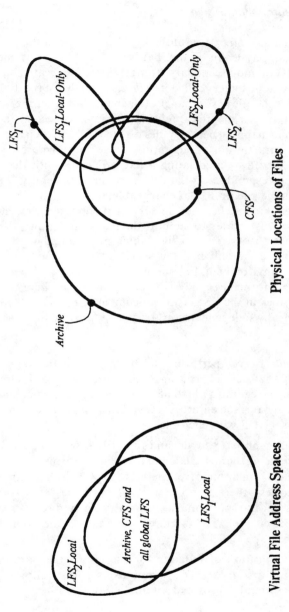

Figure 6-2. The Logical Hierarchy of File Systems.

Physical Locations of Files

LFS$_1$

LFS$_1$Local-Only

LFS$_2$Local-Only

LFS$_2$

CFS

Archive

Virtual File Address Spaces

LFS$_2$Local

Archive, CFS and
all global LFS

LFS$_1$Local

6.1.2.   The Central File System

The CFS is used as a shared resource by all the LFSs in the system and is implemented on physically secure hardware consisting of one or more processors with common secondary storage. Every file created on the CFS is identified by a unique integer called its *FileId* (FID). Most files are *invariant:* the contents of such a file never change after creation. This property of files is a consequence of the fact that the archive uses write-once media, and permits a trivial one-to-one mapping between files on the CFS and their archive copies. The classical abstraction of a long-term storage entity whose contents vary with time is achieved by associating a fixed *filename* with the FID of the invariant file corresponding to the current state of the entity. This binding between a filename and an FID is changeable, many-to-one, and orthogonal to the permanent binding between an FID and the physical collection of data it corresponds to. In order to support database operations, the CFS also supports the notion of a *variant* file, which may be updated in place. It is expected that there will only be a few such files, corresponding to the major databases in the environment. For simplicity, and in view of the fact that only a preliminary performance analysis is being attempted here, we choose to ignore variant files in the rest of this document.

Three logically independent *servers* jointly provide the functionality of the CFS:

1. The *File Server* performs the basic storage function, supporting operations such as creating a file, opening a file for reading, and writing or reading a file. It also maintains the mapping from FIDs to physical data, and enforces access restrictions by examining an access list associated with each file.

2. The mapping between filenames and FIDs is maintained by the *Name Server,* using the abstraction of a *directory.* In this system, a directory is merely a mapping from names to FIDs, other names, or other directories—there is no additional semantics associated with the appearance of a name as an entry in a directory. Directories themselves use a hierarchical naming scheme, similar to Unix [Ritchie78].

3. The verification of requests for use of the CFS are done by the *Authentication Server.* Mechanisms for specifying protection policies are also provided by this server.

Both the Name Server and the Authentication Server use the facilities of the File Server to store data needed by them for carrying out their functions. From the point of view of the File Server, the files used by these servers are treated in the same way as user files. Using the access list mechanism referred to earlier, such files are protected against access by users.

A fourth server, the *Archive Server,* manages the migration of files between the archive and the CFS and is transparent to all servers except the File Server. When a file is created on the CFS, the File Server directs the Archive Server to create a copy on the archive. Conversely, when the File Server is unable to find a file on the CFS, it requests the Archive Server to retrieve it from the archive.

It should be emphasized that the preceding descriptions of the servers are only cursory, and do not provide a complete picture of all their capabilities and functions. While this level of detail is adequate for understanding the modelling assumptions in the latter part of this chapter, a better understanding of the system can be obtained from Accetta [80].

6.1.3.   *The Spice File System*

A typical SFS node consists of a personal workstation with a processor and a megabyte or more of primary memory, secondary storage in the form of a disk, and a bit-mapped display and pointing device. For reasons of economy, or during maintenance, some SFS nodes may have to operate without local secondary storage. The design of the SFS closely resembles that of the CFS. There are three servers: a File Server, a Name Server, and an Authentication Server, each fulfilling the same role as in the CFS, and providing a similar functionality.

Files on the SFS belong to one of four *storage classes.* The storage class of a file is not a fundamental property of a file, but only a qualifying attribute, and may change with time. It is expected that in almost all cases, the assignment of a storage class to a file will be done either by a system of defaults based on the nature of the contents of the file, or by the program creating or accessing the file. Only rarely will a user explicitly specify the storage class of a file. The four storage classes are:

Local-only   These are files whose existence is known only to this SFS. They are not stored on the CFS, and are hence not accessible by the other SFSs. Most temporary files, such as intermediate outputs from compilers, document processor output en route to a printer, and other use-once-and-throw-away collections of data belong to this storage class. Local-only files which are no longer needed have to be explicitly deleted—there is no automatic garbage collection.

Direct-to-CFS   Files of this class are physically stored only on the CFS. In
(DCFS)   accessing these files, the SFS merely acts as an intermediary between a user and the CFS. A file may be assigned this

storage class either because of insufficient secondary storage at the SFS, or because system-wide synchronization of operations on it, with minimum latency, is necessary.

Cached   In situations where the size of a file exceeds the available storage on an SFS, it may be advantageous to copy frequently accessed parts of the file to local storage rather than to make it a DCFS file. By demand paging across the network to the CFS, different parts of a cached file may be brought into local storage on the SFS as the need arises. The situation is thus similar to a paged virtual memory system, with the CFS playing the role of virtual storage, and the SFS the role of real storage.

Two-copy   Files belonging to this storage class have a complete copy present on local storage in the SFS. When a file of this storage class is opened for reading, it is fetched in its entirety from the CFS, if it is not already present locally. When a user creates such a file, a copy is asynchronously created by the SFS on the CFS. Two-copy files have the advantage that they may be accessed even if the node in question is isolated from the rest of the network. Further, since all accesses after the initial fetch of a two-copy file are handled locally, the amount of network traffic is reduced. It is the responsibility of the SFS user to manage local storage by deleting local copies of two-copy files which are unlikely to be accessed in the near future.

6.2. Modelling Assumptions and Device Modules

In this section we develop the building blocks needed for constructing a simulation model of the system described in section 6.1. The first step in this process is to partition the overall model into device modules which are relatively independent of each other, and which may be parameterized to model a useful range of system configurations. The decomposition chosen here consists of five device modules, corresponding to the following entities:

- The Ethernet
- The Archive
- The CFS
- An LFS
- A Driver

The development of the device module for the driver is treated separately in chapter 7 because it requires a significant amount of explanation and discussion of experimental data. The other device modules are described in the rest of this chapter, in sections 6.2.1 to 6.2.4. Each of these sections begins with a discussion of the modelling assumptions and an overview of the corresponding device module. This is followed by an enumeration of the instantiation parameters and ports, and a brief description of their significance.* Finally, the device-specific statistics relevant to that device module are described.

6.2.1. The Ethernet Model

The Ethernet is a multiple-access packet broadcast medium incorporating a carrier-sense scheme for minimizing collisions, and an exponential-backoff retransmission algorithm to handle cases where collisions do occur [Metcalfe76]. The IPC protocol, in conjunction with lower-level protocols, uses the Ethernet to provide a collection of independent process-to-process communication paths. At this level of abstraction, the multiplexing of a single physical communication channel is manifested only as an increased transmission delay.

In the system described in section 6.1, the entities using the Ethernet are either servers of some network-wide service, or users of these services. Some servers may, of course, be users of other services. A device module that represents these server-user relationships is shown in figure 6-3. In this figure, there are M servers $S_0, S_1, \cdots, S_M$. Each server, S_i, can have up to N users, U_{i0}, $U_{i1}, \cdots, U_{iN}$. An input port and an output port are associated with each server and each user. A request received on the input port of user U_{ij} is forwarded to the server S_i after a transmission delay. The response sent by server S_i is routed back to the user U_{ij}, after another transmission delay. The routing of requests and responses is done by the device module, so servers do not need to keep track of the identity of their users.

This device module is thus a general model of servers and users communicating across an arbitrary communication medium. It is only in the calculation of the transmission delays that the specific characteristics of the medium are relevant. Incorporating other local network designs is relatively simple, and may be done without altering the external interface of the device module.

The calculation of Ethernet delays uses data presented by Almes [79]. This data is based on detailed simulations of the Ethernet and incorporates the

---

*Certain frequently occurring ports, such as those for initialization and termination, are omitted from these descriptions.

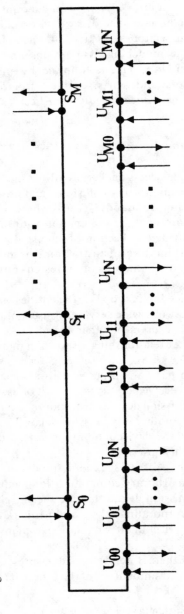

Figure 6-3. The Ethernet Server-User Device Module.

effects of the low-level phenomena, such as collisions and retrys, that affect performance. That article gives the average packet transmission delay as a function of the average load on the Ethernet, with packet size as a parameter. The average load over an interval of time is defined to be the ratio of the total number of bits transmitted in that interval to the maximum number that could have been transmitted. On the basis of experimental evidence, Almes mentions that the size of the averaging interval is relatively immaterial in computing the average load.

A piecewise linear approximation with an averaging interval of ten seconds is used for delay computation. All communications, except those involving actual data transfer, are assumed to require one packet. Write operations and the responses to Read operations are assumed to require as many packets as needed to transmit the quantity of data mentioned in the requesting message. A relatively large packet size of 2048 bits is used in all cases, since experimental evidence cited by Almes indicates that file transfers typically involve large packets.

The parameters to this device module are:

- The maximum Ethernet capacity.
- The averaging interval (fixed at ten seconds for all the simulations of chapter 8).
- The resolution of the simulation clock. This is needed in order to scale the absolute delays by an appropriate amount.
- The number of servers.
- The maximum number of users per server.

The ports of the device module are those shown in figure 6-3. The average load on the Ethernet is a device-specific performance measure, and the distribution of this quantity is maintained internally by the device module.

6.2.2. The Archive Model

As described in section 6.1.1, the archive consists of a library of videodisks, a number of read and write drives, and a mechanism for transferring videodisks between the library and the drives. Figure 6-4 illustrates the device module used to model the archive. The external interface to this module has two ports: one for archive requests, and the other for responses. Internally, the device module is decomposed into a controller and a set of read and write drives.

The total service time at the archive consists of three components: queueing for a drive (corresponding to a delay t_1), ensuring that the allocated

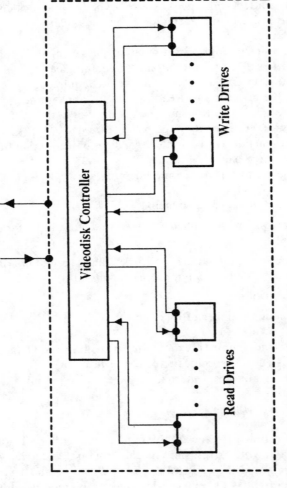

Figure 6-4. The Archive Device Module.

Note: Broken lines indicate external boundary of model.

drive has the correct videodisk (delay t_2), and actually obtaining the data from the drive (delay t_3). The factors which determine the magnitude of these delays are as follows:

t_1 The number of drives and the queueing policy obviously affect this delay. A FIFO queue is simple and equally fair to all requests. However, because the mounting of a videodisk is a relatively slow operation, a queueing policy which minimizes the total number of mounts may be better. Other optimal scheduling policies for rotating storage devices, such as those reported by Fuller [77], are also applicable. The choice of a policy depends, of course, on the specific objective function that is to be optimized.

t_2 If it is assumed that at least one drive is dedicated to write requests and that videodisks are completely filled before being dismounted, the frequency of mounts on writes will be low. For read requests, the likelihood of having a desired videodisk at a drive depends on two factors: the locality properties of the input request stream, and the queueing policy for scheduling requests. The number of drives dedicated to read requests also plays a role in determining this delay.

t_3 With a dedicated write drive, only rotational latency usually contributes to the delay for writing data on a videodisk. A seek delay occurs only when a track is full, and a mount delay is even rarer, occurring only when all the tracks have been written. For read requests, all three delays are likely to occur frequently unless the locality of the request stream is high. The calculation of these delays may be done deterministically (by assuming a storage mapping and keeping track of the coordinates of the disk head), probabilistically (viewing the delay as a random variable and assuming its statistical distribution), or statically (using constant values to represent the averages of these delays).

Since this device module is to be used only in a preliminary performance analysis, the following simplifying assumptions are made in determining delays t_1 to t_3:

• One dedicated drive each for reads and writes is present. The queueing discipline at each of the drives is FIFO.

• The probability of a mount on read requests is a constant; another constant determines this probability for write requests.

• The disk access delays are statically modelled, using average seek and latency times and a transfer time proportional to the quantity of data being transmitted.

If the need for greater realism warrants, these assumptions may be relaxed at the price of more complicated models for computing the delays.

In its typical mode of usage, it is expected that files will be transferred as a whole to and from the archive. It seems unlikely that parts of a file will be selectively sent to, or retrieved from the archive. For this reason the archive is viewed as a one-level storage system, supporting Read and Write operations on entire files. Internally, a Locate operation models a mount on a drive.

The instantiation parameters of this device module are:

- The Read and Write mount probabilities.
- The average time for a mount. This includes the time needed for dismounting the currently mounted videodisk at the drive.
- The average seek and latency times of the drives, and their data transfer rate.
- The resolution of the simulation time clock, so that delays may be scaled appropriately.

The performance statistics of interest in this model are those pertaining to queueing at the read and write drives; there are no device-specific measures.

6.2.3.   The CFS Model

Early in the development of a model for the CFS, one is faced with two critical problems. First, the set of primitives provided by the File, Name, and Authentication servers spans a broad range of functions. Many of these functions are not directly related to the storage or retrieval of data. Within the framework of the proposed methodology, it is clear that the complete functionality of the CFS cannot be captured. Second, the performance penalty associated with each CFS function depends on both hardware and software, and is difficult to estimate. If an actual implementation were available, it would be possible to experimentally measure the cost of performing each function. Since no implementation currently exists, an analytic model has to be postulated.

The device module described here assumes that the only operations of significance are those corresponding to the two-level storage model of chapter 3: opening a file for reading ($Open_R$) or writing ($Open_W$), reading a file (Read), writing a file (Write), and closing a file after reading ($Close_R$) or writing ($Close_W$). The rationale for this assumption is presented in detail in chapter 7 and is not repeated here. These operations also correspond to the most important primitives of the File Server. For purposes of performance analysis, the other File Server primitives and those corresponding to the Name and Authentication Servers are effectively ignored.

The CFS is assumed to have a single processor; this is represented as a serially reusable, nonpreemptible resource in the device module. The extension to the case of multiple processors is trivial, provided these processors are identical and processes are indifferent to the specific processor they are executing on. A processing interval is viewed as a random variable with an exponential distribution, the mean of this distribution being an instantiation parameter of the device module. If experimental data were available, an empirical distribution could be used instead.

An exponential distribution is also used to model the service time of the secondary storage devices at the CFS. These devices would typically be large-capacity disks and could be represented by an external device module such as the disk subsystem of section 4.1.4. However, such an approach would require knowledge of the mapping from file addresses to secondary storage addresses, and is avoided here for reasons of simplicity. It is assumed that there are N identical secondary storage devices, each of which is equally likely to be selected by an $Open_R$ or $Open_W$ request. All requests with the same Tag value (representing operations on one instance of an open file) are directed to the same device. Like the processor, these devices are represented internally as nonpreemptible, serially reusable resources.

Figure 6-5 shows the external interface and internal structure of the CFS device module. Requests from LFSs are received and responded to on one pair of ports, while communications with the archive take place via the other pair.

For reasons explained in chapter 7, files belong to one of three classes: *System* files, *Temporary* Files, or *User* Files. At the CFS, the class of a file is significant for two reasons. First, the probability of a requested file being at the CFS depends on the class. System and temporary files are always assumed to be available. User files may or may not be present; if absent they have to be retrieved from the archive. Second, when a system or user file is created on the CFS, a copy of it is created on the CFS. Temporary files are not copied onto the archive. The probability of a user file being absent from the CFS depends on the size of secondary storage at the CFS, the migration algorithm, and the locality properties of the request stream. A single parameter, the *hit ratio* for user files, is used in this device module to incorporate the effects of these three factors. If a hit ratio of α is specified, an $Open_R$ request for a user file requires retrieval from the archive with probability $(1 - \alpha)$.

At any instant of time, an arbitrary number of requests may be in service at this device module. The arrival of a request forks a process (modelled as a triggering of an active function) which remains in existence until the request is

Figure 6-5. The CFS Device Module.

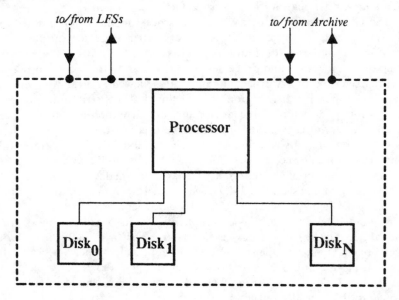

Note: Broken lines indicate external boundary of model.

serviced and its response sent. While in service, a process may be in one of five states: using the processor (S_1), using a disk (S_2), waiting for the processor (S_3), waiting for a disk (S_4), or blocked on an external event (S_5). The length of time spent in states S_1 and S_2 is exponentially distributed, as mentioned earlier. Queueing delays determine the amount of time spent in states S_3 and S_4. All cases begin with a prefix state sequence of S_3 followed by S_1, corresponding to initial processing of the request. $Open_W$ and $Close_R$ are assumed to require no further activity. For Read, Write, and $Close_W$ requests, this is followed by disk usage (states S_4 and S_2) and a cleanup sequence identical to the prefix. In the case of an $Open_R$ request with a miss, a request is sent to the archive to fetch the desired file and state S_5 is entered; after the archive response is received, the process enters the cleanup sequence. On a hit, the $Open_R$ requires no further processing. On completion of a $Close_W$ request on a system or user file, an asynchronous request is created internally to copy the file on the archive. All requests terminate by releasing the processor.

The instantiation parameters of this device module are:

- The number of disks.
- The means of the distributions for processor and disk service times.
- The user file hit ratio.
- The resolution of the simulation clock.

Since the processor and disks are modelled internally, the waiting times and queue lengths for these resources are device-specific performance statistics. The average number of requests in service is another such measure.

6.2.4. The LFS Model

In modelling the LFS, one is faced with the same pair of basic problems cited in the case of the CFS: the rich functionality of the system, and the absence of an implementation from which quantitative data can be obtained. The solution adopted here is the same as in the previous case: the only functions modelled are those corresponding to the two-level storage model of chapter 3, and analytic models are used to represent the performance penalties of the LFS hardware and software.

Given the similarity of assumptions, one might question the need for a separate LFS model. Perhaps the model described in section 6.2.3 could be used, viewing the CFS as an archive. Such an approach is not adopted here for two reasons. First, in the case of the CFS, the hit ratio for $Open_R$ operations is assumed to be an instantiation parameter. All other factors being invariant, a desired hit ratio at the CFS can be obtained by selecting an appropriate secondary storage size. However, since the LFSs are implemented on personal computers, it is likely that the cost and technology constraints on storage size are much more stringent than in the case of the CFS. It is therefore more appropriate to view the LFS hit ratio as a performance measure rather than a degree of freedom in the design specification. Second, the LFS design assumes the presence of four different storage classes for files. It would be interesting to study the performance tradeoffs associated with each of these classes. In order to do this, a more detailed model than the one developed for the CFS is needed.

Figure 6-6 shows the device module for the LFS. One pair of ports is used for user requests, while the other pair is used for communications across the network. The device module assumes that there is a processor, a storage device

Figure 6-6.   Device Module for the Local File System.

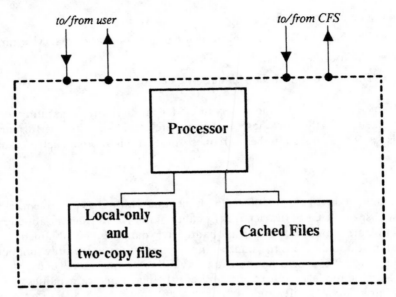

Note: Broken lines indicate external boundary of model.

for cached files, and a storage device for all other files. These components are modelled as nonpreemptible, serially reusable resources with exponential service time distributions. The separation of devices for cached files and other files makes it possible to model situations where cached file pages are stored in main memory and other files are stored on a local disk. It is possible to specify, via an instantiation parameter, that both devices are the same physical entity. This device module contains data structures to determine which two-copy and local-only files, and individual pages of cached files are currently on the LFS. The sizes of the stored files and the information needed by file and cache page replacement policies are also maintained in the device module. The need to store such detailed state information implies that an LFS device module typically has a sizable runtime memory requirement—about 1 Mbyte in the case of the simulations described in chapter 8.

The storage management algorithms on the LFS are likely to be important in determining the hit ratio. An LRU replacement algorithm, in conjunction with pure demand paging, is used for cached files. In view of the fact that most file accesses are sequential, it may be advantageous to use anticipatory paging. For simplicity, and in order to provide a reference point for comparisons of alternative page fetch policies, the current implementation of the device module assumes only demand paging.

In the case of local-only and two-copy files, the LFS design assumes that users will delete unwanted files. This deletion operation is modelled here by a threshold algorithm, conditioned on the amount of free storage. There are two limits, L and H, satisfying the relation $0 < L < H < 1$. The deletion algorithm is triggered when the amount of unused file storage falls below a fraction, L, of the total available. Files are deleted one after another until the amount of free file storage rises to a fraction H of the total, at which point the deletion algorithm is terminated. Since the actual LFS deletion process is interactive, no requests for service are likely to be made while files are being deleted. For this reason, the deletion algorithm in the device module is assumed to take no simulated time.

The driver developed in chapter 7 assumes that temporary files are never referenced later than one day after their creation. Since the local-only storage class is used exclusively for temporary files, a simple policy is used for them by the deletion algorithm: all files older than a day are deleted, while more recent files are retained.*

For two-copy files, a more sophisticated deletion policy is used. The comparison of file migration algorithms presented by Smith [81c] shows that members of the family of *space–time product algorithms* are simple to implement but yield good hit ratios. Since independent results presented in Lawrie [82] confirm this, it is used here as the two-copy file deletion policy. Each member of this family of algorithms is characterized by a constant, ϵ. If a file of size S has not been accessed for a time period T, its space-time product is given by $S \times T^\epsilon$. Files are deleted in descending order of their space-time products. On the basis of the data presented by Smith [81c], a value of 1.4 is used for ϵ and the resulting algorithm is referred to as the *STP**1.4 algorithm*.

The deletion process can be summarized as follows:

- When the amount of free storage falls below the lower threshold, L, the deletion algorithm is initiated.

- All local-only files older than a day are deleted. If the free storage fraction is now above the higher threshold, H, the deletion algorithm terminates. Otherwise two-copy files also have to be deleted.

- Two copy files are sorted in descending order of their space-time products. They are sequentially deleted until the level of free storage rises above H. At this point the algorithm terminates.

---

*The constant of one day could, of course, be made an instantiation parameter.

The device module estimates the size of a file when it is created, and each time it is copied from the CFS to the LFS. File size is assumed to be a random variable, distributed according to the empirical data presented by Satyanarayanan [81a]. On the basis of this data, a hyperexponential distribution with parameters dependent on the class of a file is used in generating file sizes.

The storage class of a file is another property that has to be determined when a file is created or copied to the LFS. This choice is made in one of three ways in the LFS: by the program creating the file, explicitly by the user, or by default. In the device module, the storage class is assigned probabilistically, using constants specified by instantiation parameters. The constants used in the simulations of chapter 8 are presented in that chapter.

Requests in service at the LFS device module go through state sequences similar to those described in section 6.2.3 for the CFS device module. On account of the increased level of modelling detail and the fact that files may be of different storage classes, the state space is much larger than in the case of the CFS device module:

S_1: Wait for processor.

S_2: Execute on processor.

S_3: Wait for local disk.

S_4: Use local disk.

S_5: Wait for cache device.

S_6: Use cache device.

S_7: This is a family of states, in which a response from the CFS is being awaited:

S_{71}: Wait for response to $Open_R$.

S_{72}: Wait for response to $Open_W$.

S_{73}: Wait for response to Read.

S_{74}: Wait for response to Write.

S_{75}: Wait for response to $Close_R$.

S_{76}: Wait for response to $Close_W$.

In comparison with the CFS device module, the transitions are more complicated. For brevity these transitions are described in table 6-1 rather than in prose.

The instantiation parameters of the LFS device module are:

- The means of the service time distributions for processor and storage devices.

- The sizes of the storage devices at the LFS.

Table 6-1.   LFS State Transitions.

	Local-Only	Two-Copy	Cached	DCFS
Open$_R$		<u>Hit:</u> <u>Miss:</u> $S_{71}S_1S_2$ $S_{73}S_1S_2S_3S_4S_1S_2$ *repeat line above for* *each page* $S_{75}S_1S_2$	$S_{71}S_1S_2$	$S_{71}S_1S_2$
Open$_W$			$S_{72}S_1S_2$	$S_{72}S_1S_2$
Read	$S_3S_4S_1S_2$	$S_3S_4S_1S_2$	<u>Hit:</u> $S_5S_6S_1S_2$ <u>Miss:</u> $S_{73}S_1S_2$ *respond* $S_5S_6S_1S_2$	$S_{73}S_1S_2$
Write	$S_3S_4S_1S_2$	$S_3S_4S_1S_2$	$S_5S_6S_1S_2$ *respond* $S_{74}S_1S_2$	$S_{74}S_1S_2$
Close$_R$			$S_{75}S_1S_2$	$S_{75}S_1S_2$
Close$_W$	$S_3S_4S_1S_2$	$S_3S_4S_1S_2$ *respond* $S_3S_4S_{74}S_1S_2$ *repeat line above for* *each page* $S_{76}S_1S_2$	$S_{76}S_1S_2$	$S_{76}S_1S_2$

Notes: All cases begin with an S_1S_2 prefix.
   Unless explicitly specified, the request is responded to at the end of the sequence.

- An indication as to whether cache file pages are stored on the same device as two-copy and local-only files.
- The constants used in the probabilistic assignment of storage classes to files.
- The low and high thresholds of the two-copy file deletion algorithm.
- The resolution of the simulation clock.

The device-specific performance measures are:

- Measures pertaining to queues at the processor and storage devices.
- The hit ratio for two-copy files. This is defined as the fraction of $Open_R$ two-copy file requests which did not require CFS access.
- The hit ratio for cached file pages. This is defined as the fraction of Read requests to cached file pages, which did not require access to the CFS.
- The frequency with which the file deletion algorithm has to be invoked.

6.3. Summary

The purpose of this chapter was to provide the motivation for the second half of the book, to describe the system being studied in detail, and to present the modelling assumptions made in the design of device modules for this system. Section 6.1 presented a high-level view of the system, stressing those aspects of its design that are likely to have a bearing on its performance. The modelling assumptions and device module descriptions were presented in section 6.2, with some forward references to chapter 7.

Chapter 7 examines the issues involved in designing a driver for file system simulations. It develops such a driver and describes the results of experiments designed to obtain parameter values for this driver. Using that driver, and the device modules described in the present chapter, the results of simulations are discussed in chapter 8.

7

A Synthetic Driver for a File System

The work described in this chapter has as its primary goal the creation of a driver for simulations of the network file system described in chapter 6. A secondary goal has been to make the driver general enough to be useful in evaluating other, broadly similar, file systems either by simulation or by queueing models.

The rich functionality of typical file systems dooms any attempt to represent the complete behavior of such a system within the framework put forth by this work. It is assumed here that the only operations which affect the performance of a file system are: (1) *opening* a file for reading or writing; (2) *closing* a file; and (3) *reading* from a file or *writing* to it. These operations map in an obvious way onto the two-level storage model described in chapter 3. The motivation for ignoring other file system functions comes from the fact that it is often the case that at least one of the following statements is true about each of them:

- It is used rarely enough to be ignored.

- It is sufficiently undemanding of computational resources that it may be ignored for the purposes of performance analysis.

- It may be represented in terms of one or more of the operations listed above.

For instance, certain file systems have a "scavenge" operation in which every disk block is examined in order to reconstruct mapping tables. Such an operation is certainly time-consuming, but occurs only rarely. Another example is a primitive on many file systems that returns information on how much secondary storage has been used by a logged-in user. The data needed to answer such a query is usually small enough that it is maintained in main memory for the duration of a user's log-in session. Consequently the use of this primitive hardly impacts file system performance. Finally, a frequently used operation such as listing a directory can often be represented in terms of more basic operations. In file systems in which directories are implemented as files, a directory listing primitive may be viewed as a read operation on the file representing the directory. It is reasonable, therefore, to restrict our attention to the operations listed earlier and to ignore all the other operations which contribute to the complexity of file systems.

While the structure of the driver developed here is quite general, its numerical parameters are based on empirical observations of an actual file system. These parameters are dependent on the activities of the user community and may not be strictly valid in other contexts. Alternatively, the same user community using a different computational environment may not generate the same kind of file system activity. However, in the absence of further information, and particularly in the case of an unimplemented file system, it is meaningful to use these parameters in a preliminary performance analysis. When empirical data is available on the file system being studied, these parameters may be reestimated and used in lieu of those provided here.

The first part of this chapter describes the structural aspects of the driver and examines the modelling assumptions used in it. Insight and some quantitative data for this driver is drawn from an earlier study on a file system [Satyanarayanan81a]. The data presented there is derived from a snapshot of the file system at one point in time, and thus corresponds to static information. Since its publication, further experimental measurements of the same file system have been made using continuous monitoring and periodic sampling. These observations, together with analytical fits to the data, are presented in this chapter and used as the basis of some design decisions. A brief concluding section summarizes the chapter.

7.1. Structure of the Driver

7.1.1. *Preliminary Design Issues*

To permit accurate performance analysis of a storage system, a driver should meet the following criteria:

- The relative frequency of use of different functions of the storage system and correlations in their usage patterns should be reflected in the requests generated by the driver.

- The interarrival times of generated requests should reflect those observed in the environment being modelled by the driver. Since the higher-order moments of interarrival time distributions can significantly affect short-term performance, it is necessary that the statistical distributions of these events be modelled as accurately as possible—postulating an arbitrary distribution is unlikely to be satisfactory.

- The requests generated by the driver should access storage addresses in a manner that accurately reflects the locality patterns observed in practice. The need for this arises from the fact that the amount of traffic in a multilevel memory hierarchy depends both on the algorithms that manage the transfer of data between different levels, as well as on the specific request stream. In the case of a file system with automatic file migration and caching of files across a network, locality of accesses to files as well as to offsets within files should be modelled accurately.

The only way to rigorously meet all these criteria is to instrument a file system and record every request made to it over a period of time. Such a trace of requests would be analogous to an instruction execution trace of a program. This approach is inadvisable for a number of reasons:

- The programming overheads involved in instrumenting a file system are nontrivial, unless such instrumentation was included as an original part of the file system design. Debugging and testing the instrumented file system has to be done stand-alone, in the absence of regular users.

- The performance penalty caused by tracing is usually high. Since the file system is a resource shared by an entire user community, imposing such overheads is rarely acceptable.

- While a trace accurately portrays the context it was recorded in, there is no obvious way to extend it to represent other situations. For instance, if a trace is made of a file system for a period of time when there are 10 users active, how does one modify it for the case when there are 20 users? In predicting performance for unimplemented systems or for anticipated loads, a trace is of questionable value.

Motivated by these considerations, the approach taken here has been to develop a synthetic driver based on an intuitive understanding of the way in which typical file systems are used. Observations of an actual file system are used to provide one set of parameter values for this driver. The driver may be extended to represent other situations by changing these parameter values. Refinements to the accuracy of the driver can be made by comparing predictions made using it with those made by using an actual trace.

In view of the fact that the network file system described in chapter 6 applies the virtual memory concept to the secondary/tertiary level, it is reasonable to ask if drivers developed for virtual memory systems may be modified for use in the present context. An example of such a driver was described earlier in section 4.1.7.

One obvious hurdle is that virtual memory systems fit a one-dimensional memory model, while file systems are more properly represented as two-dimensional storage systems. More importantly, it is not a priori evident that the locality observed in virtual memory address references is similar to the locality of file references. In fact there is reason to believe the converse. Programs exhibit both spatial and temporal locality. The spatial locality arises because of sequential execution of instructions and because data structures often span many consecutive addresses. Temporal locality arises primarily because of iterative execution of a set of instructions which access the same, or different, data in each iteration. In a file system, locality can occur at two levels: across files, and within a file. In both cases one can argue that the expected locality of reference is lower than that observed in program references to primary memory.

In the case of locality across files, there is no reason to believe that a file which has an address close to that of a recently accessed file will also be accessed in the near future—the fact that the file address space is shared across users makes this even more unlikely. Temporal locality at the file level depends on the type of file in question. Data presented by Satyanarayanan [81a] suggests that a significant fraction of files are accessed at most once after their creation. Other files, notably those containing the executable code for frequently used system programs, are accessed many times after their creation.

In the case of accesses within a file, sequential accessing certainly does imply spatial locality of accesses. On the other hand, there is little reason to believe that there is significant temporal locality of references within a file. If a subset of the data in a file is frequently used it is most likely to be read once and copied into the accessing program's address space. Repeated file accesses to the same part of a file are unlikely. In light of these observations it seems unlikely that a driver developed for a virtual memory system can be adopted for a file system.

7.1.2.   Basic Assumptions

Every file is assumed to be uniquely identified by an integer, its *FileId,* corresponding to the first-level address of a storage element in the two-level model of section 3.1.2. The file address space is initially empty, and files are alloted monotonically increasing FileIds as they are created. When a file is created, its FileId is higher than that of any other file created so far; however, its FileId need not be just one greater than that of the immediately preceding file.*

---

*This description is only partially accurate in the light of the discussion in section 7.1.4: it is strictly true only for *local* FileIds, as defined in that section.

The operations possible on a file are *Open for Read* (Open$_R$), *Open for Write* (Open $_W$), *Close, Read,* and *Write*. All files are assumed to be *invariant*, the data entered into a file at the time of its creation being never altered thereafter. This assumption of invariance is a direct consequence of the file system design described in chapter 6.** Extending this driver to the more conventional case where files may be overwritten is relatively straightforward.

It is assumed that all Read and Write accesses to files are sequential. While simplicity has been the main reason for this assumption, it is certainly true that a significant fraction of file usage in most computing environments is sequential. If experimental data on actual access patterns were available, it would be relatively straightforward to modify this driver appropriately.

Each of the five file system operations is assumed to be generated by an autonomous stochastic process, independent of the other processes. The statistical distributions of interarrival times of each operation have been studied experimentally for one file system, and are reported in section 7.2.1. However this information is available only for the file system as a whole, and not for individual files. When trace data is available, it may be feasible to model correlations in the access patterns of different types of operations to individual files, thereby removing the assumption of independence of these processes.

Each request issued by the driver is a message conforming to the format defined in chapter 3, and summarized in table 3-3. The MessageId and CreatedBy fields of the message are filled in by the simulation tool. The Action field specifies one of the five operations listed earlier: Open$_R$ and Open$_W$ map into the actions PrepareForRead and PrepareForWrite; Read and Write map onto actions of the same name; Close is mapped onto TerminateRead or TerminateWrite, depending on whether the file being closed was opened for reading or writing.

Each time an open request is generated by the driver, a new Tag value is created and is used to identify all further requests to this file. The use of a Tag value distinct from the FileId permits disambiguation between different instances of the same file being open at the same time. In this respect, the use of the Tag field is similar to that described in the transactional database system of section 4.1.6.

It is assumed that the size of each Read and Write request is a fixed quantum, which is a parameter of the driver. It would be a relatively simple matter to modify the driver so that the sizes of such requests are distributed according to a selected statistical distribution. However, in the absence of

---

**It implies that after an initial sequence of Open$_W$, series of Writes, and Close, to a file, all further accesses to it consist of sequences of Open$_R$, series of Reads, and Close.

further information, a constant size distribution assumption seems reasonable. Such an assumption is particularly appropriate for the file system whose numerical parameters are used in this driver, since its low-level software performs most input/output operations one 128 36-bit word block at a time.*

7.1.3. Modelling Locality

The sequence defined by the values in the Address field of successive requests characterizes the locality properties of a driver. Each of the five distinct, independent reference streams generated by the driver may possess different locality properties from the others. This section presents the specific locality model incorporated into the driver and discusses its rationale.

The assumption of sequential access within a file automatically determines the locality of Read and Write operations on files. The first such operation on a file after it is opened uses an address of zero. Further requests use an address which differs from the immediately preceding related request** by the fixed size quantum for Read and Write operations. If non-sequential accessing of files was being modelled, a statistical distribution would have to be used in generating the address corresponding to these operations.

The assumption of invariance simplifies the assignment of a FileId to an $Open_W$ operation—a number one higher than the FileId of the previously created file can be used. For reasons explained in section 7.1.4, a slightly more complicated address assignment is done in practice.

Modelling the locality of $Open_R$ operations is a more interesting problem. The approach taken here is motivated by the following observations presented in Satyanarayanan [81]. First, the *Functional Lifetime* (F-Lifetime) of a file is defined as the time difference between the creation of a file and the last occasion on which it was read. This quantity is a measure of the usefulness of the data in the file. Second, in general, files tend to have short f-lifetimes, of the order of a few days. However, the lengths of the tails of the f-lifetime distributions are strongly dependent on the type of file in question. Certain files, such as those corresponding to the executable object modules of commonly used programs are used long after they are created: the 90-percentile value of the cumulative distribution function of f-lifetime for this class is nearly 1500 days. On the other hand, there are files with radically different usage properties: the corresponding 90-percentile value for files containing the output from document processors is only about 80 days. More

---

*This corresponds to the size of the fixed-length data blocks on its disks.
**That is, with the same Tag value.

than 60% of such files have an f-lifetime of one day or less. Evidence presented by Smith [81b] indicates that the rate of reference to files decreases with age. This observation was made on a different file system from the one studied by Satyanarayanan [81a]. However, it seems intuitively true that older files are less likely to be used than recently-created ones. In the absence of information to the contrary, this property is assumed to be true, at least for a subset of files, on other systems too.

Based on these observations, the files modelled by the driver are postulated to fall into one of three classes:

System Files   These are files corresponding to the executable modules of system programs (such as compilers, linkers, and editors) or to files used by an operating system to maintain relatively static information (such as the list of users who may use the system, encrypted password files, and files containing documentation of system programs and commands). Files of this class are frequently read, rarely written, and usually remain in use long after their creation.

Temporary Files Many programs create files which are used at most once after their creation. For example, intermediate output created by different phases of a compiler are typically not accessed after the compilation is complete. The object files of programs being debugged, error message files created by compilers or document processors, and files generated by document processors to drive printing devices are other examples of this class. Files of this class are often created, but rarely read long after their creation.

User Files   This category corresponds to files which belong to neither of the two preceding classes. Besides the properties mentioned earlier about files in general, there is little that can be assumed about this class of files.

The locality models used for each of these three classes of files is discussed in detail in sections 7.1.3.1 to 7.1.3.3.

7.1.3.1. System Files. For the purposes of this section it is necessary to distinguish between the logical function fulfilled by a file and its FileId. The distinction between these two is best brought out by an example. Consider a typical system program, say a Pascal compiler. From the point of view of users, it is appropriate to speak of "the Pascal compiler." However this logical entity is bound to different invariant files at different instants of time, each corresponding to the executable object module of a different version of the compiler. In order to distinguish between such a logical entity and the set of invariant files that represent that entity at distinct points in time, we introduce the term *System Data Object* to stand for the former. Note that system data objects need not always correspond to programs—the non-program examples mentioned earlier (a valid user list and a login password list) are also system data objects.

At any instant of time it is assumed that there are N_{Max} system data objects identified by the integers 1, 2, $\cdots$, N_{Max}. In an actual computer system, the number of such objects typically grows with time. Since this growth is usually quite slow, it is ignored in the design of the driver. The number N_{Max} is therefore a constant, defined as a parameter of the driver. As discussed in section 7.2.2.2, the extent of usage of different system data objects varies over a significant range.* Without loss of generality, the system data objects may be ordered in non-increasing order of usage.

As figure 7-1 illustrates, the relationship between system data objects and the corresponding invariant files is analogous to that between array indices and array element values. The set of system data objects can be viewed as an array S, the element of index i representing the ith system data object. The value of $S[i]$ at any instant of time is the FileId of the invariant file which is currently bound to the ith system data object. The assumption about ordering of system data objects implies that if $i < j$, then Usage $(S[i]) \geq$ Usage $(S[j])$. Since the number of system data objects is constant over time, the size of the array S is fixed. Changing the value of element $S[i]$ corresponds to replacing the existing version of the ith system object by a new one.

If the usage of individual system data objects were known, the driver could appropriately weight the frequency of accesses to each of them. Since the number of system data objects can be quite large (typically several hundred) it becomes rather cumbersome to parameterize the driver with this usage information. A simpler alternative is therefore used. Intuitively, a small fraction of the system data objects accounts for much of the usage. For the file system considered in section 7.2.2.2, 75% of the usage is accounted for by about 4% of the system data objects; a further 20% is accounted for by about 16% of the system data objects, and the remaining 5% of the usage is accounted for by 80% of the system data objects. While these observations are strictly valid for one file system, one would expect a similar pattern of usage to be true for other file systems too. Based on this assumption, the driver

---

*The number of opens for reads is used as a measure of usage.

Figure 7-1. Relationship between System Data Objects and Their Invariant Files.

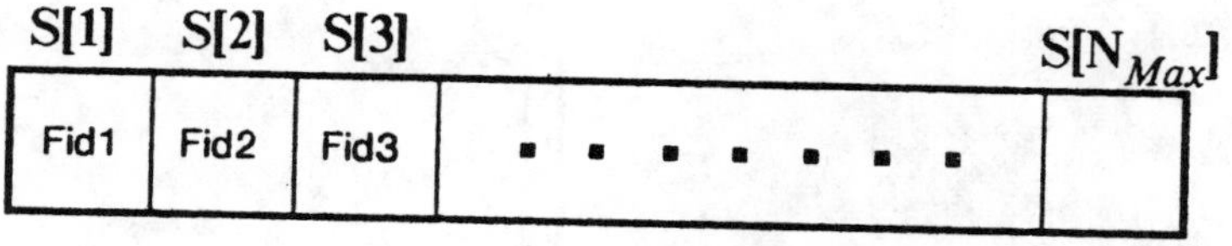

partitions the set of system data objects into three classes, with uniform probability of access within each class. The 75-fractile and the 95-fractile of the cumulative distribution function of usage are parameters of the driver. Figure 7-2 shows the assumed probability density function of accesses, N_{75} and N_{95} corresponding to the 75-fractile and 95-fractile, respectively. 75% of the accesses to system files are to system data objects in the range $S[1]$ to $S[N_{75}]$, a further 20% to objects in the range $S[N_{75} + 1]$ to $S[N_{95}]$, and the remaining 5% to objects in the range $S[N_{95} + 1]$ to $S[N_{Max}]$.

When the driver decides to generate an $Open_R$ access to a system data object, it uses the probability distribution described above to select the index of the object. The FileId corresponding to this object is used in the Address field of the generated request. On the assumption that frequently used system data objects are more likely to have new versions created, the driver also uses the same probability distribution to direct $Open_W$ accesses to system data objects—the newly created FileId is assigned to the selected system data object.

In summary, the locality model developed above for system files consists of a slowly changing set of FileIds, a small fraction of which is very frequently accessed, a slightly larger fraction being less frequently accessed, and the majority being rarely accessed.

7.1.3.2. Temporary Files. The properties that characterize temporary files are that most are never used after being created, and that the few that are used tend to be read within a very short time after creation, typically within a day. An additional assumption is that the probability of access of a file of this class falls off linearly with time. Although there is no experimental evidence to support or contradict this hypothesis, a linear falloff is the simplest and most reasonable assumption that is consistent with the observation made in section 7.1.3 that the rate of reference to files decreases with age. However, it would be relatively simple to modify the driver to incorporate a nonlinear falloff.

These assumptions are adequate to uniquely determine a locality model for temporary files. Suppose all files created are temporary files; section 7.1.4 shows how this assumption can be removed. At any instant of time τ let F_τ be the FileId of the most recently created file. Let λ be the time one day before τ,

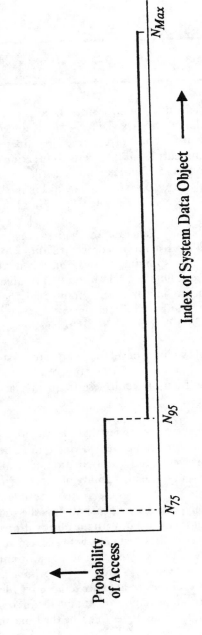

Figure 7-2. Probability Density Function of Accesses to System Files.

Note: Area under curve equals unity.

and let F_λ be the corresponding maximum FileId. Then the FileId assigned to the Address field of an Open$_R$ request generated at τ is a random variable in the range F_λ to F_τ, with a density function as shown in figure 7-3. The quantity F_λ can only be known if all the FileIds created in the course of one day are maintained. However, since the average number of temporary files created during a day, x, is known, an approximation to F_λ is given by $F_\tau - x$. Using this approximation obviates the need to keep track of a large number of FileIds. The constant of one day is, of course, arbitrary and may be made a parameter of the driver.

7.1.3.3. User Files. The primary difference between user files and temporary files is that the former tend to be accessed over a significantly longer period after their creation. By making the same assumption of linear falloff as for temporary files, the locality model for user files closely resembles that for temporary files. The only difference is that the falloff is spread over a much longer period than one day. The arguments presented in section 7.1.3.2 are valid here too, using figure 7-4 instead of figure 7-3, and $F_{\tau\,cutoff}$ instead of F_λ. The cutoff interval, $\tau - \tau_{cutoff}$ is a parameter of the driver. Since the interval τ_{cutoff} to the present time τ is quite large, it is necessary to use an approximation to $F_{\tau\,cutoff}$ rather than its exact value: $F_{\tau\,cutoff} = F_\tau - (\tau - \tau_{cutoff}) \times x$ where x is the average number of user files created per day.

7.1.4. Distinguishing File Types

In section 7.1.3.2 it was assumed that only temporary files were being generated; a similar assumption about user files was made in section 7.1.3.3. These assumptions were necessary in order to avoid having the driver maintain a history of FileId versus file type bindings. A simple way of satisfying these assumptions while generating all three types of files is to have a separate, contiguous FileId space for each file type and to map these three spaces into a global FileId space. The contiguity of the address space for each file type produces the illusion that only files of that type are being generated— all addresses from this space belong to these files.

In theory, any one-to-one mapping from local address spaces to the global space would be adequate. However, it may be of use to other device modules in the simulated memory hierarchy to be able to recognize the type of a file by merely examining the FileId. In actual file systems this information is usually available from the name of the file, or from a type field in the file header. As discussed by Satyanarayanan [81a], the type of file may be of significant value in making file migration decisions.

The mapping scheme adopted for the driver is a trivial one: the remainder obtained by dividing a FileId by 3 determines the type of the corresponding

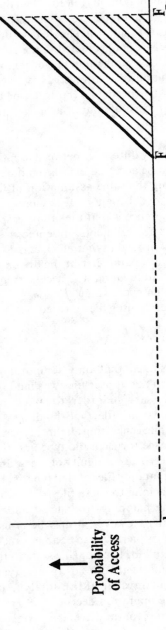

Figure 7-3. Access Probability to Temporary Files.

Probability of Access

Fileds of Temporary Files

F_λ F_τ

Note: Area of shaded portion equals unity.

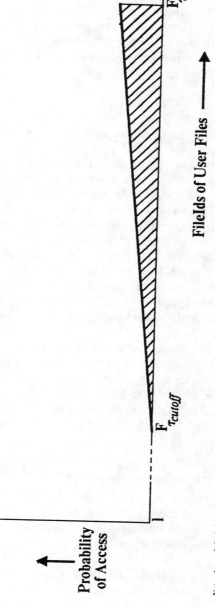

Figure 7-4. Access Probability to User Files.

Probability
of Access

FileIds of User Files

$F_{\tau_{cutoff}}$

F_τ

Note: Area of shaded portion equals unity.

file. Thus all files with FileId x such that $(x \bmod 3) \equiv 0$ are system files; those satisfying $(x \bmod 3) \equiv 1$ are temporary files, and those satisfying $(x \bmod 3) \equiv 2$ are user files. Figure 7-5 illustrates this mapping scheme. It should be noted that the local FileIds are purely local to the driver: all FileIds used outside the driver are global FileIds. Since the rate of generation of different types of files may be different, the global space may have unused FileIds below the highest FileId used; figure 7-5 shows such a situation.

7.1.5. Overall Structure of the Driver

Based on the discussions earlier, this section provides an overall view of the structure of the driver and provides the motivation for performing the experimental measurements described in the latter half of this chapter.

The driver consists of five independent event generators, one each for $Open_R$, $Open_W$, Close, Read, and Write requests. Each generator creates requests with a certain interarrival time distribution—the specific forms of these distributions are driver parameters. Once an event is generated, it has to be associated with a particular file type. The fractions of events of each kind that are directed to different file types are parameters of the driver.

If the event being generated is an $Open_R$ or an $Open_W$, a unique Tag value is created and used with all further related requests. Read, Write, and Close requests are directed to open files of a given class with equal probability. The value assigned to the Address field depends on the request being generated:

$Open_W$ The highest local FileId generated so far of the selected file type is incremented, and mapped into the global FileId space. If a request to a system file is being generated, the local FileId is assigned to a system data object selected according to the three-part distribution discussed in section 7.1.3.1.

Read or Write The address used in the most recent related request is incremented by the fixed data transfer size, and is used as the address of this request.

$Open_R$ Depending on the file type, one of the three locality models described in sections 7.1.3.1, 7.1.3.2, or 7.1.3.3 is used to generate a local FileId. This is then mapped into the global FileId space.

Building a specific instance of this driver requires the following pieces of information which have been left unspecified so far:

Figure 7-5. Encoding of FileIds.

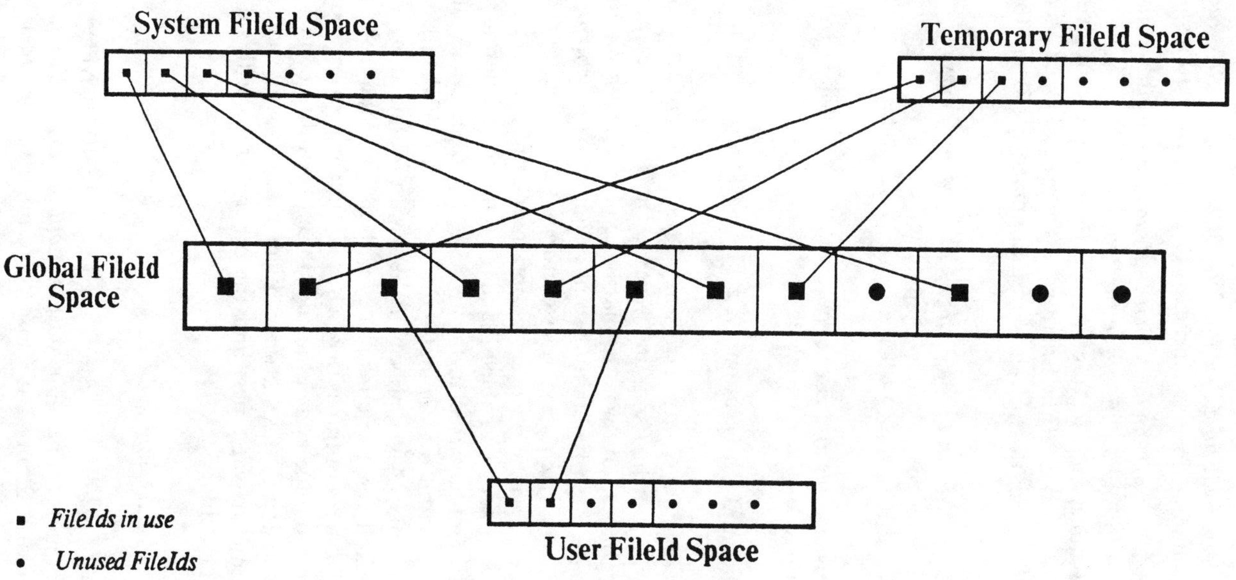

- *The interarrival time distributions of each of the five request types.*
  The functional forms and means of these distributions are needed.

- *The fraction of $Open_R$, $Open_W$, Read, and Write requests that are directed to each of the three file types.*
  It is assumed that the fraction of Close requests to a given file type is equal to the sum of the fractions of $Open_R$ and $Open_W$ requests to the same file type: this prevents an unbounded growth in the number of open files.

- *The 75-fractile and 95-fractile of the system file usage distribution.*
  This is needed in order to determine the three-part distribution discussed in section 7.1.3.1.

The rest of this chapter discusses experimental observations designed to yield one set of values for these variables.

7.2. Experimental Observations of a File System

The data presented by Satyanarayanan [81a] were collected on a PDP-10 computer system in the Computer Science Department at Carnegie-Mellon University. That study was primarily exploratory in nature, and was conducted in the hope of obtaining some insight into the properties of files in a typical file system. In contrast, the experiments described in this section were conducted for a specific purpose: to obtain quantitative data on interarrival times, usage of system data objects, and file activity for different file types. The experimental methods used in the two studies differ too. While the earlier study involved detailed examination of a snapshot of the file system at one point in time, the results presented here were obtained by dynamic data collection techniques. For consistency with the first study, and in view of the fact that this system continues to be a heavily used general-purpose computing resource, the same file system has been used for this second study.

The discussion in this section is divided into two independent parts: one concerning interarrival times, and the other dealing with usage and type-dependent file activity.

7.2.1. *Interarrival Times of Events*

The TOPS-10 operating system on the PDP-10 provides the following primitives for performing input-output: *Lookup, Enter, Close, In, Input, Out, Output.* Lookup, Enter, and Close correspond to the $Open_R$, $Open_W$, and Close operations discussed earlier in this chapter. Both In and Input correspond to Read operations; the difference between them is subtle, and may be neglected for the discussion here. In the rest of this chapter, the term

"In" will include both kinds of read operations. Similarly, Out and Output both correspond to Write operations and are jointly referred to as "Out" in the sequel.

7.2.1.1. Experimental Technique. The operating system was modified so as to intercept every input–output request to it, and to present it for examination to a metering routine before resuming normal processing of the request. The metering routine had five histogram tables, one for each of the five kinds of requests. On the basis of preliminary observations the range of the histograms was determined to be 10 milliseconds to 10000 milliseconds for all the events. On intercepting an input–output request, the metering routine noted the time elapsed since the immediately preceding request of the same kind: this quantity, t, was one sample of the corresponding interarrival time distribution. For each kind of event, the metering routine kept track of the total number of events observed, and the sums Σt, Σt^2, Σt^3, Σt^4 and Σt^5, in order to compute the first five moments of the observed distributions. It should be noted that events appeared anonymous to the metering routine: there was no information regarding which file a particular operation was being performed on. Thus the recorded data corresponded to the activity observed by the file system as a whole. Recording file-specific data, though yielding valuable information, would have involved unacceptably greater overheads.

At half hour intervals, a data collection program appended the contents of the histogram tables and moment information to a file and then cleared this data in the metering routine. The choice of a half hour was a compromise between two conflicting requirements. The first is that intervals too close together would have yielded too few sample points in each interval. Postulating statistical distributions on the basis of too few sample points is likely to lead to large errors. The second is that intervals which were too far apart might have missed significant variations in system behavior, caused by varying user activity during the course of the day. The choice of a half hour yielded 48 distinct observation intervals per day, while the typical number of Enter events* per interval was about 400. The sampling program was automatically started by the system after crashes, and the sampling epochs were the same from day to day. For instance, if a crash occurred at 12:17 P.M., the next sample would be recorded at 12:30 P.M. and not at 12:47 P.M. as the half hour sampling interval would lead one to expect. The reason for this was that it was judged to be more important to be able to correlate data from sampling intervals across different days than for every sampling interval to be exactly the same length. In practice, since the number of crashes per day was quite small, only a small fraction of the intervals were shorter than a half hour.

---

*Enters were consistently the least frequent kind of event.

Besides histogram and moment information, the information recorded by the sampling program included event identification, a time stamp, sampling interval length, and a count of the number of jobs active during the sampling interval. The data collection was carried on for a little over five weeks, after which the data reductions described in the following section were performed.

7.2.1.2.   Data Reduction. Pertaining to each of the five different events, and each of the 48 half-hour time slots, there is one observation for each day in the data collection period. It is assumed that system activity is different on weekdays and weekends, but is similar on all days within each of these two classes. The collected data can then be viewed as samples drawn from $5 \times 48 \times 2$ distinct stochastic processes. Using these samples, the observed mean and variance for each of five moments of these stochastic processes as well as their observed cumulative distribution functions can be calculated.

Figures B-1 and B-2 in appendix B show, for weekends and weekdays, respectively, the means of the five distributions as a function of the time of day. Since these are means of interarrival times, high system activity is indicated by a low ordinate on the graph. During weekdays, the period from about 10 A.M. till about 6 P.M. shows the most activity. This is indeed what one would expect, since it corresponds to the normal working day.

Rather unexpectedly, the period just after midnight shows very high activity too. As a safeguard against disk crashes, the operating staff run a program every night that copies onto tape the current copy of every file that has been created or modified since the previous night. The housekeeping activity is done when the system is otherwise lightly loaded, typically after midnight, and is the most probable cause of the high disk activity observed at this time. In systems such as the one described in chapter 6, this backing-up of files is done continuously and is not deferred until a particular time of the day. Further, input-output operations for backup are generated by the file system itself and are not caused by events external to the file system. For both reasons, it was decided to ignore this period of high file system activity after midnight and to assume that the actual user-generated activity during this period is similar to that in the morning, before the working day begins.

To model the variation in file system activity during the course of a day, two obvious alternatives present themselves. The first alternative is to model each of the 48 time slots separately for each event type. The problem with this approach is the large number of models that have to be created. The second alternative is to create a single model for each event type whose mean varies with time. Unfortunately such a model is unlikely to be a Markovian model and therefore will not be convenient for analytical modelling.

The compromise adopted was to partition the day into two periods, a

Peak Period and a *Lean Period,* and to characterize each period by one of the time slots associated with it. The peak period corresponds to the time slots in the interval 10 A.M. to 6 P.M., while the rest of the day corresponds to the lean period. For each period, the characterizing time slot is chosen to be the one at which the average rate of Lookup events attains its median value for that period: this occurs at 3 P.M. for the peak period and at 10 P.M. for the lean period. The choice of Lookup as the characterizing event is quite arbitrary— any of the other events would have been equally valid.

The partitioning into two periods could be done for weekends too. In view of the fact that the activity at peak periods on weekends is similar to the activity at lean periods on weekdays, it is assumed that weekends can be characterized by the lean period on weekdays. Though this simplification overestimates the activity in the lean periods on weekends, it was considered desirable because it reduces the number of distinct models that have to be built.

The data that has been collected has been reduced to manageable proportions on the basis of the arguments presented in this section. Clearly there is some loss of information in this process: examining the data at a more detailed level, and modelling it without the simplifying assumptions would be an extension of the work described here. For each of the five events there are two models that have to be built: one for peak periods on weekdays and the other for all other periods. The next section discusses analytical models that fit the observed data characterizing these two periods.

7.2.1.3.   Analytical Models. The means and standard deviations of the five different events during peak and lean periods are shown in table 7-1 and table 7-2 respectively. The most trivial Markovian model, an exponential, has a coefficient of variation (ratio of standard deviation to mean) equal to one, whereas the observed coefficients of variation are usually much larger than one. This indicates that exponential fits to the observed data are likely to prove unsatisfactory. Attention was therefore focussed on hyperexponentials, since they are the simplest Markovian models which can exhibit coefficients of variation greater than one. Both the moment matching method and the heuristic method discussed by Satyanarayanan [81a] were used in fitting the data. The heuristic procedure gave consistently better visual fits to the data and was used to obtain the fits presented here.

Figures B-3 to B-12 in appendix B present the cumulative distribution functions (CDFs) of the observed and fitted distributions for each of the five events during the peak and lean periods. To assess the quality of the fits, each CDF plot is followed by a P-P plot [Wilk68] which plots the fitted CDF against the observed CDF: a perfect fit would appear as a straight line at 45 degrees and the extent of the deviation from this line indicates the quality of the fit. The following comments are made with reference to these plots:

Table 7-1.   Peak Period Interarrival Time Parameters.

	Mean (ms.)	Std. Dev.	Coeff. of Var.
Lookup	345.4	622.5	1.80
Enter	2495	2918	1.17
Close	339.9	582.4	1.71
In	209.7	410.0	1.96
Out	557.4	1182.1	2.12

Table 7-2.   Lean Period Interarrival Time Parameters.

	Mean (ms.)	Std. Dev.	Coeff. of Var.
Lookup	562.1	1332.3	2.37
Enter	3389	3684.3	1.09
Close	527.1	1212.9	2.30
In	341.4	906.0	2.65
Out	1144	2341.2	2.05

- Almost all the fits are two-stage hyperexponentials. The sole exception is the distribution of Enter events during the peak period, for which a single stage (i.e., a simple exponential) gives the best fit.

- The maximum error between the observed and fitted CDFs is never greater than about 7%. Typically, the maximum error in a fit is about 3%. These fits, while adequate for practical purposes, will certainly not pass statistical tests such as the Kolmogorov–Smirnoff test or the chi-squared test [Knuth81] at the 90% or higher level. No attempt has therefore been made to obtain quantitative quality estimates for these fits.

- The maximum value of the CDF for Enter events during the lean period is only 0.9. The reason for this is that the histogram upper limit of 10000 milliseconds was determined on the basis of initial observations made during the peak period. During the lean period, however, a significant fraction (about 10%) of the Enter events are spaced further apart in time. Using the fit presented here thus overestimates Enter activity during the lean period. As discussed later in this section, the fitted distribution can be scaled to yield a lower mean rate of Enter events.

- The fits for Close events show the greatest error, close to 7%. There is reason to believe that this poor fit is not just a manifestation of the curve-fitting procedure, but is indicative of a deeper discrepancy. Many programs issue Open, Read, and Write requests sporadically in the course of their execution, but close their files only immediately prior to termination. The ensuing burst of Close requests violates the assumption, inherent in a hyperexponential model, that such requests are independent. Purely on the basis of the available data, however, it is hard to substantiate or contradict this conjecture—statistical analysis of an actual trace of requests would be the only way of testing this hypothesis.

Tables 7-3 and 7-4 present the parameters of the fitted distributions for peak and lean periods, respectively: α_i being the probabilities of selection of stages and M_i being the corresponding means.

On the assumption that only the means of these distributions change and their shapes remain unaltered, these fits can be used to model hypothetical loads. To model a load which is k times the actual load observed, the α's of the stages of the fitted distributions remain unaltered while the mean of each stage is $1/k$ times the mean specified in tables 7-3 and 7-4.* This load factor, k, can thus be made a parameter of the driver.

---

*Recall that a higher load corresponds to a lower mean interarrival time.

Table 7-3.   Fitted Parameters for Peak Period Interarrival Time
Distributions.

	Max Error	No. of Stages	α_i	M_i (ms.)
Lookup	3%	2	.9227 .077	213.2 1812
Enter	3.5%	1	1.0	2102
Close	6.5%	2	.3105 .6894	27.7 474
In	2.5%	2	.8744 .1256	112.2 863.6
Out	3.5%	2	.8530 .1453	175.6 2151

In summary, two-stage hyperexponentials with the parameters specified
in tables 7-3 and 7-4 yield reasonable fits to the interarrival times of the five
events of interest and may be extended to cover loads different from the one
actually observed.

7.2.2.   Type-specific File Data

The goal of the experiment described in this section is twofold: first, to
determine what fraction of $Open_R$, $Open_W$, Read, and Write operations are
directed to system, temporary, and user files; and second, to obtain the 75-
fractile and 95-fractile of the system file usage distribution. A single data
collection procedure yields information on both these quantities. This
procedure is described in the next section, and the collected data is examined
in section 7.2.2.2.

Table 7-4. Fitted Parameters for Lean Period Interarrival Time
Distributions.

	Max Error	No. of Stages	α_i	M_i(ms.)
Lookup	3%	2	.8988 .0966	225.2 2682
Enter	3%	2	.8658 .1342	2066 30000
Close	5%	2	.8851 .1117	209 2429
In	3.5%	2	.8802 .1187	117 1454
Out	5%	2	.7669 .2201	134.6 2376

7.2.2.1. Experimental Technique. A vendor-supplied utility to examine system status is available on the computer system being investigated. The information reported by this utility includes:

- A list of all the jobs currently in the system and the names of the programs they are running.

- A list of system programs for which the shared code ("high segment" in TOPS-10 terminology) is currently resident in primary memory. This list of high segments is a superset of the system programs being currently executed by users. Since nonsystem programs are either absent from this list, or are marked as private, there is a simple way to check if the program being executed by a user is a system program or not.

- Information on the files currently open in the system. The name of the file and the directory in which it resides, as well as information on whether the file is being read or written, and the number of read or write operations performed on it so far are also reported by the utility.

A batch program was set up to run this utility every hour and to append the data to a file. This hourly sampling of the system was carried out for about two weeks, yielding data on about 15000 files. These samples were then used as input to a program that condenses the raw data.

7.2.2.2.   Data Reduction and Observations. The data obtained from the experiment was processed by the data reduction program, described in the previous section, to extract data relevant for modelling. In this section we describe the data reduction process.

The program being run by each job is examined and classified as a system or nonsystem program. It is assumed that the running of a program involves opening the file containing its executable code and reading it in its entirety.* An $Open_R$ for system files (if this is a system program) or user files (in the case of a nonsystem program) is noted. Similarly, the number of Reads to system or user files is incremented by the estimate presented by Satyanarayanan [81a] for the average length of an object file.

Each open file is classified as a system, temporary, or user file, and the corresponding counts of $Open_R$ and Read, or $Open_W$ and Write, are incremented. The basis for this classification is as follows:

- Each file has a three-character suffix to the file name, called its *file extension,* which characterizes the contents of the file. If this extension indicates that a file is a temporary file, it is so classified.

- Non-temporary files are classified as system or user files on the basis of the directories to which they belong. A subset of the directories in the system are classified as system directories, and the rest are considered user directories.

It should be noted that this classification system is not perfect, though it works quite well in practice. In particular, users may use file extensions arbitrarily— the predefined bindings are only advisory in nature. However, since most temporary files are created by programs rather than directly by users, classifying a file as temporary on the basis of its extension is usually correct. Another source of error is that every file in a system directory need not necessarily be a system data object. A small fraction of these files correspond to what should really be considered user files. For example, the repository of

---

*The fact that the high segment of a system program may already be in primary memory is ignored here. It can be viewed as a caching strategy that reduces the average time needed to load an executable file.

Table 7-5. Fraction of Input-Output Operations to Different File Types.

	Open$_R$		Open$_W$		Read		Write	
	Count	Fraction	Count	Fraction	Count	Fraction	Count	Fraction
System	7638	.632	104	.041	535158	.240	1511	.021
Temporary	709	.059	1580	.620	24781	.011	31197	.443
User	3734	.309	865	.339	1665333	.748	37788	.536

Table 7-6.   System Data Object Usage.

Fractile	Index of Sys. Data Obj.	Fraction Of Total
75	11	3.8%
95	58	20.3%
100	288	100%

mail messages from users reporting bugs in a system program is sometimes part of the directory associated with that system program. Once again, these potential classification errors do not occur very often in practice.

A list of system data object names is maintained and each observed use of a system program or an open system file increments the usage count associated with the corresponding system data object.

The quantities of interest mentioned in the beginning of section 7.2.2 are obtained from this processed data. Table 7-5 presents the observed fraction of operations directed to system, temporary, and user files. As intuitively expected, temporary files are very often opened for writing, but hardly ever for reading. On the other hand, system files are often opened for reading, but rarely for writing. The fact that the proportion of Reads and Writes to user files are significantly greater than the proportions of $Open_R$s and $Open_W$s to them suggests that the lengths of such files are typically greater than the lengths of system and temporary files. Table 7-6 gives the 75-fractile and 95-fractile of the CDF of system data object usage. In accordance with intuition, a small fraction of the system data objects account for the lion's share of the usage. The complete data (from which table 7-6 is extracted) indicates there is a continuous falloff in the usage distribution—the piecewise uniform distribution assumed in section 7.1.3.1 is thus only an approximation.

7.3. Summary

As mentioned at the beginning of this chapter, the main purpose of this work is to develop a driver within the methodology proposed by this work for the simulations described in chapter 8. Based on observations reported in earlier work and an intuitive understanding of how file systems are used, a model of file usage has been obtained. The locality properties of this model are the combination of the locality properties of three different kinds of files. The rationale for this file classification and the individual locality models are discussed in section 7.1.3. The second part of the chapter describes experiments to obtain a set of parameter values for the driver from an actual file system. Sections 7.2.1 and 7.2.2 describe these experiments and discuss the data collected.

8

Simulation Results

Based on the modelling assumptions described earlier, this chapter presents the results of a simulation study of the performance tradeoffs in the network file system of chapter 6. The first section discusses the space of design parameters, the performance measures of interest, and the strategy employed in investigating the effects of the former on the latter. Sections 8.2 and 8.3 present the actual results of the simulations, and are to be read in conjunction with the graphs of appendix C. Section 8.4 offers suggestions for conducting further investigations, while section 8.5 discusses the practical lessons learned in using the tool and methodology. Finally, section 8.6 summarizes the work presented in this chapter.

8.1. Overview of Strategy

The design parameters of the network file system are represented in the device modules of chapters 6 and 7 in three ways:

- *Instantiation parameters,* such as the Central File System (CFS) hit ratio, size of disk on a Local File System (LFS), and request generation rate of the driver.

- *Storage management algorithms,* such as the LRU algorithm for cached file pages, the space–time product algorithm for two-copy file migration, and the algorithm for reclaiming disk storage.

- Statistical distributions, such as the service time distributions for the disks and processors at the LFS and CFS, the file size distributions, and the interarrival time distributions for driver requests.

The algorithms and distributions are already bound in the code of the device modules. However, before conducting a simulation, all instantiation parameters have to be bound to values. The space of possible combinations of these parameter values is far too large to be exhaustively examined—indeed, since many of the parameters are continuous-valued, the number of design points is unbounded. In a preliminary study such as this, the choice of design points to examine is essentially a subjective one, based on the investigator's intuition as to which paths of exploration are likely to yield the most insights. The rest of this section discusses the specific choice made and the approach taken in conducting the simulations.

The facts examined can be grouped into the following classes:

Effect of system load

How does the performance of the system degrade with increasing load? The load can be varied in two ways: by varying the number of LFSs, or by varying the rate of requests to an LFS. Only the former is investigated here.

Effect of CFS hit ratio

How sensitive are the performance measures to the $Open_R$ hit ratio at the CFS? For a given level of performance and CFS file migration algorithm, the desired hit ratio dictates the amount of secondary storage needed for the CFS.

Effect of LFS hardware

How exactly do disk and cache sizes affect performance?

Effect of driver characteristics

Chapter 7 makes many assumptions regarding the nature of file access requests. How robust are the results presented here with respect to these assumptions?

Two significant difficulties arise in investigating these issues. First, the device module for each LFS module has data structures to keep track of every file and cached file page on the LFS. Consequently, for the range of disk sizes considered, the amount of storage needed by an LFS can be as high as 1 Mbyte. This severely limits our ability to simulate the effect of a large number of LFSs on the system. Second, to evaluate the loading on the ethernet, and to account for transmission delays and CFS processor contention, the simulation clock has to have a resolution of at least 0.1 milliseconds. Since the clock is a 32-bit signed integer, the maximum simulated time period is $2^{31} - 1$ units, or 2.485 days. In view of the large amount of stored information in the LFS device modules, it seems unlikely that such a short period would be adequate for steady state to be attained.*

---

*This conjecture was, in fact, observed to be true. For the range of parameter values considered, at least 10 days were needed before the LFS attained steady state.

Both these problems were overcome by partitioning the simulations into two sets: those involving an LFS and those without any LFS. The simulations without an LFS were performed with the driver directly connected to the ethernet device module. These simulations were run at 0.1 msec resolution, and investigated the effect of system load and CFS hit ratio. On the basis of the empirically observed distribution function of response times for the heaviest load, a new device module was constructed, mimicking the response time distribution of the network for each different request type. This was then connected to a single LFS device module and simulations conducted at 1 millisecond resolution to study the other factors mentioned above. At this resolution, simulations up to 24.85 days could be performed. It is worth mentioning at this point that the structuring of the simulation as an interconnection of device modules greatly simplified (and, in fact, suggested) this partitioning scheme.

The simulations for the non-LFS case are discussed in section 8.2 and those for the LFS case in section 8.3. At least three, and sometimes four, replications with different random number sequences were performed for each design point. The results of these replications were then processed to obtain the mean and 90% confidence interval of each performance measure. The tables of sections 8.2 and 8.3 are thus summaries of these replications. Since the simulation tool automates the collection of the distributions of performance measures, actual distributions are available for much of the tabulated data and are presented whenever they appear to offer some additional insight. Confidence intervals have been omitted from graphs in order to improve their readability—unless otherwise mentioned, the width of the confidence interval of each point on a graph is a few percent of its mean value.

8.2. Simulations without Local File System

This section examines the effect of two factors: the total load on the system, and the hit ratio at the CFS. The primary performance measures of interest are the response times for each kind of operation, from the point of view of the driver. These are the times that an LFS would observe, viewing the network, CFS, and archive as a single black box. The waiting times at the CFS processor and disk, and the archive read and write videodisks are auxiliary measures of performance.

The load on the system is determined by the load factor parameter of the driver. As discussed in chapter 7, this parameter scales the means of hyperexponential distributions used to generate the arrival times between requests. A load factor of unity (denoted 1X) corresponds to the load observed on the CMUA. In all cases except section 8.2.2 (which compares peak and lean period performance) this corresponds to the load during the peak period. The average number of active users observed during the peak period on the CMUA is about 40. If a user on an LFS were to generate the same amount of file activity as on the CMUA (which is a timesharing system), a load of 1X would correspond to a network file system with 40 LFSs. Loads of 1X, 5X, and 10X were examined, the 10X load being representative of the expected maximum load in the CMU-CSD environment when the network file system is fully operational.

The range of acceptable hit ratios at the CFS is determined by the fact that the average rate of arrival of requests at the archive should be less than the rate at which these requests are serviced. Since the parameters of the archive are considered fixed in this study, this constraint implies that there is a minimum permissible hit ratio for each load. For an average archive service rate of 10 seconds per request, the minimum hit ratio is 98.9% for 10X, 97.8% for 5X, and 89% for 1X load. The actual set of hit ratios considered is close to, but greater than, these limits.

In all the non-LFS simulations the CFS is assumed to have 10 disks, with files being equally distributed among them, and each having an exponential service time distribution with a mean of 50 milliseconds. CPU process times at the CFS are assumed to have an exponential service time distribution with a mean of 1 millisecond. At the archive, 90% of the read requests and 10% of the write requests are assumed to require a disk mount. The characteristics of the archive videodisks are based on data presented by Bulthuis [79]: an average latency time of 20 milliseconds, an average seek time of 30 milliseconds, and a transfer rate of 1 Mbyte/sec are assumed. Since no automatic videodisk selection mechanism currently exists, the time for a mount has necessarily to be an educated guess. A figure of 10 seconds, which is more than two orders of magnitude larger than the time required to service an archive request not requiring a mount, is used in all the non-LFS simulations.

The results presented in sections 8.2.1 to 8.2.3 are based on simulation runs for two hours of simulated time, data collection being enabled after half an hour. Periodic snapshots of these simulations confirm that two hours is indeed adequate for the system to attain steady state.

8.2.1. Effect of Load

Table 8-1 presents the mean response time for each operation type, as a function of the load on the system, assuming a CFS hit ratio of 99.5% in all

Table 8-1. Effect of Total System Load—I.

	$Open_R$ Resp. Time		$Open_W$ Resp. Time		Read Resp. Time		Write Resp. Time		$Close_R$ Resp. Time		$Close_W$ Resp. Time	
	Mean	90% CI	Mean	90% CI	Mean	90% CI	Mean	90% CI	Mean	90% CI	Mean	90% CI
10X Load	139.6	1.82	3.18	0.02	121.8	0.66	123.8	0.76	3.3	0.01	115.9	0.79
5X Load	90.2	3.52	2.72	0.01	76.7	0.67	77.5	0.53	2.77	0.01	72.5	1.41
1X Load	72.3	2.1	2.6	0.02	58.3	0.24	58.1	0.6	2.6	0.01	57.5	1.13

Notes: All times are in milliseconds.
Resolution of simulation clock: 0.1 msec.
A load factor of 1X corresponds to the normal peak CMUA load.
Hit ratio at the CFS is 99.5% for all the loads.
These data correspond to non-LFS simulations.

cases.* Open$_W$ and Close$_R$ requests do not involve disk activity and are thus about an order of magnitude faster than the other requests. The Open$_R$ requests have a significantly larger mean response time because some of the requests have to be forwarded to the archive. Figures C-1, C-2, and C-3 present the response time distributions for Open$_R$, Open$_W$, and Read requests. The Close$_R$ distribution is similar to that of Open$_W$, while Write and Close$_W$ distributions are similar to the Read distribution. As the load on the system increases, the response times increase due to increased queueing delays at the CFS disk, CFS processor, and archive videodisks.

The effect of system load on the waiting times in various queues and the load on the ethernet is shown in table 8-2.** The mean waiting time at the CFS processor and the load on the ethernet scale almost linearly with the load. Even at a load of 10X, the ethernet load is only 30% of its maximum capacity, thus indicating that it is not a performance bottleneck. The data on waiting time at the write videodisk shows large confidence intervals, relative to the means; further replications are needed before one can make conclusive statements about this quantity.

While the mean of waiting time at the read videodisk increases with increasing load, as intuitively expected, figure C-4 shows that the actual distribution of this quantity is rather unusual. However, the shapes of these curves have a simple explanation. The y-intercept of the curves correspond to the situation where an arriving request finds no request currently in service. As the load increases from 1X to 10X, the probability of this event occurring decreases from 0.5 to about 0.3. The region of the abscissa between 0 and 10000 corresponds to the case where an arriving request waits an amount of time less than the mount time for a videodisk. This can occur in one of two ways: either because none of the requests ahead of the arriving request require a mount (unlikely, since the mount probability is 0.9), or because the arriving request enters the queue after the mount for the request currently in service is complete. The abrupt jump at 10000 occurs because a mount is modelled as a constant service time event. The region beyond 10000 corresponds to the case where one or more of the requests ahead of an arriving request require a mount.

---

*In tables 8-1 to 8-12 the columns labelled "90% CI" give the 90% confidence interval of the corresponding column labelled "Mean." The confidence interval may be interpreted as follows: if a large number of independent observations of a random variable are made, and a sample mean of M and a 90% confidence interval of C are calculated from these observations, then the probability of the actual mean of the random variable being in the range $M - C$ to $M + C$ is 0.9.

**Note that the term "waiting time" as used here refers to the time spent by a request in the body of a queue, before it is selected for service: it does *not* include the service time itself.

Table 8-2. Effect of Total System Load—II.

	Ethernet Load		Wait Time at CFS CPU		Wait Time at CFS Disk		Wait Time at Read VDisk		Wait Time at Write VDisk	
	Mean	90% CI	Mean	90% CI	Mean	90% CI	Mean	90% CI	Mean	90% CI
10X Load	0.30	0.00	0.32	0.00	67.1	1.36	8675.4	1041.8	15.1	20.5
5X Load	0.15	0.00	0.15	0.00	22.1	1.11	5918.3	520.4	5.56	12.5
1X Load	0.03	0.00	0.03	0.00	3.5	0.72	5055.1	305.2	0.05	0.04

Notes: All times are in milliseconds.
Resolution of simulation clock: 0.1 msec.
A load factor of 1X corresponds to the normal peak CMUA load.
Hit ratio at the CFS is 99.5% for all the loads.
These data correspond to non-LFS simulations.

8.2.2.   Peak and Lean Period

During the lean period, the interarrival time distributions of requests have larger means and are more skewed than during the peak period. The simulations described in sections 8.2.1 and 8.3 were performed for both peak and lean periods. In all cases the qualitative behavior of the output parameters was identical: a given load during the lean period can be viewed as a smaller load during the peak period. For the range of input and output parameters considered here, therefore, the difference in the shapes of the peak and lean distributions are not important.

Tables 8-3 and 8-4 compare the peak and lean period observations for the same load (10X) and CFS hit ratio (99.5%). The response time distributions for $Open_R$, $Open_W$, and Read, are compared in figures C-5 to C-7; the waiting time distribution at the archive read videodisk is shown in figure C-8. Comparisons of peak and lean period data for other loads and hit ratios are omitted here, since little insight is to be gained from them.

8.2.3.   Effect of CFS Hit Ratio

The hit ratio at the CFS primarily affects two output parameters: the $Open_R$ distribution, and the waiting time distribution at the archive read videodisk. Lower hit ratios can be expected to increase the means of both these distributions. Because of increased processor and disk contention at the CFS, and increased ethernet usage, the other output parameters may also be affected by the hit ratio. This, however, is only a second-order effect.

Five different hit ratios, ranging from 99.5% to 90%, were examined for a peak period load of 1X. This load was chosen so as to permit a wide range of hit ratios; as mentioned in section 8.2, a higher load would have raised the minimum admissible hit ratio. The observations tallied quite well with intuition: only $Open_R$ and the waiting time at the read videodisk were significantly impacted by varying the hit ratio. Table 8-5 shows the effect of varying the hit ratio on these two quantities. Note that the data for the 90% case has a large confidence interval relative to the mean, and should therefore be treated with caution. Figures C-9 and C-10 showing the initial and final parts of the $Open_R$ response time distributions, reveal an interesting observation that is not apparent from table 8-5. For all the hit ratios considered, these distributions are almost identical below a CDF value of 0.8; however, the tails of these distributions are significantly longer at lower hit ratios. The distributions of waiting time at the read archive are shown in figure C-11; the explanation offered in section 8.2.1 regarding the shapes of these curves is valid here too.

Table 8-3. Peak vs. Lean Period—I.

	Open$_R$ Resp. Time		Open$_W$ Resp. Time		Read Resp. Time		Write Resp. Time		Close$_R$ Resp. Time		Close$_W$ Resp. Time	
	Mean	90% CI	Mean	90% CI	Mean	90% CI	Mean	90% CI	Mean	90% CI	Mean	90% CI
Peak Period	139.6	1.82	3.18	0.02	121.8	0.66	123.8	0.76	3.3	0.01	115.9	0.79
Lean Period	112.0	2.7	2.8	0.01	96.4	0.4	96.3	0.6	2.9	0.01	88.4	0.9

Notes: All times are in milliseconds.
Resolution of simulation clock: 0.1 msec.
Load factor in both cases is 10X.
Hit ratio at the CFS is 99.5% for both cases.
These data correspond to non-LFS simulations.

Table 8-4. Peak vs. Lean Period—II.

	Ethernet Load		Wait Time at CFS CPU		Wait Time at CFS Disk		Wait Time at Read VDisk		Wait Time at Write VDisk	
	Mean	90% CI	Mean	90% CI	Mean	90% CI	Mean	90% CI	Mean	90% CI
Peak Period	0.30	0.00	0.32	0.00	67.1	1.36	8675.4	1041.8	15.1	20.5
Lean Period	0.19	0.00	0.23	0.00	41.0	2.6	7212.0	554.2	0.2	0.02

Notes: All times are in milliseconds.
Resolution of simulation clock: 0.1 msec.
Load factor in both cases is 10X.
Hit ratio at the CFS is 99.5% for both cases.
These data correspond to non-LFS simulations.

Table 8-5.   Effect of CFS Hit Ratio.

	Open$_R$ Resp. Time		Wait Time at Read VDisk	
	Mean	90% CI	Mean	90% CI
99.5% Hits	72.3	2.1	5055.1	305.2
99% Hits	89.0	1.3	5289.7	132.1
98% Hits	129.1	5.1	6454.8	378.3
95% Hits	260.0	24.5	8799.2	871.2
90% Hits	1635.8	1146.5	45808.0	33211.0

Notes: All times are in milliseconds.
Resolution of simulation clock: 0.1 msec.
Load factor is 1X, peak period.
Data correspond to non-LFS simulations.

8.3.   Simulations with Local File System

To investigate the performance tradeoffs in the presence of an LFS, one set of parameters, considered to be representative of a contemporary high-performance personal computer, was chosen as a reference point and its performance examined. Perturbations were then made about this point, in order to study the effect of various system parameters. Only one parameter was varied at a time, thus simplifying the interpretation of the observations.

The simulation results described in this section attempt to answer the following questions:

- What is the performance that can be expected of a typical personal computer connected to a network file system?
- How does the size of the local disk on a personal computer affect its file system performance?
- How does the absence of a local disk affect performance?
- How robust are the results presented here with respect to the assumptions made in designing the driver described in chapter 7?

As in the case of the non-LFS simulations, the primary measures of performance are the response time distributions for each of the six request types. Auxiliary performance measures are the waiting times at the LFS disk and processor, the number of storage reclamations required, and the hit ratios at the LFS for $Open_R$ requests of two-copy files and Read requests of cached files.

Throughout this study, a number of the LFS parameters mentioned in chapter 6 were kept constant:

- The driver load was 0.025X, corresponding to the reciprocal of the average number of active users of the CMUA during the peak period.

- The network was assumed to be operating under a load of 10X, and a hit ratio of 99.5%. This corresponds to the worst case examined in the non-LFS simulations. In conjunction with the assumption of a 0.025X LFS driver load, this corresponds to an environment with about 400 single-user personal computer systems.

- Like the CFS disk, the LFS disk is assumed to have an exponential service time with a mean of 50 milliseconds. On the assumption that the LFS processor is likely to be slower than the CFS processor, the LFS processing time distribution is assumed to have a mean of 10 milliseconds, ten times longer than the CFS.

- The low threshold for the disk storage reclamation algorithm is 0.05, and the high threshold is 0.2. In other words, reclamation is initiated when the available free space falls below 5% of the disk capacity and is terminated when it rises above 20%.

Probably the most difficult parameter values to estimate are the weights used in determining the storage class for a file: i.e., in deciding whether a file should be cached, two-copy, local-only, or direct-to-CFS. The specific set of values used is presented in table 8-6 and is based on the following criteria:

- The type of a file should play a role in determining its storage class.

- The storage class allocation algorithm should take into account the presence (or absence) of a local disk, and of cache storage.

- If possible, local files should not be stored on the CFS.

- The files stored on the local disk should be those which are the most likely to be accessed in the near future.

In the absence of quantitative measurements from an actual system, the numbers shown in table 8-6 have necessarily to be based on intuition. An

Table 8-6. Storage Class Parameters.

	Type of File	Local-Only Fraction	Two-Copy Fraction	Cached Fraction	DCFS Fraction
No Disk, No Cache	System				100%
	Temporary				100%
	User				100%
With Disk, No Cache	System	100%			
	Temporary		80%		20%
	User		50%		50%
No Disk, With Cache	System			80%	20%
	Temporary				100%
	User			50%	50%
With Disk, With Cache	System	100%			
	Temporary		80%	10%	10%
	User		50%	30%	20%

important extension of this work would be to determine how critically dependent the results presented here are on these parameter values.

All the results presented in sections 8.3.1 to 8.3.4 are based on three replications for each set of parameters, at a clock resolution of 1 millisecond. The simulations covered a period of 24 days, data collection being enabled after 20 days. Snapshots at daily intervals indicated that, for the range of parameter values considered, the system had reached steady state by that time.

8.3.1.   LFS Reference Point

The reference point assumes a local disk size of 20 Mbytes, of which 2 Mbytes is used as a cache. The response times observed for this configuration are presented in table 8-7, and are compared with the results of the non-LFS simulations for the same load and CFS hit ratio. The much larger mean $Open_R$ value for the LFS case is due to the fact that an entire file has to be copied from the CFS to the LFS when a miss occurs on a $Open_R$ for a two-copy file. $Open_W$ and $Close_R$ requests involve CPU processing but no disk activity. The assumption of a slow LFS processor causes these times to be larger in the LFS case than in the non-LFS case. In the LFS case, Read, Write, and $Close_R$ requests to local-only and two-copy files are directed only to the local disk and hence do not involve queueing delays at the CFS processor and disk. Consequently, these requests have a shorter mean response time in the LFS case. Figures C-12 to C-17 present the actual distributions of these response times.

Table 8-8 presents the auxiliary performance measures. The wait times at the LFS processor and disk are negligible, and are ignored in the following sections. Note that the value given for the number of reclamations corresponds to the number observed over the entire 24-day period, and not just over the 4-day data collection period. The value of 20% for cached file Read hit ratio seems astonishingly low, especially in comparison with the typically observed hit ratios of 98% or more in hardware caches [Smith82]. This phenomenon is examined further in the following sections. The 72% hit ratio for two-copy $Open_{RS}$ is much higher than the cached read hit ratio, but is still lower than hardware cache hit ratios.

8.3.2.   Effect of Disk Size

In virtual memory systems and hardware caches, a large increase in storage size usually improves the hit ratio significantly. Intuitively, one would expect a similar effect to be true for two-copy and cached files in the network file system considered here. In this section we examine the performance of the system for two different disk sizes: a 20 Mbyte disk, corresponding to the

Table 8-7. LFS Reference Point Data—I.

	$Open_R$ Resp. Time		$Open_W$ Resp. Time		Read Resp. Time		Write Resp. Time		$Close_R$ Resp. Time		$Close_W$ Resp. Time	
	Mean	90% CI	Mean	90% CI	Mean	90% CI	Mean	90% CI	Mean	90% CI	Mean	90% CI
With LFS	847.4	80.8	11.8	0.8	86.2	0.4	68.1	3.5	13.3	0.6	73.6	2.5
Non-LFS	139.6	1.82	3.18	0.02	121.8	0.66	123.8	0.76	3.3	0.01	115.9	0.79

Notes: All times are in milliseconds.
Resolution of simulation clock: 0.1 msec for non-LFS, 1 msec for LFS.
Network parameters: 10X, peak period, 99.5% CFS hit ratio.
LFS parameters: 18 Mb non-cache storage; 2 Mb cache storage; 0.025X load.

Table 8-8. LFS Reference Point Data—II.

	No. of Reclamations		Wait Time at LFS CPU		Wait Time at LFS Disk		Two-Copy Hit Ratio		Cached File Hit Ratio	
	Mean	90% CI	Mean	90% CI	Mean	90% CI	Mean	90% CI	Mean	90% CI
With LFS	175	7.7	0.1	0.0	1.4	0.1	0.72	0.02	0.20	0.06

Notes: All times are in milliseconds.
Resolution of simulation clock: 1 msec.
Network parameters: 10X load, peak period, 99.5% CFS hit ratio.
LFS parameters: 18 Mb non-cache storage; 2 Mb cache storage; 0.025X load.

reference point, and a 50 Mbyte disk, corresponding to the anticipated typical disk size of a large personal computer in the near future. In both cases 90% of the disk is used as two-copy and local-only storage, while the remaining 10% is used for cached files. The observed performance for these two disk sizes is shown in table 8-9.

The hit ratio for two-copy files does indeed show a statistically significant improvement with the larger disk. However the magnitude of this improvement is only about 6%, in spite of the fact that the ratio of disk sizes is 2.5:1. This change in the hit ratio is reflected as a correspondingly small decrease in the mean response time for $Open_R$ requests; the actual distributions for the two disk sizes are shown in figures C-12 and C-13. Why is the two-copy hit ratio so insensitive to the disk size? Among the modelling assumptions, the factors which seem most likely to be relevant to this question are:

- The locality properties of the reference stream from the driver.

- The policy for determining the storage class of a file. A policy which is consistently better at selecting only files with a high probability of future access for two-copy storage will have a better hit ratio.

- The file migration policy in use; all the results presented here are based on the STP**1.4 replacement algorithm discussed in chapter 6.

- The storage reclamation algorithm. The low and high threshold parameters for the current algorithm determine when files are deleted from the LFS, and how many of them are deleted at each reclamation epoch. Altering the values of the parameters as well as using a different algorithm may impact the hit ratio.

The first of these factors is examined in section 8.3.4. An important extension of the work presented here would be to investigate the effects of alternative decisions in the other three degrees of freedom.

In the case of Read operations on cached files, the hit ratio actually *decreases* from 20% to 14% when the size of the disk is increased from 20 Mbytes to 50 Mbytes. Paradoxically, the cache page replacement algorithm is LRU, which is known to possess the *Stack Property:* for a given reference stream, increasing the cache size will never yield a lower hit ratio. This apparent contradiction is resolved by observing that the storage class allocation and the storage reclamation algorithms in the LFS are stochastic in nature. Changing the disk and cache sizes changes the pattern of calls to the random number generator used in the simulation. Consequently, the reference stream presented to the cache mechanism changes when these sizes are altered, thereby violating the precondition under which the stack property holds.

Table 8-9. Effect of Disk Size.

	No. of Reclamations		Two-Copy Hit Ratio		Cached File Hit Ratio		Open$_R$ Resp. Time		Read Resp. Time	
	Mean	90% CI	Mean	90% CI	Mean	90% CI	Mean	90% CI	Mean	90% CI
20Mb Disk	175	7.7	0.72	0.02	0.20	0.06	847.4	80.8	86.2	0.4
50Mb Disk	63.3	1.0	0.78	0.01	0.14	0.08	723.0	28.0	85.5	2.0

Notes: All times are in milliseconds.
Resolution of simulation clock: 0.1 msec.
Network parameters: 10X load, peak period, 99.5% CFS hit ratio.
LFS parameters: 0.025X load; no disk.

Though not in contradiction of theory, the decreased hit ratio with increased disk size is still puzzling. What are the possible explanations for this? First, there is a significant amount of overlap in confidence intervals for the 20 Mbyte and 50 Mbyte case: the 20 Mbyte hit ratio interval is from 0.14 to 0.26, while the 50 Mbyte interval is from 0.06 to 0.22. It is thus possible that the true value of the hit ratio for the larger disk size is greater than that for the smaller disk size. Second, it is well-known that certain virtual memory page replacement algorithms, such as FIFO, occasionally exhibit anomalies of the same kind as that observed here—an increased storage size occasionally yields a diminished hit ratio. Though the existence of a precedent is not an explanation for the anomaly, it at least restores confidence in the validity of the observations. Finally, the factors which seem likely to affect the cache hit ratio are the same as those listed earlier for the two-copy hit ratio. Section 8.3.4 shows that the properties of the driver are indeed significant in determining the cache hit ratio. The effects of the other factors remain to be studied.

8.3.3. *Effect of a Cache in the Absence of a Disk*

In the absence of a disk, there are two options available to the designer of an LFS: direct all requests to the CFS, or use part of the main memory as storage for cached file pages. The non-LFS results presented in section 8.2 are applicable in the first case, provided the overheads caused by a slow LFS processor are also taken into account. For the second case, table 8-10 presents the observed hit ratios for three different cache storage sizes. The storage class allocation parameters of table 8-6 are used here too. Increasing the storage size does produce a statistically significant increase in the hit ratio, and these data do not exhibit an anomalous decrease in hit ratio with increasing storage size. However, as in the case of section 8.3.2, a large increase in cache size does not result in large hit ratios. In fact, a factor of 10 increase in size only produces a 5% increase in the hit ratio. The correspondingly minimal effect of cache size on the response time distributions of Read requests is shown in figure C-18. The absence of a disk implies that only two of the four factors listed in section 8.3.2 as likely candidates to account for the low hit ratios are applicable here: the characteristics of the driver and the storage class allocation algorithm.

8.3.4. *Effect of Driver Characteristics*

The synthetic driver developed in chapter 7 postulates the presence of three different classes of files: system, temporary, and user—each with different locality properties. Of these classes, system and temporary files already

Table 8-10.   Effect of Cache Size in the Absence of a Disk.

	Cached File Hit Ratio		Open$_R$ Resp. Time		Read Resp. Time	
	Mean	90% CI	Mean	90% CI	Mean	90% CI
1Mb Cache	0.34	0.01	126.5	0.9	103.7	1.3
2Mb Cache	0.36	0.01	126.7	0.7	102.1	1.1
10Mb Cache	0.39	0.01	126.5	1.0	99.0	0.6

Notes: All times are in milliseconds.
Resolution of simulation clock: 0.1 msec.
Network parameters: 10X peak load, 99.5% CFS hit ratio.
LFS parameters: 0.025X load; no disk.

possess a high degree of locality of reference. The access probability of user files, however, falls off linearly over the relatively long period of 800 days, this number being obtained from experimental observations. A simple way to increase the locality of the driver request stream is to decrease this constant of 800 days; doing so increases the probability that a recently accessed user file is accessed again in the near future.

Maintaining all other parameters at their reference point values, table 8-11 shows the effect of varying the cutoff point, τ_c, for user files over two orders of magnitude. A τ_c of 80 days shows a modest improvement in hit ratio, while a τ_c of 8 days shows a dramatic improvement. Figures C-19 and C-20 show the effect of τ_c on the Open$_R$ response time distribution, while figure C-21 shows its effect on the Read response time distribution. A value of 8 days for τ_c seems too low to be realistic. Data in Satyanarayanan [81a] indicates that many references are made to files which are 100 days or older. Consequently, assuming that a linear falloff is realistic, the data in table 8-11 establishes that the results presented in this chapter are relatively robust with respect to the assumptions made in the driver design. An obvious extension of this work would be to investigate the effects of nonlinear falloffs in the driver.

Another source of inaccuracy in the driver is the fact that on the computer system on which the experimental observations of chapter 7 were made, the same operating system primitive ("LookUp") is used for opening a file for reading as well as for obtaining directory information on that file.

Table 8-11. Effect of Locality in Reference Stream.

	No. of Reclamations		Two-Copy Hit Ratio		Cached File Hit Ratio		$Open_R$ Resp. Time		Read Resp. Time	
	Mean	90% CI	Mean	90% CI	Mean	90% CI	Mean	90% CI	Mean	90% CI
$\tau_c = 800$ days	175	7.7	0.72	0.02	0.20	0.06	847.4	80.8	86.2	0.4
$\tau_c = 80$ days	162	5.8	0.76	0.04	0.28	0.05	735.5	117.6	84.3	2.2
$\tau_c = 8$ days	102.7	6.4	0.93	0.01	0.69	0.03	245.0	26.7	70.2	0.7

Notes: All times are in milliseconds.
Resolution of simulation clock: 1 msec.
Network parameters: 10X load, peak period, 99.5% CFS hit ratio.
LFS parameters: 0.025X load, 18Mb non-cache storage, 2Mb cache storage.

Unfortunately, there is no information available to the measurement routines described in chapter 7 to distinguish between these two cases. As a result the measured rate of $Open_R s$ is an overestimate, while the rate of Reads is underestimated. To gauge the seriousness of this inaccuracy, the driver was modified so that a fixed percentage of its $Open_R$ requests were converted internally into Read requests. Table 8-12 compares the reference point with the case where 20% of the $Open_R s$ are converted to Reads. The two-copy hit ratio is hardly affected, while the cache hit ratio is improved slightly. Figures C-22 and C-23 show that the corresponding $Open_R$ and Read response-time distributions are barely distinguishable. For the range of parameters considered, therefore, the results presented in this chapter seem quite robust with respect to minor overestimates of $Open_R$ rates and underestimates in Read rates.

8.4. Suggestions for Further Exploration

Of the results presented in preceding sections of this chapter, probably the two most unexpected are the low cache file hit ratio and the relative insensitivity of two-copy and cached file hit ratios to the storage size. Probing the underlying causes for these observations by modifying some of the assumptions made so far is probably the best way to further one's understanding of the performance tradeoffs in this system.

The driver generates strictly sequential Read and Write requests to an open file; yet no anticipatory paging is done by the LFS. It would appear that relaxing the assumption of strict demand paging would improve the cache hit ratio. Is this really the case? Of course, the use of anticipatory paging implies the presence of an algorithm to decide when to page ahead, and which pages to fetch. The form of this algorithm as well as its numerical parameters are degrees of freedom whose effects on performance need to be studied.

The storage reclamation algorithm attempts to mimic a human user deleting files when the available free space on the disk is low. The effects of different parameter values need to be examined. Would an entirely different algorithm change the performance significantly? For example, what would be the effect of an algorithm that is periodically activated, rather than threshold-triggered?

The replacement algorithm used for cache pages is simple LRU, while the one used for two-copy files is the STP**1.4 algorithm described in 6. How sensitive are the results presented here to these assumptions?

The locality characteristics of the driver request stream is clearly a very important factor in determining performance. In section 8.3.4, locality was altered by varying the cutoff interval for user requests. It would be interesting to observe how other ways of changing locality affect the performance. For

Table 8-12.   Effect of Non-Open$_R$ Lookups.

	No. of Reclamations		Two-Copy Hit Ratio		Cached File Hit Ratio		Open$_R$ Resp. Time		Read Resp. Time	
	Mean	90% CI	Mean	90% CI	Mean	90% CI	Mean	90% CI	Mean	90% CI
100% Open$_R$	175	7.7	0.72	0.02	0.20	0.06	847.4	80.8	86.2	0.4
80% Open$_R$	157	1.7	0.71	0.03	0.28	0.07	839.4	116.9	83.3	1.0

Notes: All times are in milliseconds.
Resolution of simulation clock: 1 msec.
Network parameters: 10X load, peak period. 99.5% CFS hit ratio.
LFS parameters: 0.025X load. 18Mb two-copy storage, 2Mb cache storage.

instance, a linear access probability falloff is assumed for two-copy and local-only files. Nonlinear falloffs are likely to be more realistic and may yield significantly different results. Another assumption made in the driver is that Read and Write requests are directed with equal probability to all open files. How critical is this assumption? A completely different approach to this problem would be to collect file reference traces and drive the simulations with them; this would also serve as a means of calibrating the driver.

The questions posed in the previous paragraphs are, of course, only a small subset of the totality of such questions. However they form a good basis on which to begin a more extensive investigation of performance issues in a network file system.

8.5.   Experience with Tool and Methodology

The work reported in the second half of this book was conducted for two reasons: to investigate the performance of an interesting, real-life memory system, and to gain hands-on experience in the use of the proposed methodology and tool. The preceding sections of this chapter have focussed on the first of these two issues. This section stresses the practical aspects of using the methodology and tool using, where applicable, actual quantitative data gathered during the development and production phases of the simulation case study.

Probably the most valuable information obtained by actual use of the tool is a realistic estimate of the overheads imposed by it. The measurements in chapter 5 indicate that it takes about 1500 microseconds to perform a Send Message operation which triggers an active function. Unless one knows the frequency of communication between device modules, however, this number is not in itself adequate to decide what fraction of the total running time of a simulation is due to the tool. An alternative approach, which is the basis of the discussion here, is to obtain an execution time profile of an actual simulation and to estimate the overheads directly from it.

Four of the simulations presented in sections 8.2 and 8.3 were selected, and their execution profiles obtained. The routines involved in the simulations can be partitioned into four classes:

Unix Routines	These correspond to routines providing operating system support, or library functions such as those for finding square roots and logarithms.
Task Subsystem. *Routines*	The essential function of these routines is to support a co-routine style of programming, and to provide the basic functions needed in a discrete-event simulation system.

Tool Routines   Running on top of the task subsystem routines, these routines provide the runtime support for the tool. Typical of the functions provided by these routines are the transmission of messages, the triggering of active functions, and the collection of data.

User Routines   The bodies of active functions and user procedures fall into this class. Since they embody the essential characteristics of the devices being modelled, they would be present regardless of the environment in which the simulations are performed.

In all four of the examples considered, approximately 75 routines accounted for 99% of the total time required for simulation. A simple estimate of the tool overhead is given by summing the contributions of each tool routine to the total execution time. This is slightly inaccurate, because some of the calls to Unix and task subsystem routines would not occur if the tool were absent. At the same time, however, many of the functions performed by the tool routines, such as data collection, would have to be provided anyway. Ignoring these as second-order effects, table 8-13 presents the fraction of the time spent in each class of routines for each of the four samples profiles. The entries marked "p020" and "p024" refer to non-LFS simulations at loads of 10X and 1X, respectively, with the CFS hit ratio constant at 99.5%. Entry "p104" corresponds to the LFS reference point, while "p112" refers to the non-disk simulation with a 1 Mbyte main memory cache. As table 3-13 shows, the overheads due to the tool routines are in the range of 29% to 38%. Chapter 5 mentions there is good reason to believe that the SendMessage time can be reduced by a factor of 4, given the right hardware and a more efficient tool implementation. In that case one can expect to see much lower overheads, perhaps in the range of 10% to 15%.

The design of the device modules described in chapter 6 took approximately one man-month, while their coding and debugging took about two man-months. It is unlikely that these times would have been significantly shorter if a monolithic simulation strategy had been used. In fact, the need to express the external interface of a device module in terms of ports and instantiation parameters was quite useful during the modelling phase, since it provided a framework within which to express the essential characteristics of a device. As was mentioned earlier, this approach facilitated the partitioning of the simulations into those with an LFS and those without an LFS. The modularization implicit in the proposed methodology is of value in the coding and debugging phases too. All the benefits usually attributed to modular decomposition are relevant here: the need for shared data is minimized,

Table 8-13.   Tool Overhead Measurements.

	Unix Routines		Task Subsystem		Tool Support		User Routines	
	Count	Fract.	Count	Fract.	Count	Fract.	Count	Fract.
p020	9	15.2%	20	25.7%	34	38.4%	12	19.9%
p024	14	17.9%	21	24.3%	32	36.3%	11	20.8%
p104	12	20.2%	22	27.3%	29	28.9%	14	22.5%
p112	9	15.2%	19	25.9%	27	32.8%	16	25.1%

Notes: The data for each row accounts for at least 99% of the total execution time.

The number of routines of a given type are specified by the corresponding Count field.

The contribution of a given class of routines to the total execution time is given by the corresponding Fract field.

changes within one module are transparent to other modules, understandability and maintainability are enhanced, and so on.

The syntax restrictions in the tool implementation mentioned in chapter 5 were hardly found to be a handicap—at worst, they were mild irritants. A number of minor features were added to the tool in order to facilitate the actual running of simulations. Many of these are in the form of runtime switches:

–r <*value*>   sets the seed of the random number generator to <*value*>. This provides a means of performing independent replications of simulations.

–i <*value*>   sets the initial value of the simulation clock to <*value*>. This ability was needed in order to compare the peak and lean period of performance, but it is useful whenever the behaviour of one or more device modules depend on the absolute value of the simulation clock.

–c <*value*>   disables data collection until the clock value exceeds <*value*>. This permits initial transients to be ignored, and is necessary if the stead-state characteristics of a system are to be studied.

-s \<*value*\>   defines a snapshot interval of \<*value*\> simulated time units. Automatically collected statistics are output at periodic intervals of \<*value*\> time units after the initial data collection delay. In order to obtain snapshots of device-specific statistics, the name "SNAPSHOT" is assumed to be distinguished, and an empty message is sent by the runtime system to each input port with this name at every snapshot epoch. The active functions corresponding to these ports may then output device-specific statistics.

-ct \<*value*\>   forks a Unix process at intervals of \<*value*\> simulated time units, in order to display the current simulated time and statistics of memory and processor usage. This proved to be a great help in monitoring the progress of long simulations, typically taking about four hours of elapsed time.

The fact that the tool is implemented as a composition of a number of preprocessors hindered debugging significantly. Because of the many levels of preprocessing, it was sometimes quite difficult to relate an error message to its cause in the device module source code. To aggravate the problem, the use of these preprocessors precluded the use of the standard Unix source-level debugger *sdb*. Three kinds of errors were particularly difficult to track down: deadlocks, cases where an active function failed to respond to its requestor, and instances of a fatal error (such as an invalid memory address error) occurring after a large amount of processing time had elapsed. To assist debugging in such situations, a message-tracing mechanism was added to the runtime system. After a user-specified delay, details of every message sent is appended to a circular buffer; a similar buffer traces all received messages. Upon fatal termination or deadlock detection, the contents of these buffers are printed out in chronological order, thereby providing a limited history of events prior to termination. This simple mechanism proved invaluable in debugging. However, it is clear that better error-handling is an issue to be addressed in building a production version of this tool.

For the proposed methodology to be really useful it should be possible to use the same set of device modules in many different contexts. How versatile are the device modules developed here? The ethernet connection module, the videodisk archive modules, and the driver seem to offer the most potential for use in other system models. If a simple hit ratio characterization is adequate, the CFS module seems to be quite general-purpose too—for greater generality, its disk subsystem should be modelled as a distinct entity. Of the modules, the LFS device module seems to be the least versatile. Many important design assumptions are expressed as algorithms in the bodies of the active functions. Although these algorithms are parameterized, there are a number of interesting alternative designs which can only be modelled by changing the algorithms themselves.

The automated data collection facilities in the tool, particularly the ability to record actual distributions of performance measures, proved very useful. Operation-specific response times and queue waiting times were the two most frequently used performance measures. The support for device-specific data collection was also heavily used—data on hit ratios and storage reclamation counts were obtained in this way. Processor and disk contention at the LFS and CFS were also treated as device-specific variables. Data collection on disk contention could be automated in both cases by making the disk a distinct entity connected to its parent file system. Unfortunately there seems to be little scope for automating data collection on the other device-specific variables.

8.6. Summary

The purpose of this chapter was twofold: to present the results of a preliminary study of the performance tradeoffs in a network file system, and to discuss the lessons learned in the course of using the proposed methodology and tool.

Material pertinent to the first of these concerns was presented in sections 8.2 and 8.3, and suggestions for extending this work offered in section 8.4. What reasonable extrapolations can a network file system designer draw from the information presented there?

One significant observation is that the expected hit ratios for two-copy and cached files are lower than typically observed hardware cache hit ratios. For two-copy files an $Open_R$ hit ratio of about 70% can be expected; this figure improves only slightly with an increase in local disk capacity. In the case of cached files the hit ratio on Reads is about 25%. One cause for this low hit ratio is the use of pure demand paging in an environment where requests are predominantly sequential. It is likely (but has not been shown here) that anticipatory paging algorithms will yield improved hit ratios.

Another important observation concerns the usefulness of a local disk. There are two reasons for incorporating a local disk: to provide a secondary storage facility when a node is isolated, and to improve performance by minimizing the frequency of accesses to a shared node across the network. With identical local and shared disks, the relative performance figures for LFS and non-LFS cases show that the presence of the local disk improves performance only under very heavy loads. However, for economic reasons, a local disk is likely to have poorer performance than the large-capacity, high-performance disks of a shared file facility. Consequently, for light to medium loads in a reliable network, it is probably wise to omit the local disk altogether.

Practical experience with the tool and methodology, together with measurements on tool overheads, were discussed in section 8.5. What are the main insights on the design and implementation of the tool?

One important item of information relates to the overheads imposed by the use of the tool: for this application, the simulation costs were about 30% higher than they would have been if a monolithic simulation model of the same level of detail had been used. Different applications will, of course, yield a different number for this quantity. However, unless the decomposition results in a large number of frequently communicating device modules, the overheads are likely to be of the same order of magnitude as that of the current application. The application also shows deficiencies in the error reporting and debugging aspects of the tool. As it stands, the current tool implementation is usable but non user-friendly. Both problems can be rectified in a production version of the tool.

Part IV

Conclusion

9

Conclusion

The primary purpose of this concluding chapter is to restate the thesis of this book and to summarize the steps taken in its proof. Section 9.1 and 9.2 fulfill this function.

Rarely is a single piece of research the last word on its topic. There are usually unexplored paths and alternative assumptions worthy of close examination. Section 9.3 discusses extensions and refinements to the work presented here, thereby motivating further research in a number of directions. Finally, section 9.4 summarizes the contributions of this work.

9.1. The Thesis

The major claim of this study is as follows:

> *It is possible to develop simulation models for the performance of memory devices independently of the environment in which they will be used. The term "memory devices" encompasses hardware-only devices as well as storage subsystems employing a significant amount of processing and software control. The models so developed may be interconnected in a variety of ways to model a wide spectrum of complex memory systems.*

Why is this thesis significant? A large amount of time is currently spent in modelling and developing code for simulating memory systems. Design engineers often use simulation as a means of evaluating alternative memory system designs, while researchers use it both as a performance evaluation tool and as a means of validating alternative performance analysis techniques. The thesis shows a way of reducing the amount of human effort spent in these activities by allowing models and code to be reused in a variety of simulation studies.

The development of the thesis in chapter 3 implicitly provides guidelines for developing models of memory systems, motivating a particular style of modelling. Further, as section 9.3.1 suggests, it may be possible to formalize the input–output characteristics of a device module. Such a formalism would be a significant advance in the modelling of memory systems.

9.2. Overview of Proof

Chapter 2 establishes the fact that the thesis is significant and merits serious attention. The substantiation of the thesis occurs in three steps:

1. A methodology that embodies the thesis is proposed.
2. Playing the role of devil's advocate, arguments are offered against this methodology.
3. These arguments are shown to be specious.

Chapter 3 describes the methodology. Based on the idea of abstract data types in programming languages, two levels of modelling are proposed: the *device module* level, where device-specific modelling assumptions are made, and the *hierarchy description* level, which describes the structure of a complex memory system in terms of its constituent device modules. Each of these levels supports a certain degree of flexibility. By deferring the binding of parameters until instantiation, a given device module may model a family of memory devices whose members differ only in detail. At the hierarchy description level, flexibility exists in the interconnection structure as well as in the choice of device modules for the nodes of a given interconnection structure.

Two potential objections to this methodology are that it is not versatile enough and that it is computationally too expensive. Intuitive reasons refuting both arguments are offered in chapter 3. One- and two-level storage models are developed to account for the behavioral characteristics of memory devices. The existence of a compact abstract characterization of memory devices, and the fact that address translation can be represented as a device module lend credibility to the belief that a wide variety of storage systems may be modelled within the framework of the methodology. The main potential source of computational overheads in using the methodology is the communications between device modules. It is shown that the amount of information that has to be exchanged between device modules is small, and that existing communication mechanisms are quite efficient in such situations. On the basis of these arguments, the design of a language-independent tool incorporating the methodology is presented.

The material presented in chapters 4 and 5 offers evidence directly contradicting the two objections mentioned above. In chapter 4, device modules for a large number of memory devices are developed. These device modules are then used in various configurations, representing a wide spectrum of memory systems. The material presented in this chapter corroborates the claim that the methodology is versatile. Chapter 5 describes the implementation of one instance of the tool described in chapter 3. Measurements made on this implementation substantiate the claim that computational overheads are not excessive.

Thus the proof of the thesis is essentially complete at the end of the first half of the book. The work described in chapters 6, 7, and 8 serves mainly to reinforce the proof. The practicability of the proposed ideas is demonstrated by their successful application to a real-life memory system, while the low cost of applying them in that context is established by the tool overhead measurements of chapter 8.

9.3. Directions for Future Research

The work presented here can be extended along three dimensions. First, one can make modifications to the methodology itself. Second, improvements can be made to the tool design and implementation. Third, one can make refinements to the network file system simulation models and driver, and conduct further explorations of the performance tradeoffs of this system.

A little reflection will show that these three dimensions are not strictly orthogonal to each other. The design of the tool, for instance, clearly depends on the methodology. However, the extent of the overlap is relatively small, and the effect of changes along a particular dimension can be discussed assuming that the other dimensions are invariant. Consequently, each of the following three sections focusses exclusively on one of these dimensions.

9.3.1. Methodology

A hierarchy description currently consists of a one-level composition of device modules. If multilevel compositions of device modules were allowed, it would be possible to define a device module for a memory subsystem out of more primitive device modules. Originally, there did not seem to be practical situations where it was useful for the added complexity of multilevel composition to be warranted. The models of chapter 4, for example, are all based on one-level compositions. However, experience with the device modules for the network file system indicates that multilevel compositions are indeed useful, because better use of the automatic data collection facilities may be made. The device module for the videodisk archive of section 6.2.2, for instance, actually consists of three device modules: one for the controller and one each for the read and write drives. Queueing statistics at the drives are automatically collected by the tool; if a monolithic device module were to be used, device-specific data collection code would have to be present to gather these statistics. By providing a mechanism to encapsulate intermediate interconnections of device modules, the internal structure of models for memory subsystems could be hidden from higher-level hierarchy descriptions. There do not seem to be any fundamental problems in permitting such compositions; however, the details of the mechanism need to be worked out.

In the present scheme, address translation is viewed purely as a performance penalty and is represented as a device module. An alternative approach would be to associate a *type* with each address, and to view address translation as a coercion from one address type to another. The advantage of such an approach is the protection offered by typing: meaningless interconnections of device modules can be checked for by the tool. For example, if ports were associated with specific address types, and if the device module for a driver generating main memory references were to be connected to the device module for a file archive, a simple examination of the hierarchy description by the tool would reveal the error. The problem with this approach is that significant additional machinery is needed to support typing; it is not clear that the benefits warrant this complexity. A further objection is that the performance penalty caused by address translation would be associated with the type coercion functions, and no longer explicitly represented in the hierarchy description. Further investigation is needed before one can comment decisively on the usefulness of this approach.

A considerable body of work exists on the formal specification of abstract data types in programming languages. Since device modules are analogous to abstract data types, it is reasonable to ask if formal specifications can be developed for them too. In the case of an abstract data type, formal specifications precisely and unambiguously define the external behavior of the abstract data type, and serve as a constraint on its implementation. Both device modules and abstract data types contain private state information. However, they differ in the degrees of freedom available to them. For abstract data types, the set of functions which may operate on private data is a degree of freedom. For device modules, this set of functions is fixed and corresponds to the primitives (such as Read and Write) of the one- and two-level storage models. The degrees of freedom in this case are the set of ports available, the sequence of messages sent out on output ports as a consequence of a message arriving at an input port, and the time delays associated with the servicing of a request. Thus, abstract data types and device modules are based on the same philosophy but differ in important details. An attempt to formalize the specifications of device modules would therefore be a nontrivial exercise. The use of formal specifications instead of prose would permit greater precision in the description of a device module.

If a number of different device modules are available for a given memory device, a natural question is: How accurately do each of these alternatives model the delay characteristics of the memory device? In the case of an isolated device, it is relatively easy to conceive of a suitable figure of merit. For example, the accuracy in response time would be a reasonable measure for a device module that models a single-ported main memory. However, it is often the case that a request to a device module triggers other requests, all of which must be serviced before the original request can be responded to. The accuracy of the response time to the original request clearly depends on the accuracies of the responses to the triggered requests. The latter in turn depend on the actual memory hierarchy, and cannot be specified at the time a device module is created. A possible solution to this problem arises from the observation that an analogous problem exists in numerical analysis. In that context, the accuracy of results produced by an algorithm depends on both the algorithm as well as on the magnitude of errors in the input data. The view adopted in that case is to characterize the dependence of the algorithm on its input data by a *Condition Number* [Dahlquist74], which is a measure of the error in the output produced by a small perturbation in the input data. Perhaps a similar approach would be useful in characterizing the dependence of a device module on the accuracy of the other device modules to which it is connected. The feasibility and usefulness of this line of thinking remains to be studied.

This book has concerned itself exclusively with memory systems. The reason is that device modules are constructed independently of the hierarchies in which they are used. In order to use a device module in a variety of circumstances, the functionality demanded has to be limited and known a priori. The one- and two-level models of chapter 3 show that these properties hold for memory systems. This observation, together with the considerable importance of memory in computing systems, has motivated the scope of this work. However, it may perhaps be possible to export the methodology to other domains, where the constituent elements have a simple abstract characterization. For example, it may be possible to represent the reliability model of a system in terms of the reliability models of the individual devices in the system. The viability of such extensions needs to be investigated in depth before conclusive statements can be made about the portability of these ideas.

9.3.2. Tool

The tool design described in chapter 5 was oriented toward ease of implementation, with limited attention paid to efficiency. An obvious extension of the work presented here would be to refine and reimplement this tool. Such an implementation should remove the syntax restrictions mentioned in chapter 5, and pay much greater attention to the issue of efficiency. As chapter 8 indicated, the reporting of errors at compile-time and runtime is rather poor in the current implementation. In addition, this implementation provides only minimal support for debugging. Both shortcomings should be addressed in the design of a production version.

Another direction of investigation would be to explore the use of microcode for enhancing the efficiency of the tool. There are three aspects of the tool which would benefit significantly by microcoding. One is task-switching. Each time a task relinquishes control and a new task is scheduled, a context-switching overhead is incurred. Microcoding may reduce this overhead significantly. A second area is in the message subsystem. By embedding primitives such as SendMessage and ReceiveMessage in microcode, the cost of communications between device modules can be reduced. Finally, the measurements of chapter 5 show that the most expensive tool overhead is the triggering of an active function by the arrival of a message at an input port. Any reduction in the cost of this operation would significantly reduce the overall cost involved in using the tool. Microcode is an obvious candidate for this purpose.

The proposed methodology results in the modular decomposition of a complex simulation model, with no shared data between the constituent modules. The amount of information communicated between the modules is relatively small. During one instant of simulated time, there is rarely a need to synchronize operations between device modules, even though significant computation occurs within device modules during this period of real time. These characteristics are precisely those which are desirable when decomposing a problem for implementation on a multiprocessor. It appears therefore, that the proposed methodology naturally provides the needed problem decomposition. An interesting research project based on this observation would be the design and implementation of a multiprocessor version of the tool. Actual experiments would be necessary to gauge the available parallelism accurately. If nontrivial speedup is possible, the total elapsed time for simulations could be significantly reduced. This would be a significant achievement because the speedup would be obtained without explicit programming effort in the development of code for device modules.

9.3.3. *Application*

The simulations described in chapter 8 only examine a subset of the performance tradeoffs in a network file system. Examining the effect of a number of other factors on performance, as suggested in section 8.4, would be an interesting and useful extension of the work presented here. The cause of low cache and two-copy hit ratios, the usefulness of anticipatory paging, the sensitivity of the results to the storage class allocation probabilities, and the effect of alternate storage management algorithms are some of the questions which should be addressed by such an investigation. In addition, the simulations could be expanded to cover a wider range of parameter values: for example, larger disk sizes, lower hit ratios, and a greater range of locality in the driver reference stream.

The design of the driver is another area where further experimental work is called for. The most valuable contribution in this area would be the collection of an actual trace of file system references, preferably from the same system on which the data of chapter 7 and in other work by Satyanarayanan [81a] were collected. Obtaining such a trace would be expensive for reasons discussed in chapter 7, but it would be worthwhile since no published data on this topic is currently available, and since it would serve as a means of verifying the modelling assumptions in the driver. The results of the calibration procedure may suggest modifications to some aspects of the driver, such as the assumption of a linear rate falloff for accesses to temporary and user files. One refinement of the experimental results presented in chapter 7 would be to model the interarrival time distributions of each type of request by a single distribution with a time-varying mean; the present model assumes separate distributions, with fixed means, for peak and lean periods.

Finally, there are other distributed file systems whose performance could be analyzed using the tools and techniques described in this book. Examples of such systems for which actual implementations exist at the present time are Locus [Walker83], the Cedar File System [Schroeder85] and the Andrew File System [Satyanarayanan85]. Comparison between the observed performance of these systems and the performance predicted using the methodology described here would help refine and improve our analysis techniques.

9.4. Contributions of the Study

The formulation and substantiation of the thesis stated in section 9.1 is the major contribution of this work. In the course of demonstrating the validity of these ideas, a number of incidental advancements have also been made. The design and implementation of a simulation tool for memory systems is one such contribution. The development of a driver for file system simulations based on static and dynamic experimental data from an actual file system is another. Finally, there have been insights into the performance tradeoffs in a network file system. While secondary to the thesis, these are significant and useful contributions in themselves.

Appendix A

Device Module for Section 4.1.2

Cache: **Device** (Size, LineWidth, SetAssoc, ReplaceAlgorithm,
                   UpdateAlgorithm, DataWidth: **integer**);

Size	*in bytes, power of 2*
LineWidth	*in bytes, multiple of DataWidth*
DataWidth	*of requests on CPUIn, power of two, typically word width*
SetAssoc	*power of 2*
ReplaceAlgorithm:	*1 = Random*
	2 = Fifo
	3 = LRU
UpdateAlgorithm	*1 = WriteThrough*
	2 = WriteBack

begin *Cache*

Port – Declaration
    CPUIn: (**Input**, Blocksize=DataWidth, ResponsePort=CPUOut,
              ActiveFn=Fn1);
    CPUOut: (**Output**);
    MainOut: (**Output**);
    MainIn: (**Input**);
    Invalidate: (**Input**, ActiveFn=Fn2);

State – Declaration
    TotalSlots, SlotsPerSet, TestSlot, CorrectSlot, MemOutSize: **integer**;
    AccessCount, HitsOnRead, HitsOnWrite, NoOfReads, NoOfWrites: **integer**;
    DataSlots[0:(Size/LineWidth)-1] **of**

> **record**
> Dirty, Valid: **boolean**;
> Address, ReplaceInfo: **integer**;
> **end**;

    CacheBusy(1,1): **semaphore**;

Procedure – Declaration
    boolean procedure MainAccess(DoWrite: **boolean**;
                      WhichAddr, HowManyBytes: **integer**);
    If DoWrite is true, writes out HowManyBytes starting at WhichAddr,
    performing as many operations as warranted by the block size of the port
    connected to MainOut. If any response other than Success is received,
    that response is conveyed to CPUOut and false is returned. Otherwise
    true is returned without any response on CPUOut. If DoWrite is false,
    the preceding description holds, with "read" substituted for "write".

```
begin  MainAccess
OutMsg: Request;
InMsg: Response;
i, NoOfAccesses: integer;

if DoWrite
then OutMsg.Action := Write
else OutMsg.Action := Read;
if MemOutSize < 0
then
    begin  block size unspecified
    OutMsg.Address := WhichAddr;
    OutMsg.DataSize := HowManyBytes;
    NoOfAccesses := 1;
    end    block size unspecified
else
    begin block size specified
    OutMsg.Address := (WhichAddr DIV MemOutSize)*MemOutSize; start of block
    OutMsg.DataSize := MemOutSize;

        NoOfAccesses := (CEILING((WhichAddr+HowManyBytes)/MemOutSize)*MemOutSize
                                    - OutMsg.Address) DIV MemOutSize;
        end;   block size specified


    for i := 0 to NoOfAccesses-1 do
        begin Request/Response Loop
        SENDMESSAGE(MainOut, OutMsg);
        InMsg := RECEIVEMESSAGE(MainIn);
        REMOVEMESSAGE(MainIn);
        if InMsg.Response NEQ Success
        then
            begin
            SENDRESPONSE(CPUOut, InMsg.Response);
            return(false);
            end;
        else OutMsg.Address := OutMsg.Address + MemOutSize;
        end; Request/Response Loop

        return(true);
    end; MainAccess
```

ActiveFn – Declaration

```
    Initialize: ActiveFn;
        begin Initialize
        i: integer;
        TotalSlots := Size/LineWidth;
        SlotsPerSet := TotalSlots / SetAssoc;
        MemOutSize := RemoteBlockSize(MainOut);
        AccessCount := 0;
        HitsOnRead := 0;
        HitsOnWrite := 0;
        NoOfReads := 0;
        NoOfWrites := 0;
        for i := 0 to TotalSlots-1 do
            DataSlots[i].Valid := false;
        end; Initialize
```

```
Terminate: ActiveFn;
    begin Terminate
    Print('Total Number of Read Accesses = ', NoOfReads);
    Print('Hit Ratio on Reads = ', HitsOnRead/NoOfReads);
    Print('Total Number of Write Accesses = ', NoOfWrites);
    Print('Hit Ratio on Writes = ', HitsOnWrites/NoOfWrites);
    Print('Total Number of Accesses = ', AccessCount);
    Print('Overall Hit Ratio = ', (HitsOnReads+HitsOnWrites)/AccessCount);
    end; Terminate


Fn2: ActiveFn
    begin Fn2          invoked by request on Invalidate port
    InMsg: Request;
    i: integer;

    InMsg := RECEIVEMESSAGE(Invalidate);
    if InMsg.Action = Write
    then
        begin
        P(CacheBusy);
        TestSlot := (InMsg.Address DIV LineWidth) MOD SlotsPerSet;
        for i := 0 to SetAssoc-1 do
            if DataSlots[i*SlotsPerSet+TestSlot].Valid AND
                DataSlots[i*SlotsPerSet+TestSlot].Address =
                        (InMsg.Address DIV LineWidth)*LineWidth

            then
                begin
                DataSlots[i*SlotsPerSet+TestSlot].Valid := false;
                exitloop;
                end;
        V(CacheBusy);
        end;
    end; Fn2


Fn1: ActiveFn;
    begin Fn1
    i: integer;
    InMsg, OutMsg: Request;

    P(CacheBusy);
    InMsg := RECEIVEMESSAGE(CPUIn);
    if (InMsg.Action NEQ Read) AND (InMsg.Action NEQ Write)
    then
        begin
        SENDRESPONSE(CPUOut, Success);
        goto Quit;
        end;

    if (InMsg.DataSize NEQ DataWidth)
    then
        begin
        SENDRESPONSE(CPUOut, ErrorInOperation);
        goto Quit;
        end;
```

```
Now check for a hit.
TestSlot := (InMsg.Address DIV LineWidth) MOD SlotsPerSet;
CorrectSlot := -1;
for i := 0 to (SetAssoc-1) do
    if DataSlots[i*SlotsPerSet+TestSlot].Valid AND
        DataSlots[i*SlotsPerSet+TestSlot].Address =
                 (InMsg.Address DIV LineWidth)*LineWidth
    then
        begin
        CorrectSlot := i*SlotsPerSet+TestSlot;
        exitloop;
        end;

CorrectSlot = -1 at this point implies a cache miss.
DELAY(logic delay to account for checking);
AccessCount := AccessCount+1;

if InMsg.Action = Write
then
    if CorrectSlot GEQ 0  AND UpdateAlgorithm = 2 WriteBack
    then
        begin WriteBack and Hit on Write
        NoOfWrites := NoOfWrites + 1;
        HitsOnWrite := HitsOnWrite + 1;
        DELAY(Cache Write Delay);
        DataSlots[CorrectSlot].Dirty := true;
        if ReplacementAlgorithm = 3 LRU
        then DataSlots[CorrectSlot].ReplaceInfo := AccessCount;
        SENDRESPONSE(CPUOut, Success);
        end; WriteBack and Hit on Write

    else
        begin Miss or WriteThrough on Write

        NoOfWrites := NoOfWrites + 1;
        if CorrectSlot GEQ 0
        then
            begin Hit and WriteThrough
            HitsOnWrite := HitsOnWrite + 1;
            DELAY(Cache Write Delay);
            if ReplacementAlgorithm = 3   LRU
            then DataSlots[CorrectSlot].ReplaceInfo := AccessCount;
            end; Hit and WriteThrough
        if MainAccess(true, InMsg.Address, InMsg.DataSize)
        then SENDRESPONSE(CPUOut, Success);
        else write failed; response already done within MainAccess.

        end Miss or WriteThrough on Write


else we have a Read
if CorrectSlot GEQ 0
then
    begin Hit on Read
    NoOfReads := NoOfReads + 1;
    HitsOnRead := HitsOnRead + 1;
    DELAY(Cache Access Time);
    if ReplaceAlgorithm = 3 LRU
    then DataSlots[CorrectSlot].ReplaceInfo := AccessCount;
    SENDRESPONSE(CPUOut, Success);
    end Hit on Read
```

```
else
    begin  Miss on Read
    Check for an empty slot.
    for i := 0 to SetAssoc-1 do
        if NOT(DataSlots[i*SlotsPerSet+TestSlot].Valid)
        then
            begin
            CorrectSlot := i*SlotsPerSet+TestSlot;
            exitloop;
            end;
    if CorrectSlot < 0
    then
        begin  No empty slots
        Find a slot to replace
        case ReplacementAlg of
            begin  case
            1:  begin  Random
                i := SetAssoc*RANDOM;
                CorrectSlot := i*SlotsPerSet+TestSlot;
                end;  Random

            2,3:  begin  FIFO, LRU
                  CorrectSlot := TestSlot;
                  for i := 1 to SetAssoc-1 do
                      if DataSlots[CorrectSlot].ReplaceInfo >
                          DataSlots[i*SlotsPerSet+TestSlot].ReplaceInfo
                      then CorrectSlot := i*SlotsPerSet+TestSlot;
                  end;  FIFO, LRU
            end;  case

        if UpdateAlgorithm = 2 AND DataSlots[CorrectSlot].Dirty
        then
            begin  Write back dirty line of bytes
            if NOT MainAccess(true, DataSlots[CorrectSlot].Address,
                                                        LineWidth)
            then goto Quit;       write back failed. MainAccess has
                                        already responded with failure
            end;  Write back dirty line of bytes

            end;  No empty slots

        Now CorrectSlot corresponds to a really empty slot.
        if NOT MainAccess(false,
                (InMsg.Address DIV LineWidth)*LineWidth, LineWidth)
        then goto Quit;       Read from device failed

        Read successful; update housekeeping information.
        SENDRESPONSE(CPUOut, Success);
        DELAY(Cache Write Delay);
        DataSlots[CorrectSlot].Valid := true;
        DataSlots[CorrectSlot].Dirty := false;
        DataSlots[CorrectSlot].Address :=
                (InMsg.Address DIV LineWidth)*LineWidth;
        DataSlots[ReplaceInfo] := AccessCount;

        end;  Miss on Read

    Quit: V(CacheBusy);
    end;  Fn1

end;  Cache
```

Appendix B

Interarrival Time Data for Chapter 7

Figure B-1.   Mean Interarrival Rate of Events on Weekdays.

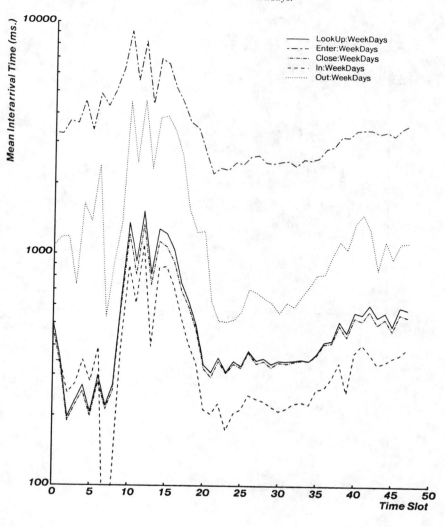

Figure B-2.   Mean Interarrival Rate of Events on Weekends.

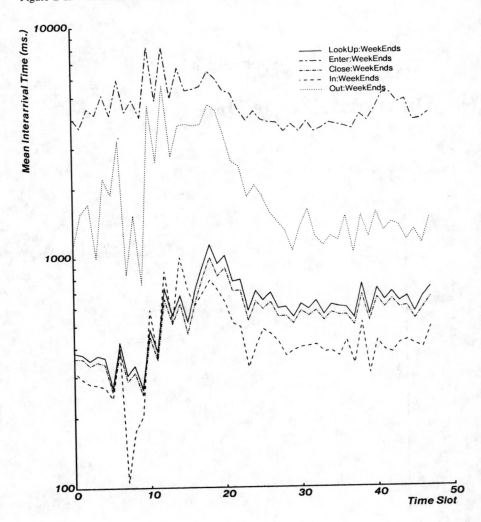

Figure B-3. Fit to Interarrival Times of Lookups (Peak Period).

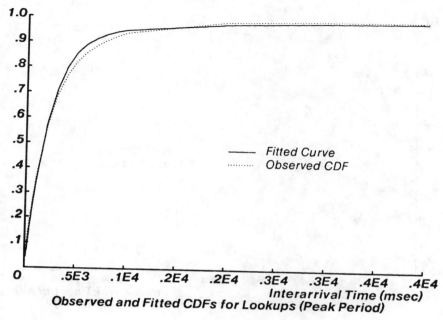

Observed and Fitted CDFs for Lookups (Peak Period)

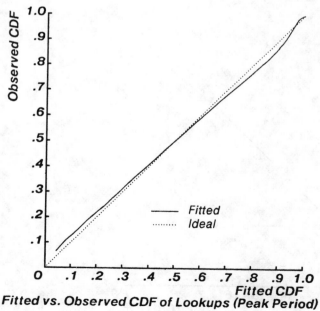

Fitted vs. Observed CDF of Lookups (Peak Period)

Figure B-4.   Fit to Interarrival Times of Lookups (Lean Period).

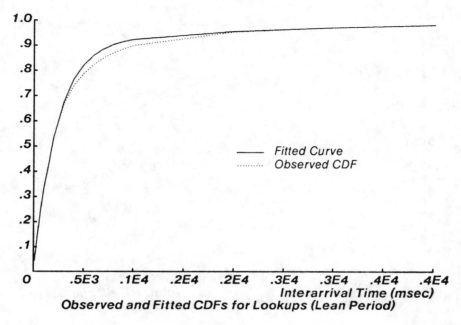

Observed and Fitted CDFs for Lookups (Lean Period)

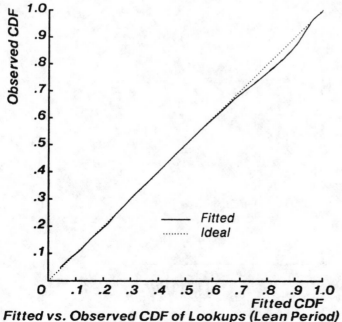

Fitted vs. Observed CDF of Lookups (Lean Period)

Figure B-5.   Fit to Interarrival Times of Enters (Peak Period).

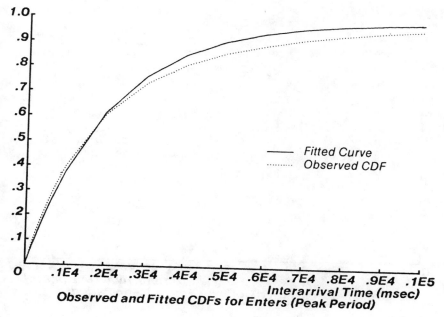

Observed and Fitted CDFs for Enters (Peak Period)

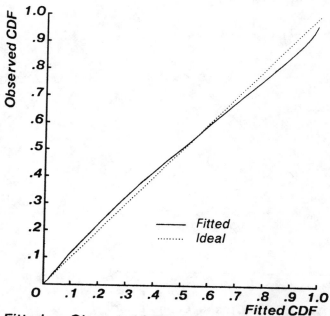

Fitted vs. Observed CDF of Enters (Peak Period)

Figure B-6.   Fit to Interarrival Times of Enters (Lean Period).

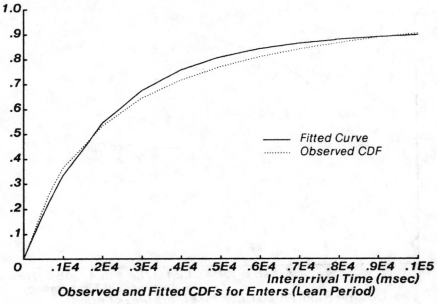

Observed and Fitted CDFs for Enters (Lean Period)

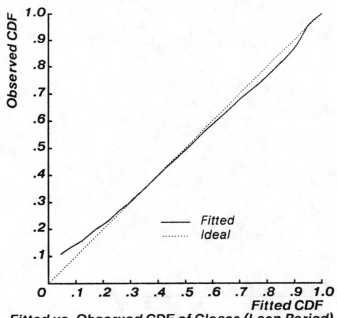

Fitted vs. Observed CDF of Closes (Lean Period)

Figure B-7.   Fit to Interarrival Times of Closes (Peak Period).

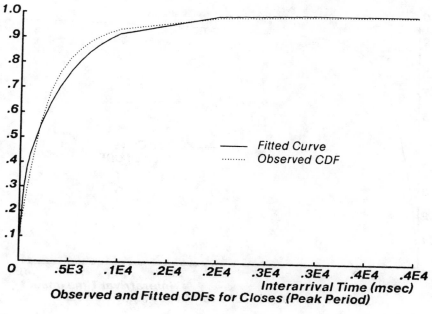

Observed and Fitted CDFs for Closes (Peak Period)

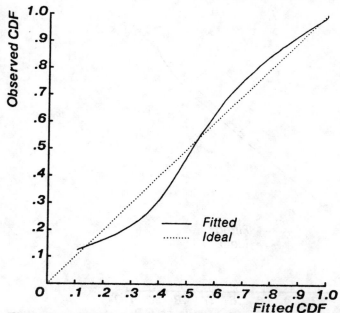

Fitted vs. Observed CDF of Closes (Peak Period)

Figure B-8.   Fit to Interarrival Times of Closes (Lean Period).

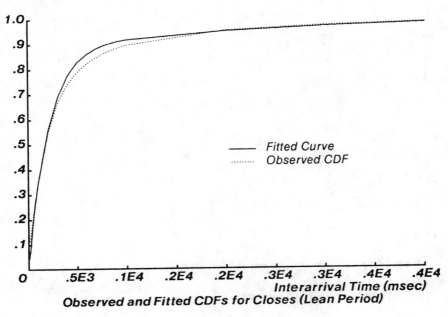

Observed and Fitted CDFs for Closes (Lean Period)

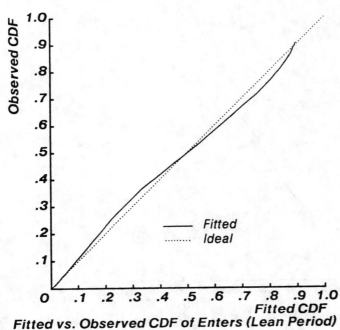

Fitted vs. Observed CDF of Enters (Lean Period)

Figure B-9.　Fit to Interarrival Times of Ins (Peak Period).

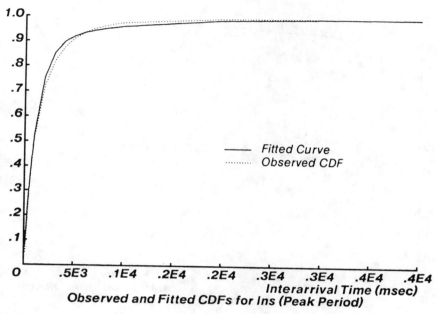

Observed and Fitted CDFs for Ins (Peak Period)

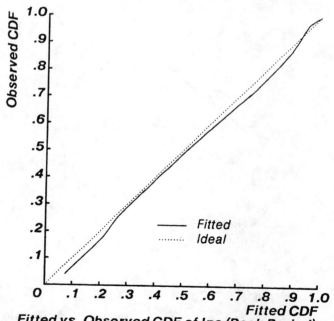

Fitted vs. Observed CDF of Ins (Peak Period)

Figure B-10.   Fit to Interarrival Times of Ins (Lean Period).

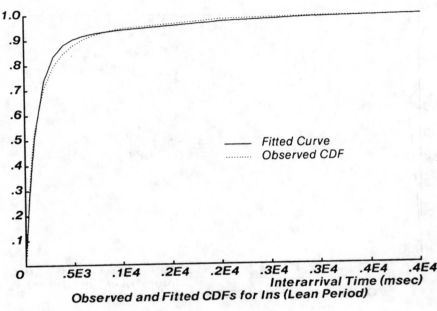

Observed and Fitted CDFs for Ins (Lean Period)

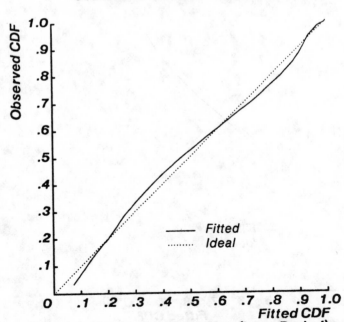

Fitted vs. Observed CDF of Ins (Lean Period)

Figure B-11.   Fit to Interarrival Times of Outs (Peak Period).

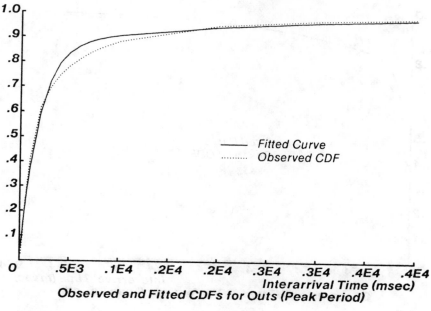

Observed and Fitted CDFs for Outs (Peak Period)

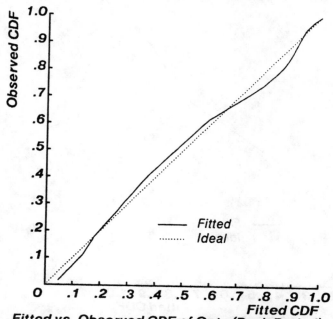

Fitted vs. Observed CDF of Outs (Peak Period)

Figure B-12.   Fit to Interarrival Times of Outs (Lean Period).

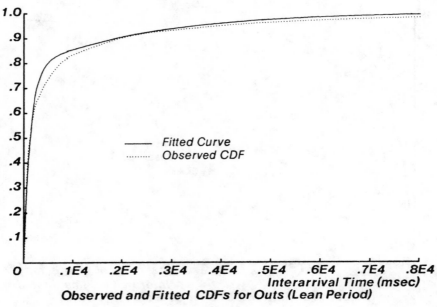

Observed and Fitted CDFs for Outs (Lean Period)

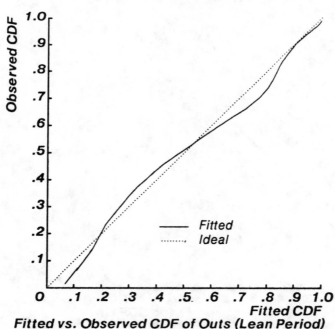

Fitted vs. Observed CDF of Outs (Lean Period)

Appendix C

Graphs for Chapter 8

Figure C-1.   Effect of Total System Load—I.

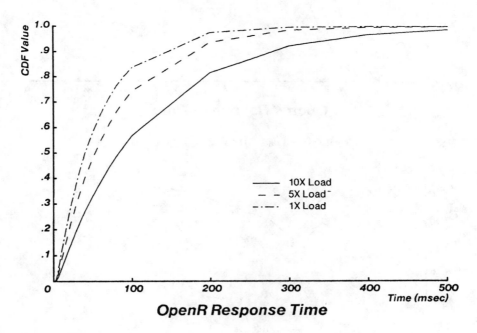

Figure C-2.   Effect of Total System Load—II.

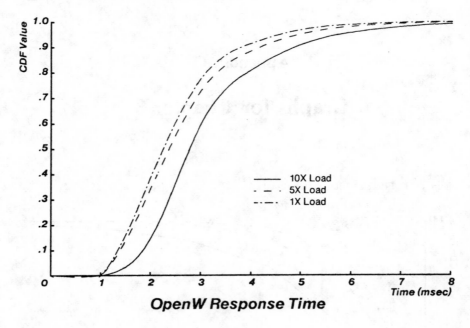

OpenW Response Time

Figure C-3.   Effect of Total System Load—III.

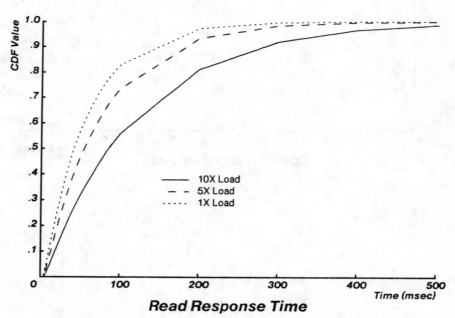

Read Response Time

Figure C-4.   Effect of Total System Load—IV.

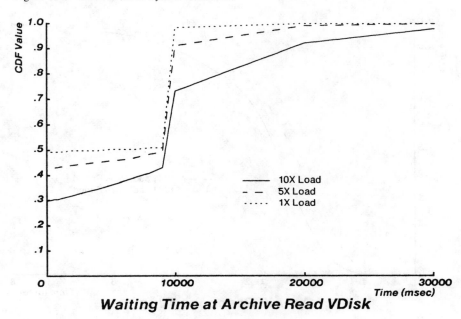

Waiting Time at Archive Read VDisk

Figure C-5.   Peak vs. Lean Period—I.

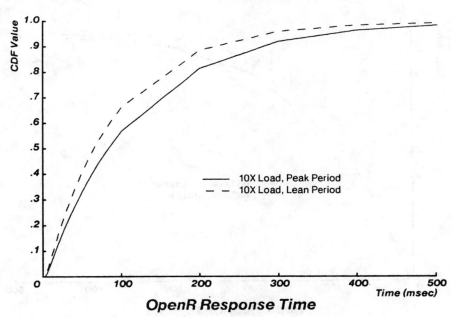

OpenR Response Time

Figure C-6. Peak vs. Lean Period—II.

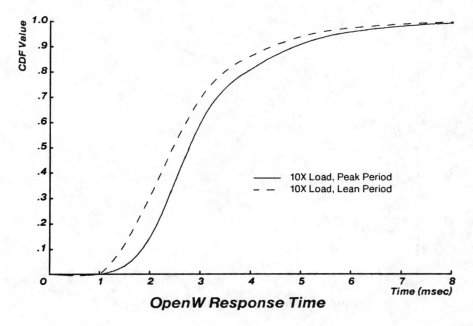

OpenW Response Time

Figure C-7. Peak vs. Lean Period—III.

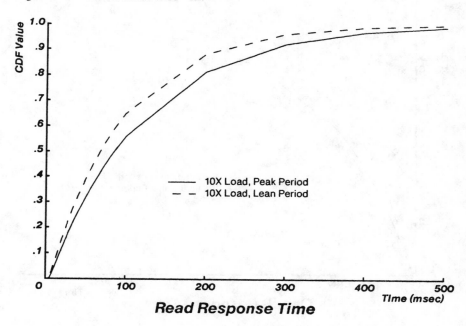

Read Response Time

Figure C-8.   Peak vs. Lean Period—IV.

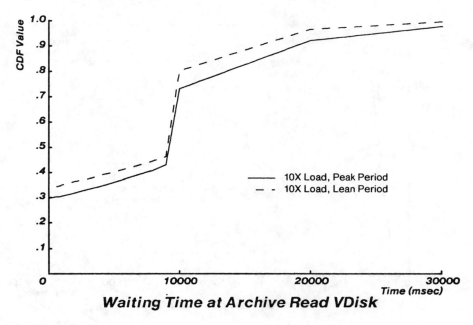

Waiting Time at Archive Read VDisk

Figure C-9.   Effect of Hit Ratio—Ia.

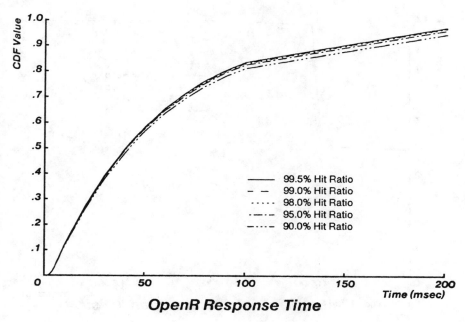

OpenR Response Time

Figure C-10.   Effect of Hit Ratio—Ib.

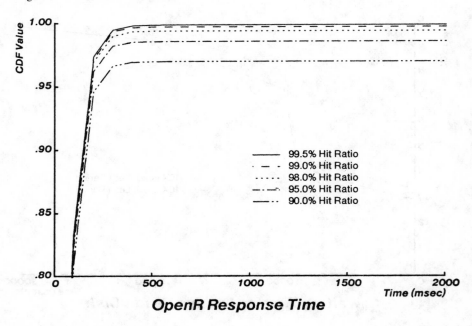

OpenR Response Time

Figure C-11.   Effect of Hit Ratio—II.

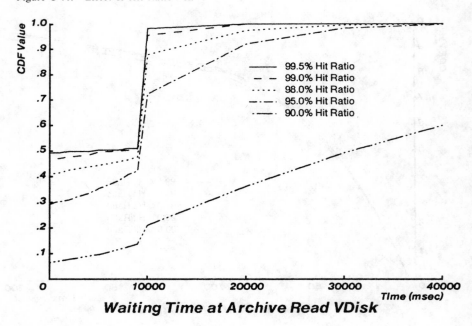

Waiting Time at Archive Read VDisk

Figure C-12.   LFS Reference Point—Ia.

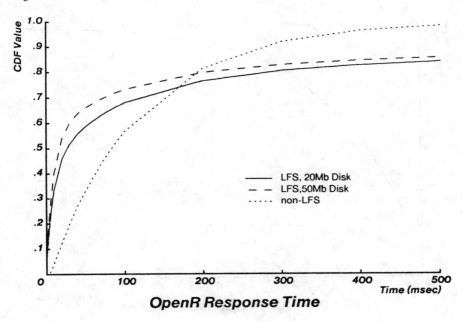

Figure C-13.   LFS Reference Point—Ib.

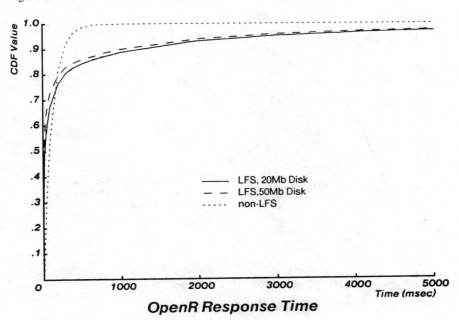

Figure C-14.   LFS Reference Point—II.

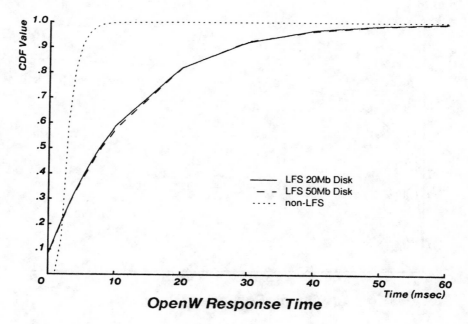

OpenW Response Time

Figure C-15.   LFS Reference Point—III.

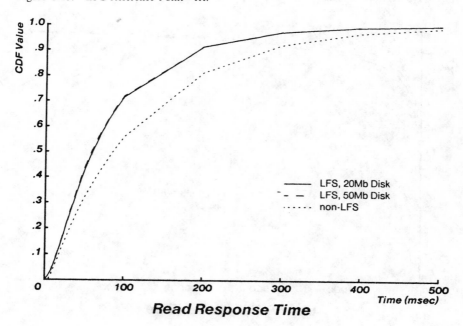

Read Response Time

Figure C-16.   LFS Reference Point—IV.

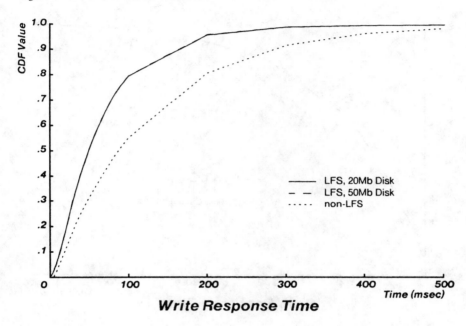

Figure C-17.   LFS Reference Point—V.

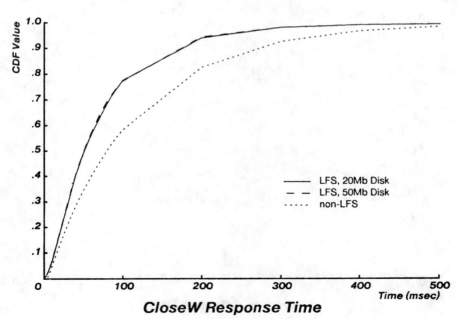

Figure C-18.   Effect of Non-Disk Cache Size.

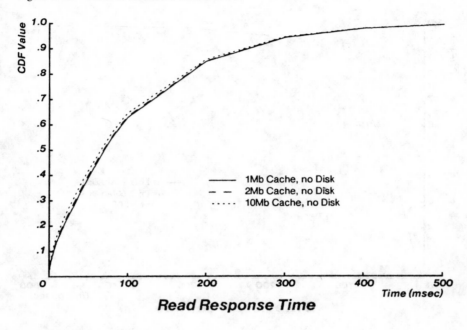

Read Response Time

Figure C-19.   Effect of Driver Locality—Ia.

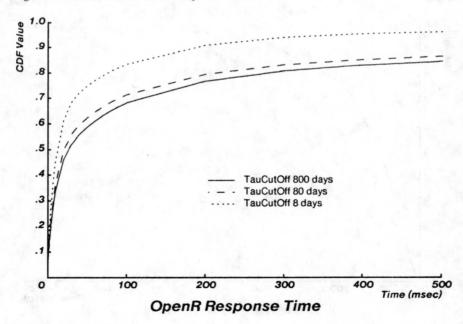

OpenR Response Time

Figure C-20. Effect of Driver Locality—Ib.

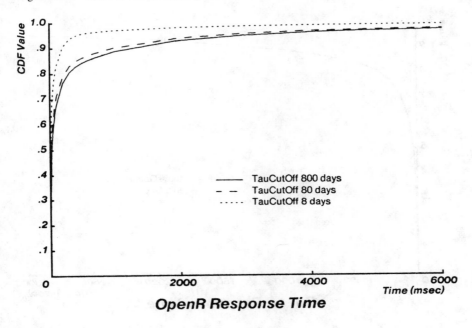

OpenR Response Time

Figure C-21. Effect of Driver Locality—II.

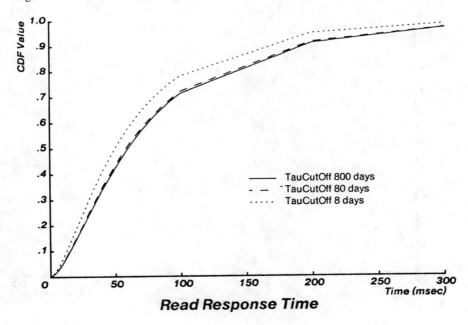

Read Response Time

Figure C-22.   Effect of Overestimating Open$_R$ Rate—I.

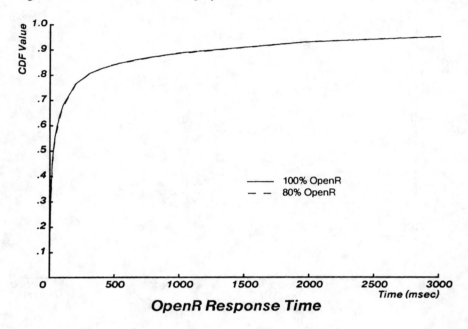

Figure C-23.   Effect of Overestimating Open$_R$ Rate—II.

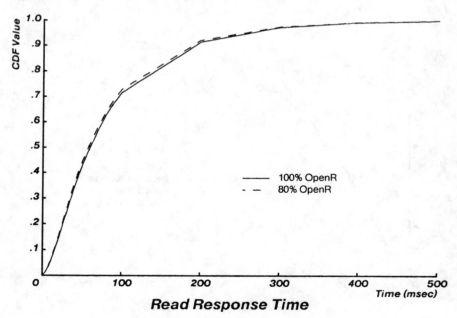

Bibliography

[Abate68]   Abate, J.; Dubner, H.; and Weinberg, S.B.
                 Queueing Analysis of the IBM 2314 Disk Storage Facility.
                 Journal of the ACM 15(4):577–589, October 1968.

[Accetta80]   Accetta, M.; Robertson, G.; Satyanarayanan, M.; and Thompson, M.
                 The Design of a Network-Based Central File System.
                 Technical Report CMU-CS-80-134, Computer Science Department, Carnegie-
                     Mellon University, August 1980.

[Agrawal77]   Agrawal, O.P.; Zingg, R.J.; and Pohm, A.V.
                 Applicability of "Cache" Memories to Dedicated Multiprocessor Systems
                 In *Proceedings of the 14th IEEE Computer Society International Conference,*
                     pp. 74–76. San Francisco, February–March 1977.

[Allen78]   Allen, A.O.
                 Probability, Statistics, and Queueing Theory.
                 Academic Press, New York, 1978.

[Almes79]   Almes, G.T., and Lazowska, E.D.
                 The Behavior of Ethernet-like Computer Communications Networks.
                 In *Proceedings of the Seventh Symposium on Operating System Principles,* pp.
                     66–81. Asilomar, CA: Association for Computing Machinery, 1979.

[Bard78]   Bard, Y.
                 The VM/370 Performance Predictor.
                 Computing Surveys 10(3):333–342, September 1978.

[Bell74]   Bell, J., and Bell, C.G.
                 An Investigation of Alternative Cache Organizations.
                 IEEE Transactions on Computers C-23(4):346–351, April 1974.

[Bhandarkar75]   Bhandarkar, D.P.
                 On the Performance of Magnetic Bubble Memories in Computer Systems.
                 IEEE Transactions on Computers C-24(11):1125–1129, November 1975.

[Bulthuis79]   Bulthuis, K.; Carasso, M.G.; Heemskerk, J.P.J.; Kivits, P.J.; Kleuters, W.J.;
                     and Zalm, P.
                 Ten Billion Bits on a Disk.
                 IEEE Spectrum 16(8):26–33, August 1979.

[Chandy69]   Chandy, K.M., and Ramamoorthy, C.V.
                 Optimization of Information Storage Systems
                 Information and Control 13:509–526, 1968.

[Chanson80]   Chanson, S.T., and Sinha, P.S.
                 Optimization of Memory Hierarchies in Multiprogrammed Computer Systems
                     with Fixed Cost Constraint.
                 IEEE Transactions on Computers C-29(7):611–618, July 1980.

[Chow74]   Chow, C.K.
                An Optimization of Storage Hierarchies.
                IBM Journal of Research and Development 18(3):194–203, May 1974.

[Dahlquist74]   Dahlquist, G., and Bjorck, A.
                Numerical Methods
                Prentice-Hall, Englewood Cliffs, NJ, 1974.

[Denning70]   Denning, P.J.
                Virtual Memory.
                Computing Surveys 2(3):153–189, September 1970.

[Doran76]   Doran, R.W.
                Virtual Memory.
                Computer 9(10):27–37, October 1976.

[Feldman78]   Feldman, S.I.
                Make—A Program for Maintaining Computer Programs.
                Technical Report Computing Science Technical Report No. 57, Bell
                    Laboratories, Murray Hill, NJ, August 1978.

[Finnin78]   Finnin, G.R.
                A Queueing Model of a Disk Subsystem.
                In *Proceedings of the Seventh Texas Conference on Computing Systems.*
                    IEEE, Houston, TX, October–November 1978.

[Foster75]   Foster, D.V.
                Channel Balancing in a Memory Hierarchy—a Case Study.
                In *1975 Winter Computer Simulation Conference, Sacramento, CA,* pp.
                    505–509. Infotech International, Maidenhead, England: December 1975.

[Fuller77]   Fuller, S.F.
                Direct Access Device Modelling.
                In *Performance Modelling and Prediction, State of the Art Report,* pp.
                    125–161. Infotech International, Maidenhead, England, 1977.

[Gaver74]   Gaver, D.P.; Lewis, P.A.W.; and Shedler, G.S.
                Analysis of Exception Data in a Staging Hierarchy.
                IBM Journal of Research and Development 18(5):423–435, September 1974.

[Gecsei74a]   Gecsei, J.
                Determining Hit Ratios for Multilevel Hierarchies.
                IBM Journal of Research & Development 18(4):316–327, June 1974.

[Gecsei74b]   Gecsei, J., and Lukes, J.A.
                A Model for the Evaluation of Storage Hierarchies.
                IBM Systems Journal 13(2):163–178, 1974.

[Harding75]   Harding, W.J.
                Hardware-Controlled Memory Hierarchies and their Performance.
                Ph.D. thesis, Arizona State University, November 1975.

[Harris75]   Harris, J.P.; Rohde, R.S.; and Arter, N.K.
                The IBM 3850 Mass Storage System: Design Aspects.
                Proceedings of the IEEE 63(8):1171–1176, August 1975.

[Hoagland79]   Hoagland, A.S.
                Storage Technology: Capability and Limitations.
                Computer 12(5):12–18, May 1979.

[Hulten77]   Hulten, C., and Soderlund, L.
                A Simulation Model for Performance Analysis of Large Shared Data Bases.
                In *Proceedings on Very Large Data Bases, Tokyo, Japan,* pp. 524–532. October
                    1977.

[Johnson75a]   Johnson, C.T.
The IBM 3850: A Mass Storage System with Disk Characteristics.
Proceedings of the IEEE 63(8):1166–1170, August 1975.

[Johnson75b]   Johnson, C.T.
Yacc: Yet Another Compiler Compiler.
Technical Report Computing Science Technical Report No. 32, Bell
Laboratories, Murray Hill, NJ, 1975.

[Joseph70]   Joseph, M.
An Analysis of Paging and Program Behaviour.
The Computer Journal 13(1):48–54, February 1970.

[Kazar80]   Kazar, M.
Echoes.
In *The Cm* Multiprocessor Project: A Research Review*, ed. A.K. Jones and
E.F. Gehringer, pages 171–182. Department of Computer Science, Carnegie-
Mellon University, 1980.

[Kernighan78]   Kernighan, B.W., and Ritchie, D.M.
Prentice-Hall Software Series: The C Programming Language.
Prentice-Hall, Englewood Cliffs, NJ, 1978.

[Keyes81]   Keyes, R.W.
Fundamental Limits in Digital Information Processing.
Proceedings of the IEEE 69(2):267–278, February 1981.

[Kho72]   Kho, J.W.
Optimal Organization of I/O Operations in Multiprogrammed Systems.
Ph.D. thesis, University of Wisconsin, October 1972.

[Kleinrock75a]   Kleinrock, L.
Queueing Theory. Volume 1: *Theory.*
John Wiley & Sons, New York, 1975.

[Kleinrock75b]   Kleinrock, L.
Queueing Theory. Volume 2: *Computer Applications.*
John Wiley & Sons, New York, 1975.

[Knuth81]   Knuth, D.E.
The Art of Computer Programming.
Addison-Wesley, Reading, MA, 1981.
Second Edition, pp. 45–52.

[Kumar80]   Kumar, B., and Davidson, E.S.
Computer System Design Using a Hierarchical Approach to Performance
Evaluation.
Communications of the ACM 23(9), September 1980.

[Lavenberg73]   Lavenberg, S.S.
Queueing Analysis of a Multiprogrammed Computer System having a
Multilevel Storage Hierarchy.
SIAM Journal of Computing 2(4):232–252, December 1973.

[Law82]   Law, A.M., and Kelton, W.D.
Simulation Modelling and Analysis.
McGraw-Hill Book Co., New York, 1982.

[Lawrie82]   Lawrie, D.H.; Randal, J.M.; and Barton, R.R.
Experiments with Automatic File Migration.
Computer 15(7):45–55, July 1982.

[Lesk75]   Lesk, M.E.
                Lex—A Lexical Analyzer Generator.
                Technical Report Computing Science Technical Report No. 39, Bell
                    Laboratories, Murray Hill, NJ, October 1975.
[Lewis73]   Lewis, P.A.W., and Shedler, G.S.
                Empirically Derived Micromodels for Sequences of Page Exceptions.
                IBM Journal of Research and Development 17(2):86–100, March 1979.
[Lin72]   Lin, Y.S., and Mattson, R.L.
                Cost-Performance Evaluation of Memory Hierarchies.
                IEEE Transactions on Magnetics Mag-8(3):390–392, September 1972.
[Liptay68]   Liptay, J.S.
                Structural Aspects of the System/360 Model 85 II. The Cache.
                IBM Systems Journal 7(1), 1968.
[Lyons74]   Lyons, N.R.
                A Model for Testing Allocation Policies for On-Line Disk Storage.
                Bulletin of the Operations Research Society of America 22(suppl. 1):B73, 1974.
[Matick77]   Matick, R.E.
                Computer Storage Systems and Technology.
                John Wiley & Sons, New York, 1977.
[Mattson70]   Mattson, R.L.; Gecsei, J.; Slutz, D.R.; and Traiger, I.L.
                Evaluation Techniques for Storage Hierarchies.
                IBM Systems Journal 9(2):78–117, 1970.
[McBride79]   McBride, E.J.; Tonik, A.B.; and Finnin, G.R.
                System Considerations for Predicting Mass Storage Subsystem Behavior.
                In *AFIPS Proceedings of the 1979 National Computer Conference, New York,*
                    vol. 48, pp. 749–759, June 1979.
[Mead80]   Mead, C., and Conway, L.
                Introduction to VLSI Systems.
                Addison-Wesley, New York, 1980.
[Metcalfe76]   Metcalfe, R.M., and Boggs, D.R.
                Ethernet: Distributed Packet Switching for Local Computer Networks.
                Communications of the ACM 9(7), July 1976.
[Misra81]   Misra, P.N.
                Capacity Analysis of the Mass Storage System.
                IBM Systems Journal 20(3):346–360, 1981.
[Mortenson76]   Mortenson, J.A.
                Computer Storage Hierarchy and Analysis.
                Ph.D. thesis, Stanford University, June 1976.
[Nahouraii74]   Nahouraii, E.
                Direct-Access Device Simulation.
                IBM Systems Journal 13(1):19–31, 1974.
[Nakamura78]   Nakamura, F.; Kimura, A.; and Yoshida, I.
                Performance of Channel and Disk Subsystems.
                In *Proceedings of the 3rd USA-Japan Computer Conference,* pp. 28–34.
                    AFIPS, San Francisco, October 1978.
[Oleinick78]   Oleinick, P.N.
                The Implementation and Evaluation of Parallel Algorithms on C.mmp.
                Ph.D. thesis, Carnegie-Mellon University, CMU-CS-78-151, November 1978.

[Pohm81]   Pohm, A.V., and Smay, T.A.
               Computer Memory Systems.
               Computer 14(10):93–110, October 1981.

[Powell77]   Powell, M.L.
               The DEMOS File System.
               In *Proceedings of the Sixth Symposium on Operating Systems Principles,* pp.
                    39–40. Association for Computing Machinery, November 1977.

[Puthuff78]   Puthuff, S.H.
               Technical Innovations in Information Storage & Retrieval.
               IEEE Transactions on Magnetics MAG-14(4):143–148, July 1978.

[Ramamoorthy70]
               Ramamoorthy, C.V., and Chandy, K.M.
               Optimization of Memory Hierarchies in Multiprogrammed Systems.
               Journal of the ACM 17(3):426–445, July 1970.

[Rashid80]   Rashid, R.F.
               An Inter-Process Communication Facility for Unix.
               Technical Report CMU-CS-80-124, Dept. of Computer Science, Carnegie-
                    Mellon University, March 1980.

[Rau79]   Rau, B.R.
               Program Behavior and the Performance of Interleaved Memories.
               IEEE Transactions on Computers C-28(3):191–199, March 1979.

[Rege76]   Rege, S.L.
               Cost, Performance and Size Tradeoffs for Different Levels in a Memory
                    Hierarchy.
               Computer 9(4):43–51, April 1976.

[Revelle75]   Revelle, R.
               An Empirical Study of File Reference Patterns.
               Technical Report RJ 1557, IBM Research, San Jose, April 1975.

[Ritchie78]   Ritchie, D.M., and Thompson, K.
               The UNIX Time-Sharing System.
               Bell System Technical Journal 57(6, Pt. 2):1905–1930, July–August 1978.

[Rose78]   Rose, C.A.
               A Measurement Procedure for Queueing Network Models of Computer
                    Systems.
               Computing Surveys 10(3):263–280, September 1978.

[Salasin73]   Salasin, J.
               Hierarchical Storage in Information Retrieval.
               Communications of the ACM 16(5):291–295, May 1973.

[Saltzer74]   Saltzer, J.H.
               A Simple Linear Model of Demand Paging Performance.
               Communications of the ACM 17(4):181–186, April 1974.

[Satyanarayanan81a]
               Satyanarayanan, M.
               A Study of File Sizes and Functional Lifetimes.
               In *Proceedings of the Eighth Symposium on Operating System Principles.*
                    Asilomar, CA: Association for Computing Machinery, December 1981.

[Satyanarayanan81b]
               Satyanarayanan, M., and Bhandarkar, D.P.
               Design Trade-Offs in VAX-11 Translation Buffer Organization
               Computer 14(12), December 1981.

[Satyanarayanan85]
Satyanarayanan, M.; Howard, J.; Nichols, D.; Sidebotham, R.; Spector, A.; West, M.
The ITC Distributed File System: Principles and Design.
In Proceedings of the Tenth ACM Symposium on Operating System Principles, pp. 35–50. Orcas Island: Association for Computing Machinery, December 1985.

[Scherr67]
Scherr, A.L.
An Analysis of Time-Shared Computer Systems.
MIT Press, Cambridge, MA, 1967.

[Schroeder85]
Schroeder, M.; Gifford, D.; Needham, R.
A Caching File System for a Programmer's Workstation.
In *Proceedings of the Tenth ACM Symposium on Operation System Principles,* pp. 25–34. Orcas Island: Association for Computing Machinery, December 1985.

[Smith76]
Smith, A.J.
A Locality Model for Disk Reference Patterns.
In *Digest of Papers of the 10th IEEE Computer Society International Meeting* San Francisco, pp. 109–112. February 1976.

[Smith77]
Smith, A.J.
Two Methods for the Efficient Analysis of Memory Address Trace Data.
IEEE Transactions on Software Engineering SE-3(1):94–101, January 1977.

[Smith78a]
Smith, A.J.
Directions for Memory Hierarchies and their Components: Research and Development.
In *Proceedings of the COMPSAC 78 Computer Software and Applications Conference, Chicago,* pp. 704–709. IEEE, November 1978.

[Smith78b]
Smith, A.J.
Bibliography on Paging and Related Topics.
Operating Systems Review 12(4):39–49, October 1978.

[Smith81a]
Smith, A.J.
Bibliography on File and I/O System Optimization and Related Topics.
Operating Systems Review 15(4):39–54, October 1981.

[Smith81b]
Smith, A.J.
Analysis of Long Term File Reference Patterns for Application to File Migration Algorithms.
IEEE Transactions on Software Engineering SE-7(4):403–417, July 1981.

[Smith81c]
Smith, A.J.
Long Term File Migration: Development and Evaluation of Algorithms.
Communications of the ACM 24(8):521–532, August 1981.

[Smith82]
Smith, A.J.
Cache Memories.
Computing Surveys 14(3):473–530, September 1982.

[Spice80]
Proposal for a Joint Effort in Personal Scientific Computing.
Dept. of Computer Science, Carnegie-Mellon University, August 1980.

[Strecker76]
Strecker, W.D.
Cache Memories for PDP-11 Family Computers.
In *Proceedings of the 3rd Annual Symposium on Computer Architecture,* pp. 155–158. IEEE, Clearwater, FL, January 1976.

[Strecker78]   Strecker, W.D.
                  Optimal Design of Memory Hierarchies.
                  In *Proceedings of the Twelfth Hawaii International Conference on System
                  Sciences, Pt. III, Honolulu,* pp. 45–56. IEEE, Western Periodicals Ltd.,
                  North Hollywood, CA, January 1979.
[Stritter77]   Stritter, E.P.
                  File Migration.
                  Ph.D. thesis, Stanford University, March 1977.
                  Stan-CS-77-594.
[Stroustrup80]   Stroustrup, B.
                  A Set of C Classes for Co-Routine Style Programming.
                  Technical Report Computing Science Technical Report No. 90, Bell
                  Laboratories, Murray Hill, NJ, November 1980.
[Stroustrup81]   Stroustrup, B.
                  Classes: An Abstract Data Type Facility for the C Language.
                  Technical Report Computing Science Technical Report No. 84, Bell
                  Laboratories, Murray Hill, NJ, August 1981.
[Teorey72]   Teorey, T.J., and Pinkerton, T.B.
                  A Comparative Analysis of Disk Scheduling Policies.
                  Communications of the ACM 15(3):177–184, March 1972.
[Thompson81]   Thompson, M.T.; Robertson, G.R.; Accetta, M.; and Satyanarayanan, M.
                  The Spice File System.
                  Internal Working Document, Dept. of Computer Science, Carnegie-Mellon
                  University, April 1981.
[Tsuruho78]   Tsuruho, S.; Matsuda, K.; Ohminami, M.; and Ito, Y.
                  Mass Storage Systems Performance Analysis using a Queueing Model.
                  In *Proceedings of the 3rd USA-Japan Computer Conference Proceedings,*
                  San Francisco, pp. 320–324. October 1978.
[Turner77]   Turner, R., and Strecker, B.
                  Use of the LRU Stack Depth Distribution for Simulation of Paging Behavior.
                  Communications of the ACM 20(11):795–798, November 1977.
[VAXVMS]   Digital Equipment Corp.
                  VAX11 Software Handbook.
                  Maynard, MA, 1978.
[Walker83].   Walker, B.; Popek, G.; English, R.; Kline, C.; and Thiel, G.
                  The LOCUS Distributed Operating System.
                  In *Proceedings of the Ninth ACM Symposium on Operating System
                  Principles,* pp. 49–70. Bretton Woods: Association for Computing
                  Machinery, October 1983.
[Welch78]   Welch, T.A.
                  Memory Hierarchy Configuration Analysis.
                  IEEE Transactions on Computers C-27(5):408–413, May 1978.
[Welch79]   Welch, T.A.
                  Effects of Sequential Data Access on Memory Hierarchy Design.
                  In *Proceedings of Spring Compcon 79,* pp. 65–68. IEEE, San Francisco,
                  February 1979.
[Wilhelm77]   Wilhelm, N.C.
                  A General Model for the Performance of Disk Systems.
                  Journal of the ACM 24(1):14–31, January 1977.

[Wilk68]   Wilk, M.B., and Gnanadesikan, R.
            Probability Plotting Methods for the Analysis of Data.
            Biometrika 55(1):1–17, 1968.

[Woolf71]   Woolf, A.M.
            Analysis and Optimization of Multiprogrammed Computer Systems Using
               Storage Hierarchies.
            Ph.D. thesis. University of Michigan 1971.

Index